Advance Praise for The Way of Love

"This excellent volume edited by Dr. York thoughtfully connects a long tradition of Islamic sciences to contemporary discourse in the field of modern psychology. I recommend this book to practitioners and imams alike - it provides new and interdisciplinary insights into the beautiful teachings of Islam regarding human behaviour."

- IMAM MOHAMED MAGID - Executive Imam – ADAMS Center and Commissioner – United States Commission on International Religious Freedom

"Dr. York and colleagues have provided a unique contribution that challenges us to find the best version of ourselves by combining the principles of Positive Psychology, the pursuit of virtue and character development, and the tenets of the Islamic faith. In doing so, the authors convincingly offer Islamic Psychology as a fascinating and novel line of inquiry into what it means to be human. Anyone interested in mental health theory, the meeting of Faith and Reason, and intersectional inquiry should read this volume."

- SUZANNE NORTIER HOLLMAN, PSY.D, PH.D. Dean Emeritus, Associate Professor, Institute for the Psychological Sciences Affiliated Clinical Faculty, The George Washington University

"In a time when self-hate and a deficit of love poison human relationships, isn't it refreshing to have a study that positions love as the bedrock of psychology? Dr. Carrie and her colleagues, through this work, beckon us on a transformative journey centered on healing through love. The book illuminates the profound role love can play in addressing myriad personal and societal challenges. I am firmly convinced that we should allow love its due chance to work its wonders within us."

- SÜLEYMAN DERIN, PHD Professor of Sufism, Faculty of Theology. Marmara University. Istanbul, Turkey. Author of *Divine Love in Sufism*

"In *The Way of Love: Towards an Islamic Psychology of Virtues and Character Development*, Dr. Carrie York and her team of Islamic scholars have assembled a much needed and important contribution that thoughtfully considers the intersection of Islamic psychology, positive psychology, ethics, and character development. Few articles or books have successfully integrated and articulated a state-of-the-art understanding of how Islamic psychology can help us to understand and integrate the wisdom of these various influences. The book will likely be a terrific resource for many and will surely help scholars and practitioners alike."

- THOMAS G. PLANTE, PH.D., ABPP, Augustin Cardinal Bea, S.J. University Professor, Santa Clara University and Adjunct Clinical Professor, Department of Psychiatry, Stanford University School of Medicine

"A truly welcome and greatly needed volume – not only for therapists to help re-align those they are treating with their theomorphic essences but for anyone consciously making the Sacred Journey intended by the blessing of human life."

- VIRGINIA GRAY HENRY, Director – Fons Vitae

"A collection of fine essays on the role of spirituality in Islamic Psychology and the editor's reflections that surrendering to God and His Plan is the only way to peace. The contributors' genuine attempts to promote Islamic values in the modern context are commendable."

- AMBER HAQUE, PH.D. - Director, Muslim Family Services, ICNA Relief, USA Non-Resident Faculty, Islamic Psychology Program - Cambridge Muslim College, UK

"This book will be a sunrise onto the fields of psychology and human development. It opens the treasure chest of Sufi knowledge about the nature of the human being, from the earthly soul levels to the divine level where the human manifests the divine reality, shining as the Face of God. As this knowledge flows into our creative western culture we will witness and participate in a new civilization of divine humanity."

- SHAYKHA FARIHA FATIMA AL-JERRAHI - Spiritual Guide of the Nur Ashki Jerrahi Community

THE WAY OF
LOVE

*Towards an
Islamic Psychology of Virtues
and Character Development*

EDITED BY

Carrie M. York, PhD

ALKARAM
PRESS

This book first published November 2023
Alkaram Press
Virginia, USA
Copyright © 2023 by Alkaram Press

Printed in the Unites States of America

FOR LOVERS AND
SEEKERS OF GOD EVERYWHERE

Table of Contents

ACKNOWLEDGMENTS

———— ❧ ————

Putting this book together required the help, contribution, and patience of many people. Before I thank them, I first want to thank God who makes all things possible. He puts things in our heart to pursue and I'm so honored He entrusted me with this project. It took a long time to get it done because of a devastating personal situation He had written into my life, but He has been holding me through it all and has allowed the project to finally reach completion – alhamdulillah.

In terms of thanking people - I would first like to thank the Board of Directors of the Alkaram Institute - Farah Lodi and Anjali Kapil - for believing in the idea of Alkaram Press. This book is our first publication. We are a small Board but big on vision, perseverance, patience, and faith. Their dedication and support for all things Alkaram as well as their support and friendship to me personally is deeply appreciated, greatly needed, and no doubt a divine gift!

I would next like to thank the chapter contributors. Simply put, this book would not have been possible without their expertise and willingness to share it here. I am incredibly honored and lucky to work with such amazing scholars: Shaykh Dr. Hasan Awan, Dr. Anisah Bagasra, Dr. Ghena Ismail, Dr. Muhammad Tahir Khalily, Dr. Maneeza Dawood, Sarah Mohr, Haseena Sahib, Shahid Ijaz, Salua Omais, Dr. Misbah Rafiq, Dr. Shawkat Ahmad Shah, Dr. Manoel Antonio dos Santos, and Eman Tarif. I thank them all and pray that God blesses and increases them in goodness.

I would next like to thank our amazing administrator - Raabia Haque – who did the cover design and basically put the entire book together, including necessary elements like buying ISBNs and other administrative matters related to setting up Alkaram Press. Raabia wears many hats at the Alkaram Institute and I am so grateful for all that she does. A special thank you is also in order to our wonderful copyeditor – Dr. Jennifer Hill.

Trying to get work done, which included this book, while going through an extremely painful life-changing situation would not have been possible without the love and support of many people behind the scenes in my life including family, friends, and others who loved, prayed for, and supported me. These *ansar* (helpers) helped keep me together and that helped me keep this project together.

First, my love, appreciation, and respect for my parents – Nathan "Bud" York and Glenda Duell. Sometimes God uses life's most painful experiences to show us how much our parents love us. I thank them as well as my step-mom Cheryl York and step-father Kent Duell for the gazillion ways they have all supported me now and throughout my life. I also thank my 98-year-old paternal grandmother Lois York who is still praying for me every single day.

Next, I want to express love and gratitude to other family members: A special thank you to my brother Luke and his wife Amanda and my brother Karl and his wife Karen. Thank you also to my step-sister Reigan and her husband Joel and my step-sister Jude and her husband Jeff. Thank you also to my Aunt Starr, Aunt Claudia, cousin Allison and her husband Chris and cousin Krissy and her husband Will. The unique ways each person has loved and supported me has been greatly healing.

I also want to thank many beautiful friends – some of whom I've known for ages and others who entered my life during this most difficult time. You are all beautiful gifts God has placed along my path of life: Syazana Durrani, Ilham Totonji (and her husband Dr. Ahmed Alwani), Dr. Marwa Assar, Dr. Khalid Elzamzamy, Jane Fatima Casewit, Farhat Awan, Dr. Mahrukh Mustansar (and her husband Dr. Laeeq Butt), Dr. Farah Zahir, Dr. Anisah Bagasra, Alia Ellen Wertheimer, Naz Georgas, Ameer Abuhalimeh, Haseena Sahib, Dr. Jennifer Hill, Dr. Rebecca Maschka, Jonathan Bethony, Maryam Bacchus, Khadijah Nassiry, Darrell Blakeway, Aisha Gray Henry, Jen Cedeno, Juan Polit, and Rehaan Khan.

I also want to thank and express love and gratitude to some of my teachers and pastoral caregivers. I have learned much about virtue and character development from them as well as many other things: Imam Mohamed Magid, Dr. Zainab Alwani, Shaykh Dr. Hasan Awan, Shaykh Hicham Hall, Shaykha Fariha Fatima al-Jerrahi, and Shaykh Al-Bashir Moore.

Lastly, I want to acknowledge the love of my life and most precious gift of all – my 12-year-old daughter Lina. Being her mom is the best job on earth and is by far the most joyful reminder to live The Way of Love every single day.

PREFACE

I once wrote a paper in graduate school entitled "When Research Becomes Me-Search". It was a self-reflection paper where I was asked to examine how various psychological concepts and theories applied to my own life. Since then, over the past nearly twenty years, almost all of my academic work as a psychologist has been "Research as Me-Search" – me trying to understand or make sense of something that happened to me and looking for ways to heal it, which has usually involved some kind of spiritual practice or intervention. Separating my professional life from my own personal psychological and spiritual journey is impossible. In fact, it's the exact opposite! Trying to make sense of my life is what has given birth to and fueled virtually all of my scholarly endeavors. This book is no different.

At first glance, *The Way of Love* appears to be a book about advancing the fields of Islamic psychology, positive psychology, and domains related to virtue and character development. The contributors and I have put forth a rationale and framework and offered some suggestions on ways forward. However, the *concept* of The Way of Love is an entirely different affair. For me, The Way of Love is about getting on board with the plan God has for our life. One can study *about* virtues or *about* character development or *about* wellbeing or *about* how to be happy, but that is a different endeavor than trying to establish love, patience, wisdom, gratitude, or contentment in your own soul. To do this requires complete surrender to God and His plan. This is not easy because often His vision is not at all what we have in mind and sometimes, His plan can be painful when it requires us to let go of what we want and replace it with what He wants for us. But it's the only way, and it is none other than a Way of Love – God's love – even if we don't like it or understand.

I have put together this book from the perspective of need and struggle. In terms of need, I could see from a personal and professional standpoint that Islam and Islamic spirituality had so much to offer the field of psychology and scholarship related to virtues, character development, and wellbeing. It felt logical and extremely needed to do a project that highlighted this obvious gap and to make some recommendations for ways forward to jumpstart this line of inquiry.

In terms of struggle, I am simply trying to get on board with God's plans after a devastating experience that shattered my entire life. For me, The Way of Love has been a *process* of coming to know God, trusting Him, surrendering to Him and His plans, and the love story with Him that is unfolding as a result of it all. Said differently, it's about making God the center of your life. Developing virtues, good character, happiness, or wellbeing are merely side-effects.

It is an honor and privilege to have been a steward of this project and to bring it through to completion. I pray that the work presented here is useful and beneficial. Any mistakes or shortcomings are entirely my own.

Carrie M. York, PhD
September 2023
The Great Falls Zawiya
Great Falls, Virginia. USA.

INTRODUCTION

The field of positive psychology, which began in the late 1990s and was spearheaded by former president of the American Psychological Association (APA) Martin Seligman, has sought to understand the nature of well-being, happiness, positive inner states, positive individual traits, virtues like love, wisdom, and generosity, and institutions that enable positive experiences and positive traits (Seligman & Csikszentmihalyi, 2000). One central aspect of this field as it relates specifically to virtue and character development is on understanding the fundamental nature of what virtues even are. Are they something that we *do* or are they something that we *have* or *are* (Cantor, 1990)?

Positive psychology was essentially born as a criticism of "mainstream" psychology, namely that it was a field that purported to help people, but did so by focusing exclusively on disease, distress, and illness. It was argued that understanding and treating mental disorders and psychopathology is not the same thing as understanding happiness or wellness. Removing a person's symptoms of depression does not necessarily mean they will become happy and thrive. Rather, being happy or well, or developing virtues like patience or gratitude, is something that needs to be cultivated.

Despite positive psychology's demonstrated efficacy (Bolier et al., 2013; Schueller & Parks, 2014; Sin & Lyubomirsky, 2009), a caveat remains: the field is admittedly western and thus, heavily culture-bound (Bermant, et al., 2011; Lambert, et al., 2015; Pandey, 2011; Wong, 2013), prompting a need to explore and expand our understanding of well-being (Lambert, et al., 2015) as well as virtue and character development.

In their seminal book *Character Strengths and Virtues: A Handbook and Classification (CSV)*, Peterson & Seligman (2004) identify and describe 24 character strengths which underlie six broad virtues that facilitate thriving. However, the authors admit that it is likely that the structures of those virtues differ across cultures, that other virtues not included on their list were worthy of consideration, and that they hoped others would examine such potential virtues in future iterations of the CSV. These gaps in the positive psychology domain, the call to fill them, and a desire and need to advance the re-emerging field of Islamic psychology, are all central to what has given rise to this book.

Of course, positive psychology is not the only domain that seeks to understand such things. For most of human history, such topics have been the domain of ethics, philosophy, and religion. Indeed, part of the point of almost all organized religions is to help its adherents be happy, virtuous people of good character. As this relates to Islam specifically, Prophet Mohammed said he came to teach one thing – good character – and the Islamic tradition has an entire science dedicated to this. It goes by a number of names including Islamic spirituality, Sufism (*tasawwuf*), the science of the self (*ilm al-nafs*), the science of beautification/excellence (*ihsan*), purification of the self (*tazkiyat al-nafs*), manners (*akhlaq*), and Islamic psychology (for example, see York Al-Karam, 2018; 2020; 2021), amongst a number of other terms. This science is similar to positive psychology in that it, too, deals with the cultivation of health, wellness, positive states, virtues, and good character, and it is also similar to "mainstream" psychology in that it is interested in removing psychopathology, negative inner states, and changing negative behavior. Until now though, this science has been primarily the domain of religion and spirituality and not one of psychology. The other central purpose of this book, therefore, is to bring the Islamic science of virtue and character development into the domain of modern (positive) psychology and thereby expand the field of Islamic psychology and the various domains upon which each chapter touches.

The Chapters

The chapters in this book provide a broad introduction to various types of scholarship that could exist in the aforementioned fields and beyond. In chapter one - *Purification, Gratitude, or Love: Models of Spiritual Transformation and Virtue Development in Sufism* – Shaykh Dr. Hasan Awan discusses the diversity of approaches to spiritual purification and character transformation in Islamic and Sufi contexts. He explains that such approaches are either through the purification of the ego-self or in the context of gratitude for being aware of God's nearness. He argues that these two ways can be found at the very origins of Islam, and that the difference between them lies in the distinctive starting point and emphasis of each path. Whereas the way of purification starts with the ego-self, which requires purification in order to be worthy of the spiritual opening that leads to further character transformation, the way of gratitude (or presence) starts with the recognition of the immediacy of the spiritual opening to God's grace, and seeks to purify the self in order to increase a sense of gratitude for the opening to God. He continues to say that a third way, which integrates these two ways, is what is called the way of love, which can also be called love's way. Love's way aligns with the divine secret of human consciousness and being, and allows life and living to unfold as God's loving secret within the human heart. He asserts that it is a secret because only the individual can experience his or her unique secret with God. No one can know that or do that for anyone else. Yet the secret is one and the same for all. This chapter examines these approaches and concludes with recommendations for ways forward with this line of inquiry.

In chapter two - *Acquiring the Character Traits of God (Takhalluq bi Akhlāq Allah) and Character Development Through Cognitive Reappraisal* – Haseena Sahib and Maneeza Dawood examine how acquiring and embodying the character traits of God (His names and attributes) is a fundamental component of Islamic spirituality. They explore how this process of *Takhalluq bi Akhlāq Allah* involves developing one's character and behavior to mirror the attributes of God, such as mercy, forbearance, wisdom, and justice. The authors explore how this can be achieved through cognitive reappraisal, a psychological technique that involves changing, or reframing, one's thoughts and perceptions about a situation. They contend that challenging life experiences are opportunities for people to examine the spectrum of divine names, and imbibe those that speak most to those unique circumstances. They conclude with a discussion and recommendations for the future use of cognitive reappraisal as a technique for character development and embodying the divine names.

In chapter three - *Extreme Altruism as a Manifestation of Islamic Virtues* - Anisah Bagasra examines the role of Islamic virtues in the lives and actions of Muslims who have engaged in extreme altruism. Altruism is considered a distinct form of prosocial behavior that involves helping with no benefit to the helper, and in some cases, helping may actually be detrimental to the helper. Extreme altruism is altruistic acts that meet these qualifications, but also involve great risk or self-sacrifice on the part of the altruist. Little research has sought to examine altruism from the perspective of religion and spirituality, especially within the Islamic tradition. This chapter highlights the qualities found in individuals who have engaged in altruism, and how others can foster these virtues in their own lives.

In chapter four – *Sufi Ethical Discourse: The Relationship Between Self-Transcendence, Compassion, and a Beatific Vision* – Ghena Ismail tackles the question of how one can transcend oneself. She begins by showing the link in Sufism between the theme of self-transcendence, and a beatific vision that entertains the possibility of an encounter with God or essence within. Love and a deep longing to realize one's authentic self is presented as the motive force in Sufi ethics. After discussing this, she shows the paradoxical relationship between ascetic practices and feeding one's ego. She also discusses different (hidden) forms of egoism as detected in Sufi literature. Self-compassion is presented as an antidote to egoism, as well as an appreciation of the significant, yet limited, role of the individual will. The centering function of the heart and its connection to purifying or making clear one's intention is highlighted. Overall, she presents Sufism as a science that holds direct encounter with one's innermost essence as its ultimate aspiration. Mindfulness of one's intentions, motives, and values, as opposed to being pre-occupied with positive or negative self-appraisals, are given due attention in Sufi ethical discourse in a manner that resonates with Buddhist psychology. She also examines primary and secondary Sufi sources in conjunction with contemporary psychological discourse, and ancient sources that may not be known to the contemporary reader of psychology. She then discusses implications on the contemporary practice of psychotherapy and our understanding of what it means to be human.

In chapter five - *Jihad-an-nafs and the Twelve Steps: Addiction Treatment as Development of Virtue and Purification of Character* - Sarah Mohr explores the similarities and differences between the Sufi practice of *jihad-an-nafs* (purification of the self) and the Twelve Step program. Refining one's character in Twelve Step programs involves practicing spiritual principles that closely resemble the descriptions in Sufi texts on the work to purify the *nafs*, including practices like surrender, faith, intention, refinement of character, repentance, and service. Practices of community meetings, writing practices ranging from journaling to calligraphy, speaking with those who have more experience such as a shaykh or sponsor, and prayer and meditation are among the means in both paths to improve character, develop virtues, and cultivate a happy life. A closer look at similarities, as well as differences, between Twelve Step programs and Sufi practices reveals deep parallels between the two paths, which suggests these practices can support recovering individuals to progress in the development of good character and overall wellness if used in conjunction. The chapter concludes with a case study and suggestions for clinical applications.

In chapter six - *Spiritual Virtues: Linguistic Definitions and Counselling Applications* - Misbah Rafiq and Shawkat Ahmad Shah explore the linguistic definitions of spiritual virtue in the Quran in order to facilitate their incorporation into counselling and psychotherapeutic spaces. They explore questions such as: what is spirituality, how does spirituality feature in Islamic psychology, what is the nature of the relationship between psychological and spiritual well-being, what are spiritual virtues, and why is it important in the context of Islamic counselling to furnish linguistic definitions of spiritual virtues. They then examine various spiritual values and their definitions such as gratitude (shukur), patience (sabr), reliance (tawakkul), hope (rajaa), reverence (taqwa), sincerity (ikhlas), love (hub), benevolence (ihsan), and abstinence (ijtinaab). They then provide practical ways of incorporating these spiritual virtues into counselling practices by setting them as goals and devising techniques of contemplation, meditation, and a few other practices to instil them. They conclude by offering a brief summary and recommendations for applying the techniques in order to evaluate their effectiveness.

In chapter seven - *Ethics, Morals, Virtues and Character Strengths: A Comparison Between Islamic Psychology and Positive Psychology* - Sálua Omais, Eman Tarif, and Manoel Antônio dos Santos examine and attempt to build a theoretical discussion that includes examining the similarities and differences between elements in positive psychology and Islamic psychology, pointing to some conceptualizations in each of these approaches. They also highlight the direct connection between spirituality, morals, and virtues in Islam, identifying some virtues addressed by primary Islamic sources as a way to contribute to the expansion of the theoretical framework linked to this theme.

Lastly, in chapter eight - *Maladies of the Nafs (Self)* - Shahid Ijaz, Muhammad Tahir Khalily, and Carrie M. York examine the concept of maladies of the self (spiritual diseases of the heart) within the Islamic tradition, focusing on their ontological composition and relevance to the tazkiya process (self-purification). The chapter begins with an introduction to the subject, providing an overview of the significance of comprehending and treating these maladies. It then examines the Islamic view of the self, including the roles of the ruh (soul), qalb (heart), and nafs (self) in spiritual development. They then provide a detailed definition and analysis of nine specific maladies: lying, backbiting, anger, avarice, arrogance, slander, envy, ostentation, and sarcasm. Each malady is analysed in terms of its manifestation and effect on a person's personality and spiritual health. In addition, the chapter investigates the global ramifications of these maladies. It emphasizes the necessity of addressing them for the betterment of society by discussing their effects at the individual, familial, social, and global levels. The contemporary relevance of these maladies is also emphasized, highlighting the need for additional research and investigation in this area. They conclude by calling for continued research and the development of effective strategies to treat maladies and promote spiritual health.

These chapters cover much diverse ground and give insight into various types of scholarship that could emerge from an "Islamic positive psychology" field. However, such works represent a beginning only, and by no means an end or arrival of what the field could be. Some work in this field has already been done (for example, see Pasha-Zaidi, 2022) but much more is needed. In terms of moving forward, a few suggestions are given in the next section.

Moving Forward

The field of positive psychology is vast, and the field of Islamic psychology is rapidly growing (for example, see Abu-Raiya, 2012; Assar, 2023; Awaad & Ali, 2014, 2015; Awaad et al. 2020; Badri, 2009; Bakhtiar, 2019; Keshavarzi et al., 2020; Rothman, 2018; Rothman & Coyle, 2018; Rothman & Coyle, 2020; York Al-Karam, 2018, 2020, 2021). Of course, the study of virtues and character development spans many domains and not just (positive) psychology or social psychology, although that is where much work is being done (for example, see the large and impressive body of work by Sarah Schnitker, 2023). In terms of potential ways forward within an Islamic positive psychology context amongst other domains, the following are a few suggestions on important and necessary lines of inquiry. This list is not at all exhaustive, but merely potential focus points for these growing and/or emerging fields. Examples of scholarship could include:

- How the constructs of "virtues" and "character development" are defined or conceptualized in the Islamic tradition, including primary Islamic sources such as the Quran and hadith, or secondary sources such as classical or modern scholars.

- How specific virtues like wisdom, love, generosity, gratitude, patience, contentment, and others are defined or conceptualized according to primary Islamic sources like the Quran and hadith, as well as how classical or contemporary scholars have defined or conceptualized them within an Islamic context.

- Ways to expand the current list of virtues recognized in the positive psychology literature by proposing new ones from the Islamic tradition. Examples could include, but are not limited to: God-consciousness (*taqwa*), reliance on God (*tawwakul*), self-vigilance (*muraqaba*), self-accounting/examination (*muhasaba*), and more.

- Novel virtue or character development interventions – historical or current ones.

- Islamic spirituality and/or spiritual practices that lead to virtue/character development.

- Theoretical and/or philosophical similarities/differences between the science of Islamic virtues/character development and that of positive psychology.

- Measuring (Islamic) virtues. Discussion could include examining psychometric scales or other qualitative ways to measure virtues/stations of the soul from the perspective of spiritual or psychological development as well as challenges in doing this.

- Treatments for spiritual diseases and disorders or psychological disorders, with an emphasis on virtue development.

- Other topics or themes related to virtues and character development that bridge Islam and psychology, broadly speaking.

Final Thoughts

The purpose of this book is to spark a new line of inquiry about ways Islam and Muslim thinking can contribute to scholarship on virtue and character development, happiness, wellbeing, and related topics, primarily within the social, positive, and Islamic psychology domains. Of course, these topics are not new – Muslims have been examining them for centuries. What is perhaps new is the context and ways in which they can be studied and applied. This is important because of the potential impact it can have on people and society, as well as perceptions and understandings of Islam. Developing a knowledge economy rooted in an Islamic worldview, especially in a Western and non-Muslim context, elevates Muslims from being merely consumers of psychological science to *creators* of it. This is vital and necessary, contributes to the further rooting of Islam into the fabric of American life and all of its diversity, and is in line with the vast and rich Islamic tradition of making the societies in which it comes into contact flourish. This track record of contribution and excellence is none other than a beautiful example of The Way of Love.

INTRODUCTION

References

Abu-Raiya, H. (2012). Towards a systematic Qur'anic theory of personality. *Mental Health, Religion & Culture, 15*(3), 217–233.

Assar, M. (2023). *The Compass Home*. The H.O.M.E. Institute.

Assar, M. (2017). *An Islamic psychological approach to psychotherapy* [Unpublished doctoral dissertation]. Chicago School of Professional Psychology.

Awaad, R., & Ali, S. (2014). Obsessional disorders in al-Balkhi's 9th century treatise: Sustenance of the body and soul. *Journal of Affective Disorders, 180,* 185–189. https://doi.org/10.1016/j.jad.2015.03.003

Awaad, R., & Ali, S. (2015). A modern conceptualization of phobia in al-Balkhi's 9th century treatise: Sustenance of the body and soul. *Journal of Anxiety Disorders, 37,* 89–93. https://doi.org/10.1016/j.janxdis.2015.11.003

Awaad, R., Elsayed, D., Ali, S., & Abid, A. (2020). *Islamic psychology: A portrait of its historical origins and contributions.* In H. Keshavarzi, F. Khan, S. Ali, & R. Awaad (Eds.), *Applying Islamic principles to clinical mental health care* (pp. 69-95). Routledge.

Badri, M. (2009). The Islamization of psychology: Its "why", its "what", its "how" and its "who." In N. Noor (Ed.), *Psychology from an Islamic perspective* (pp. 13–41). IIUM Press.

Bakhtiar, L. (2019). *Quranic psychology of the self: A textbook on Islamic moral psychology.* Chicago: Kazi Publications.

Cantor, N. (1990). From thought to behavior: "Having" and "doing" in the study of personality and cognition. *American Psychologist, 45,* 735–750.

Bermant, G., Talwar, C., & Rozin, P. (2011). To celebrate positive psychology and extend its horizons. In K. M. Sheldon, T. B. Kashdan, & M. F. Steger (Eds.), *Designing positive psychology: Taking stock and moving forward* (pp. 430–438). Oxford University Press.

Bolier, L., Haverman, M., Westerhof, G. J., Riper, H., Smit, F., & Bohlmeijer, E. (2013). Positive psychology interventions: A meta-analysis of randomized controlled studies. *BMC Public Health, 13,* 119.

Keshavarzi, H., Khan, F., Ali, B., & Awaad, R. (Eds.). (2020). *Applying Islamic principles to clinical mental health care: Introducing traditional Islamically integrated psychotherapy.* Routledge.

Lambert D'raven, L., Pasha-Zaidi, N., Passmore, H.A., & York Al-Karam, C. (2015). Developing an indigenous positive psychology in the United Arab Emirates. *Middle East Journal of Positive Psychology, 1*(1), 123.

Pandey, S. (2011, Nov 22-24). *Positive psychology: Blending strengths of western, eastern and other indigenous psychologies.* [Paper presentation]. 1st International Conference on Emerging Paradigms in Business & Social Sciences (EPBSS-2011), Middlesex University, Dubai, United Arab Emirates.

Pasha-Zaidi, N. (2022). *Towards a positive psychology of Islam and Muslims: Spirituality, struggle, and social justice.* Springer.

Peterson, C., & Seligman, M. E. P. (2004). *Character strengths and virtues: A handbook and classification.* Oxford University Press.

Rothman, A. (2018). An Islamic theoretical orientation to psychotherapy. In C. York Al-Karam (Ed.), *Islamically integrated psychotherapy: Uniting faith and professional practice* (pp. 25-56). Templeton Press.

Rothman, A., & Coyle, A. (2018). Toward a framework for Islamic psychology and psychotherapy: An Islamic model of the soul. *Journal of Religion and Health 57*(50), 17311744.

Rothman, A., & Coyle, A. (2020). Conceptualizing an Islamic psychotherapy: A grounded theory study. *Spirituality in Clinical Practice 7*(3), 197–213. https://doi.org/10.1037/scp0000219

Schnitker, S. (2023). *Science of Virtues Lab.* Baylor University. Retrieved September 20, 2023, from https://sites.baylor.edu/science-of-virtues/who-we-are/dr-sarah-schnitker/

Schnitker, S. (2023). Some of her publications retrieved on Sept 20, 2023 from https://scholar.google.com/citations?user=RpcnBYMAAAAJ&hl=en

Schueller, S. M., & Parks, A. C. (2014). The science of self-help: Translating positive psychology research into increased individual happiness. *European Psychologist*, 19, 145155.

INTRODUCTION

Seligman, M. E. P., & Csikszentmihalyi, M. (2000). Positive psychology: An introduction. *American Psychologist, 55*(1), 514.

Sin, N., & Lyubomirsky, S. (2009). Enhancing well-being and alleviating depressive symptoms with positive psychology interventions: A practice-friendly meta-analysis. *Journal of Clinical Psychology: In Session, 65*(5), 467487.

Wong, P. T. P. (2013). Cross-cultural positive psychology. In K. Keith (Ed.), *Encyclopedia of Cross-cultural Psychology.* Wiley Blackwell Publishers.

York Al-Karam, C. (2018). Islamic psychology: Towards a 21st century definition and conceptual framework. *Journal of Islamic Ethics, 2*(2018), 97–109.

York Al-Karam, C. (2020). Islamic psychology: Expanding beyond the clinic. *Journal of Islamic Faith and Practice, 3*, 111–120.

York Al-Karam, C. (2021). Islamic Psychology in the United States. In Haque and Rothman (Eds.), *Islamic Psychology Around the World* (pp. 308-323). International Association of Islamic Psychology.

CHAPTER 1

———————— ••••• ————————

Purification, Gratitude, or Love: Models of Spiritual Transformation and Virtue Development in Sufism

Shaykh Hasan Awan, MD

"Oh God, you have made my physical creation beautiful, so make my character beautiful as well!"—Prayer of the Prophet Muḥammad (s)

Verily with Hardship there is ease, indeed with hardship there is ease.
(Qur'ān 94:5–6)

Sufism, or Islamic spirituality, is the spiritual heart of Islam. It is, in fact, the essential perspective of the Holy Prophet Muhammad (s), who taught his Companions about spiritual purification and character development as a foundational element of the religion of Islam. Revelation as such is understood in Islamic teachings to be a "reminder" of God's oneness (*tawḥīd*) as well as a reminder of our original presence and covenant with God bearing witness to this oneness. In order to live the reminder, purification from the effects of our existential forgetfulness is necessary. Such purification is not possible without faith and requires following the Prophetic example and integrating the teachings of Islam into the fullness of our souls and character. In order for our Prophetic obedience to be fully established and able to flower in our being, character transformation or virtue development must be realized in this lifetime.

1

This process of virtue development and character transformation deals not only with a spiritual intimacy in seeking the Divine, but also with gaining knowledge of the effects of the psychological conditioning of the ego-self (*nafs*) that either veils or supports the spiritual journey of the heart to the divine presence. For this reason, the spiritual heart (*qalb*) is the subject of the disciplines of both Islamic spirituality and Islamic psychology. When the heart is considered from the standpoint of the conditioning of the ego-self that veils it from its higher possibilities, purification of the heart is needed through discipline and refinement of the ego-self. This process of personal purification is predominantly the subject of Islamic psychology (as *tazkiyah*), that is, the discipline within Islam that primarily seeks to refine and integrate the various parts (conscious and unconscious) of the human psyche or soul into its innate divinely created nature (*fiṭrah*). When the heart is considered from the standpoint of its origin in the Spirit (*Rūḥ*), or the divine spark placed in the inmost recesses of the heart by God, an awakening to spiritual virtues such as gratitude is effected. This process is predominantly the subject of Islamic spirituality (as Sufism or *sulūk*), which is primarily interested in the process of awakening the presence of the spirit within the center of the human psyche, and secondarily in personal purification. While both Islamic psychology and Islamic spirituality work with character transformation, each approaches character transformation from a different (but complementary) angle. This chapter will focus primarily on the approach Islamic spirituality (or Sufism) takes to character transformation and virtue development.

Islamic spirituality, which includes purification and self-realization as God's knowing and loving presence in the heart, is contained within and embodied by virtuous perfection in the very being and sanctified presence of Prophet Muhammad (s). This Prophetic spirituality has its source in the divine and sacred revelation that he received and that has been passed down from the time of his generation to the current day through continuous chains of transmission. While the spirit and form of the teachings have remained intact, they have also gone through modes of adaptation to meet the needs of various times and climes. This dimension of Islam that concerns purification and transformation has mainly been the purview of Sufis and Sufism, although all Muslims as believers are called by God to purify their souls. It is in the domain of Sufism that the highest aims of Islamic psychology, as it concerns character transformation, may be found. When considered in this manner, Islamic psychology is nothing other than Islamic spirituality.

In the Islamic and Sufi contexts, there is a diversity of approaches to spiritual purification and character transformation. These approaches to character transformation can be in essence, likened to appreciating spiritual purification in the context of *seeking* God or in the context of *being aware* of God's nearness to us. These two essential ways can be found at the very origins of Islam. For the purposes of this discussion, when spiritual purification is related to removing the effects of sins and egoic (nafs) conditioning and other psychological obstacles that prevent one from worshiping sincerely and realizing God's good pleasure (riḍwān) through obedience to the sacred law, this is the way of purification (tazkiyah) or the way of striving (riyāḍāt). The wisdom in this is best characterized by verses such as,

> "Indeed he succeeds who purifies his self; and he loses who corrupts his self" (Qur'ān 91:9–10).

When spiritual purification is related to realizing and embodying more fully God's ever-present loving nearness to us, this is the way of gratitude (*shukr*) or the way of presence (*ḥuḍūr*). Such heart-presence as a genuine Islamic approach is best indicated by verses such as,

> "This [Judgment] Day wherein neither wealth nor sons will avail; except him who brings forth to God a sound [spiritual] heart" (Qur'ān 26:88–89).

In Islamic spirituality, these two approaches (the ways of striving/purification and gratitude/presence) are not mutually exclusive. Each, in fact, complements and reinforces the other in some way. The way of gratitude procures some element of purification; however, the intention is purification not for its own sake, but for the sake of humbled gratitude for the grace of insight into the ever-present nearness of the divine presence. The way of purification *may* (but does not necessarily) lead to gratitude for the grace of a spiritual opening to intimacy with God that results in character transformation. In other words, as shall be clarified, the difference between the way of purification and the way of gratitude lies in the distinctive starting point and emphasis of each path. Whereas the way of purification starts with the ego-self, which requires purification in order to be worthy of the spiritual opening that leads to character transformation, the way of gratitude (or presence) starts with the recognition of the immediacy of the spiritual opening to God's grace and seeks to purify the self in order to increase a sense of gratitude for the opening to God. Hence, the way of gratitude starts with a sense of gratitude for the transmission of the grace of deep insight into an awareness of God's already-present nearness, while the way of striving or purification starts with striving for purification of the ego-self's sense of separation from God in order to attain the grace of nearness to God.

Sufism and the Body-Mind-Heart Dimensions of Religion

It is important to briefly clarify Sufism's connection to Islam as a revealed religion before proceeding to a discussion of the different models of virtue and character development in Sufism. The *Ḥadīth* Jibrīl (a *ḥadīth* is a particular tradition or statement of the Prophet) is connected to the Archangel Gabriel's encounter with the Prophet of Islam (s) (as found in Imām Nawawī's manual of *Forty Hadiths*). This *ḥadīth* outlines four dimensions of revealed religion. Each dimension emphasizes a particular approach to the religion and acknowledges in some way the other approaches or dimensions. These dimensions of religion can be related to the body, mind, and heart dimensions of the human being. Just as the human being needs the body, mind, and heart dimensions to work in unison to create the fullness of human experience, religion needs the integration of all three dimensions in order to realize the fullness of the religious experience.

The first dimension of religion, the body aspect, corresponds to the first question asked by Jibrīl to the Prophet (s): "What is *Islām*?" The response the Prophet (s) gives aligns with five comprehensive bodily activities as found in the well-known five pillars of Islam. This dimension of religion emphasizes the submission of our will to God; it engages the body and its willful acting out of revealed ritual—from the testimony of faith to the ritual ablution and performance of various modes of worship, including prayer, paying the alms-due, fasting, and the great pilgrimage to Makkah.

The second dimension, or mind aspect, is described when Gabriel asks the Prophet (s), "What is *īmān*?" The Prophet (s) responds by proclaiming six articles of faith—that is, six concepts or ideas relating to an Islamic understanding of the unseen (*al-ghayb*). These include belief in the reality of God, angels, scriptures, messengers, the Day of Judgment, and the good and evil of that which is ordained in this life. This dimension corresponds with Islam's engagement with the mind and emphasizes how conceptual knowledge or mental understanding informs faith and the practice of religion.

Next, Gabriel asks, "What is *iḥsān*?" This is the third dimension of Islam, or the heart aspect. *Iḥsān* has many positive connotations in the Islamic understanding, including beauty, virtue, mastery, and spiritual excellence in religion. When *iḥsān* is understood as relating to the inner nature of our relationship with God, this is precisely the territory of Sufism. The Prophet (s) defines *iḥsān* in this way: "It is to worship God as if you see Him; and if you do not see Him, verily He sees you." This definition emphasizes a heart-orientation to religion, even a methodology of awakening the spiritual heart in order to realize more deeply and embody

4

more fully the consequences of engaging with religion with sincerity of heart. Such heart-orientation to religious worship facilitates or awakens a witnessing presence of heart with God in one's worship—and not just ritual worship, but in the worship and service to God that is the life of the believer. This spiritual heart-witnessing of God in worship and mindful awareness of the Divine Witness over all things, including the heart, is only possible when the spiritual-heart dimension of one's inner self is awakened and deeply connected to the inner dimensions of the revealed religion. This is *iḥsān* as Sufism.

For completeness's sake, it should be noted that the fourth dimension of the religion of Islam mentioned in this *ḥadīth* concerns the signs of the end of time as they relate to the eschatological fate of humanity on a global scale. This chapter, however, focuses on the first three dimensions of religion—*islām*, *īmān*, and *iḥsān*—and especially on the third. As suggested, to say Sufism is to say *iḥsān*—it is the heart dimension of Islam. One approaches God in a direct and immediate sense through engagement with religion by awakening to the dimension of heart-presence. The awakened heart is the essence of Sufism, and it is clear that sensitivity to the spiritual heart as it pertains to religion is already embedded in the sayings of Prophet Muḥammad (s) at the origin of Islam, although the implications of this heart-orientation for one's religion with God as Islam may not be as obvious until the tradition unfolds them.

When Islamic history is examined, the crystallization of the schools of religious law, or *madhhabs*, can be seen. The schools of law concern the body dimension of religion: the method for performing the ablutions or the prayers, for example, or the dietary laws. These different schools are well known, as it is imperative that Muslims follow to a great extent the methodology and rulings of one of them. Yet this is only the body dimension of Islam—the first qualification of Islam transmitted through the *Ḥadīth Jibrīl*. There are also the mind and heart dimensions that, when practiced, complete the religion or allow one to live in a more holistic or integrated manner.

At the same time that the legal or body dimensions of Islam were being formulated and canonized in the tradition, the mind and heart dimensions of Islam were also being formulated and transmitted. Often, in fact, the body and the mind dimensions were developed together. For example, adherents of the Ḥanafī school of law or religious praxis would most likely be Māturīdī in their conceptual and dogmatic theology, and those following the Malakī school of religious praxis would be Ashʿarī in their creedal understanding. But just as the different *madhhabs* have been linked to the mind dimensions of religion, so have they often been linked to spiritual perspectives or heart dimensions of religion. For example, a traditional Malakī in sacred law is likely also a Shādhilī or Tijanī in spirituality. But such explicit body-mind-heart connections to religion would manifest their possibilities or applications in these ways a bit later in the unfolding of the Islamic tradition as the need to clarify access to these dimensions of religion grew.

For any Muslim spiritual seeker who is of a more contemplative temperament, the essential question has always been: How do I conform or orient my heart-presence, the very core (*lubb*) of my pure being and essential knowing, to the divine presence? The answer to this question is the vocation and the point of departure of Sufism, of Islamic spirituality. Such conformity to the divine presence involves an awakening of latent faculties of the inner heart, the center of our being and knowing, which usually occur through a process of purification of the psychological and physical self (*nafs*) connected with practices of the invocation of litanies, themselves connected to revelation and other forms of remembrance of God (*dhikr Allāh*). In this regard, one-way abiding character transformation can occur is as a result of the embodiment of prophetic virtues, which are awakened and actualized through practicing modes of *dhikr* and keeping a spiritual connection with awakened teachers and realized guides within the traditional disciplines of Sufism, which form an unbroken chain of transmission through realized masters back to the person and presence of Prophet Muḥammad (s).

Sufism, Virtue, and Character Development

Sufism is about virtue and character development as a corollary to sincerely worshiping God through beautiful character traits (*khuluq*). Such cultivation of beautiful character is ultimately the result of a deepened awareness of God's merciful nearness to us and His connection to our spiritual hearts, and of a balanced integration of this awareness in our souls and characters. To say beauty or perfection of character is to say perfection of our intimate knowing of God as the ultimate loving presence in our life. When the Prophet (s) states, "I have come only to perfect and ennoble character" (Mālik, *Muwaṭṭa'*, *ḥusn al-khulq*, 8; Aḥmad, Vol. 2, 381), he is speaking to the greatest possibility of every human being: to fully embody the gnosis of God's presence of nearness and to live it in the most beautiful and prophetic way. This latter understanding is the very definition, goal, and reality of Sufism.

If the outer dimension of Islam focuses on the schools of law, and the intellectual aspects of Islam concern theology, then Sufism is primarily about how to existentially participate in the prophetic virtues that ultimately belong to God's nature that we must actualize within ourselves. Sufism is, thus, primarily a heart-orientation to the divine presence, and through this orientation, it is to awaken to God's true nature and embody and "acquire the character traits of God," (Chittick, 2013, pp. 210, 461) according to a well-known definition of Sufism by one of the earliest authorities of this sacred science, Imām al-Junayd. Each of us has a body, a mind, and a heart, and they all come together to make the human being, which is a unified expression of our spiritual presence that stands beyond these dimensions yet operates within or through them. In the manifested realm, these three dimensions of the human being must be integrated sufficiently to recognize or awaken to our spiritual potential as vicegerent (*khalīfah*) of God on earth.

All three dimensions—body, mind, and heart—must be cultivated in some way, but throughout the history of Islamic spirituality, precedence has always been given to the inward dimension of religion, which is identified with the spiritual heart. A person may perform the formal rituals perfectly, but if they are not sincerely present in worship with God in their heart, then their religious worship is incomplete. This sense of cultivating a more complete, sincere, intimate, and loving presence with God is what Sufism is all about. This emphasis on the inward, without neglecting or contradicting the outward of religion, is embodied in the following Prophetic tradition as found in *Ṣaḥīḥ al-Bukhārī*:

> "There is a part of the body that if ill, the whole body is ill, and if sound in well-being, the whole body is sound. That thing is the heart" (Bukhārī, *Saḥīḥ*, *īmān* 39).

The Islamic science and art of promoting the health and well-being of the spiritual heart is none other than Sufism.

Sufism focuses in a special way on virtue because virtue is directly connected to the heart dimension of the human being, even though the mind or intellect and will are necessary to bring about its full fruition. Virtue in Sufism is an embodiment of the Prophetic nature and presence, or the living reality of the character of the Prophet that is transmitted from his speech, behavior, and comportment in the *hadīth* literature, as well as through the exemplars of those who have embodied these Prophetic virtues most beautifully and thereby most authoritatively. Such embodiment and transmission of virtue has been the special purview of the Sufis. Interestingly, many, if not all, of those who are named in the chains of narration of *hadīth* were considered righteous saints, ascetics, or Sufis. They were recognized as deeply pious and morally upright individuals, and they lived their lives to the fullest by virtue of the wisdom and presence contained in these Prophetic sayings. According to the traditional science of *hadīth* transmission, the recognition of the authenticity of an *isnād* (chain of narration) of a Prophetic tradition was in part due to the veracity of character of its transmitters and their degree of embodiment of Prophetic virtue. The Sufis who transmitted the sayings of the Prophet were recognized as saints because in effect, they were transmitting the sanctified presence of the Prophet (s) through a sense of transparency of their realized presence, actions, and words—and who better to do this than those who were more fully realized as the embodiment of Prophetic virtues?

Sufism has many meanings, as appreciated through the many definitions given to it. Among these definitions is the saying "Sufism is *adab*" (*adab* means courtesy). Courtesy with what? Courtesy with God, first and foremost, but also courtesy with oneself, as well as other human beings; courtesy with the sacred law (*sharī'ah*); and courtesy with an understanding of religion (*fiqh*). Notice that to be courteous with anything, one must be in a state of conscious presence with it, and this leads to virtue. So Sufism as *adab* is a beautiful formulation because it includes being in a state of loving presence with the body, mind, and heart dimensions of the religion, along with the divine presence, all of which are connected in some way to character development and virtue embodiment.

Another important definition of Sufism is as *akhlāq*, or character. This resonates even more directly with the focus on Sufism's connection with virtue embodiment. An early anonymous saying regarding Sufism is "The best in character or the best amongst you is the best in Sufism"—with the understanding that the one who had the best character was the Prophet (s), along with those who follow him (s) the most—inwardly and outwardly. The idea of having good or the best character is also found in the following *ṣaḥīḥ ḥadīth* found in al-Tirmidhī:

> "The best among the believers are those with the best character" (Abu Dāwūd, Sunnan, sunnah 14, 15 jīhād, 15; Bukhārī, Saḥīḥ, īmān 1; Tirmidhī, Jāmi 'a, riḍā', 11; īmān 6, qīyāma 60; Dārimī, Sunan, riqāq 74; Aḥmad, Vol. 2, pp. 250, 472, 528).

There is another ḥadīth found in Ibn Majah, in which the Prophet (s) states,

> "The best among you are those who are best to their family, and I am the best to my family" (Tirmidhī, Jāmi 'a, manāqib 63; Ibn Mājah, Sunan, nikāḥ 50; Dārimī, Sunan, nikāḥ 55).

This is to say, he was best in character—in how he responded to his most intimate family members, even in apparently mundane situations, in courtesy, love, and intimacy, all the while being aware of God with selfless and loving virtue, which is the highest modality of conscious courtesy. It was the hope and prayer of the Prophet (s) that his followers would follow him in beautifying and ennobling character, which is demonstrated in the following *ṣaḥīḥ ḥadīth* also found in Ibn Hibbān:

"Verily, the most beloved of you and closest to me in the hereafter are those with the best character" (Tirmidhī, Jāmi 'a, birr 71).

This is all to say that the best in religion and most beloved by God and His Messenger (s) are those among the followers of Muḥammad (s) who are best in character. If Sufism is centered upon spiritual transformation and character development in a very specialized way within Islam, then those Sufis who actually follow through with the perspective and practice of Sufism as the heart of Islam are among the best of Muslims with regard to character.

Perhaps the greatest definition of Sufism as it concerns true spiritual transformation could be said to be the Prophet's prayer as found in the *ṣaḥīḥ* collection of the Musnad of Ahmad ibn Hanbal:

"Oh God, you have made my physical creation beautiful, so make my character beautiful as well" (Aḥmad; Muslim).

If we apply the content and wisdom of this Prophetic prayer to construct a definition of Sufism, we could say: "Oh God, you have made the outward of my religion with you very beautiful as you have revealed it, so make the inward of my religion just as beautiful as you inspire it!"

As already mentioned, another definition of Sufism is *al-taṣawwuf al-takhallaq bi akhlāqiLlāh*: Sufism is acquiring the character traits of God. This is a profound statement because it refers to what it means to embody virtue in the Islamic understanding: as human beings we are acquiring or participating in the divine qualities through purification. Purification itself is the basis of one of Sufism's etymologies. The Arabic term for Sufism comes from *taṣawwuf*, which is etymologically related to the terms *ṣāf* and *ṣafā*, meaning both purity and wool—for early Sufis wore wool. Another cognate for Sufism is through the term *ṣuffah*, as in the *aṣḥāb al-ṣuffah*, or "people of the bench": those early Companions in the time of the Prophet (s) who were always engaged in contemplation of and meditation upon God. In addition to their explicit mention in various *ḥadīth*, God implicitly mentions these blessed individuals in the Qur'ān in a passage in which the Prophet (s) is commanded to give these individuals his full, heartfelt attention:

"Do not turn away from those who invoke their Lord in the morning and evening, seeking only His face (*wajh*)" (Qur'ān 6:52).

Those among the early Companions of the Prophet (s) who sat for long periods of time, "seeking only the presence of their Lord" through contemplative worship, shunned the extravagances of this world and sat in poverty solely for God—contemplating God's signs and meditating deeply for God's sake, or *wajh*. Interestingly, *wajh* is another cognate for presence, for *wajh* means face, purpose, or essential being—in this context, that of God's intimacy or presence. Such individuals among the Companions of the Prophet (s) who sought the face or presence of God were, after the Prophet (s), the first "Sufis" of Islamic history, who "sat for God" in a state of yearning (*irādah*) and remembrance (*dhikr*). The Prophet (s) was the first of them, as he sat for God's sake in the cave of Ḥirāʾ for a period of time, in isolation, until the revelation of the Qurʾān descended upon his sacred heart and being, and the Prophetic mission began. God commands the Prophet (s) to honor these as his most worthy followers. These early Companions of the Prophet as contemplatives are the prototypes of the Sufis in Islamic history. They were honored by God for the purity of heart and selfless virtue they cultivated through sitting meditation and ritual worship. And it is through this honor that Sufism receives its most noble name. Thus, from the very beginning of Sufism is to be found the indispensable element of spiritual transformation through meditative presence with God and virtue embodiment.

The Process of Virtue Embodiment in Sufism

How does one go about acquiring the character traits or the virtues of God and eliminating human vices? The short answer is in evoking and actualizing the divine love inherent within one's hearts as awakened through the grace of the Muḥammadan presence (*barakah/ḥaḍrah Muḥammadīyah*): for he (s) is the perfect, most loving, and most praiseworthy embodiment of the virtues that belong to God alone. These traits are acquired by following his "most excellent and beautiful model" according to the Qurʾān (33:21), as he is the *uswat al-ḥasanah*. Note that *ḥasanah* is etymologically related to *iḥsān*. This is a process of both attracting and "presencing" the divine love through following the Prophet (s) and of purifying oneself from all that resists this "presencing" and locus of the divine love. This process of virtue embodiment in Sufism is essentially awakening the spiritual heart (*qalb*) and purifying the lower self (*nafs*) and more consciously abiding as presence of heart with God through the medium of the prophetic model.

In this context it may be stated that virtue is an existential meeting in the human spiritual heart between the qualities of divine being and the attitudes of prophetic living. As mentioned, aligned with *ḥadīth* transmission, the early Sufis focused on virtue development—not just with regard to behavior but especially in cultivating a deeply loving relationship and intimate knowing (*maʿrifah*) with God: being present with God in one's heart-presence in every moment of interaction in life, which in turn transforms one's living experience naturally.

As found in Sufi literature on the science of the soul, most of the earliest treatises by Sufis were regarding sincerity in religion, spiritual development, and character transformation. In the context of what has just been said about the Sufi understanding of the nature of virtue, these treatises on virtue or character development were simply pointers to God's presence and how to relate to God through connecting with His qualities and embodying them as Prophetic virtues, within an Islamic context. And indeed, if we stay connected to or in a conscious state of God's presence by Sufi methodologies, the most essential of which is the *dhikr* of Allah, the process itself will guide us to knowing how to act with God and be courteous to Him in any situation. This is the essence of virtue—that is, of acquiring or embodying the divine attributes or qualities of God's being— His *wujūd*—as our being through the cloak of the Muḥammadan virtues. This evokes the Qur'ānic verse,

> "Have *taqwá* [conscious, reverent awareness] of God, and God will teach you" (2:282).

The greatest realization of this verse is the reported (but not authentically established) statement of the Prophet (s), whose meaning and reality is well established: "My Lord taught me *adab* directly." It is for these reasons that the medium and model of this embodiment of virtue is the Prophetic presence and his *sunnah*, which the Sufis understood not just as his outward behavior and actions, but also his speech and internal states of being in God's presence. A well-known saying of the Prophet (s) captures practically everything written here thus far in one line. It is quoted by many Sufi authors in their treatises to describe the Prophet's sublime exemplar and character: "The *sharī'ah* [sacred law] is my words, the *ṭarīqah* [spiritual way] is my acts, and the *ḥaqīqah* [ultimate reality] is my states." (Schimmel, 1975 pp. 99) In order for Muslim seekers to embody religion fully in all its dimensions—body, mind, and heart—they must follow the Prophet (s) in word, act, and state—that is, to follow the Prophet (s) in virtue. This is true and complete courtesy in our religion with God.

The Prophetic virtues go hand in hand with the spiritual stations upon the path to the divine presence, the *maqāmāt*. These virtues are like the outward embodiments of the inward stations of divine presence that is the Prophetic path of Sufism. Certain schools of Sufism may tend to emphasize virtue as outer comportment, but there is also an inner comportment that is the very essence of virtue, what some Sufis have called "the inner *sunnah*." The inner *sunnah* of the Prophet (s) is this subtle heart-meeting of divine Being and the human being through the form or being of the Prophetic nature, or *khuluqin 'aẓīm*, as God describes the Prophet (s) in the Qur'ān (68:4). The Prophetic nature or Muḥammadan presence becomes the celestial model, spiritual bridge, and existential isthmus between our being and God's Being. The Prophetic nature is the authoritative personification and the revealed objectification of our spiritual realization as the primordial or innate norm (*fiṭrah*) upon which God has created all of mankind (see Qur'ān 30:30).

Sincerity as Virtuously Embodied Purification

There are two foundational principles that inform Sufism as a methodology of Islamic spirituality. The first could be described as the objective pole: the knowledge of the reality of God's oneness, of the immediacy of God's presence as beyond (or transcendent) yet within (or immanent in) us and in the world. The subjective pole of Sufism, as understood and articulated by the early sources, is *ikhlāṣ*, an inexhaustible and central term in Islamic spirituality that is usually translated as "sincerity." From this perspective, Sufism is sincerity in worship, sincerity in intention, sincerity in interaction, sincerity in knowing God, and sincerity as inner and outer transparency in one's relationship with oneself and one's loved ones, as well as others, and most importantly, God. To be sincere in Sufism, then, is to embody selfless and Prophetic virtue in a manner that procures spiritual purification of all that is insincere toward God's constant presence. The question is: How does one go about practicing the presence of God and being sincere or embodying this presence in one's character virtuously? In Sufi history, there are two essential ways. The first way is the way of spiritual works. Those who want to reach God need to work to purify themselves of all those things that they are attached to or identified with that lead them away from God's guidance and presence. Second, there is the way of presence that consists of embodying gratitude as a response to the recognition or realization of God's immediate presence or Nearness to oneself.

There is an abundance of stories about the piety of saints and their asceticism. It is important to understand that this asceticism was practiced in the context of the intention of being sincere with God and attaining his good pleasure (*riḍwān*) and for no other reason. Islam as a civilization found itself going from a purely Bedouin society to a predominantly urban one, along with the many luxuries that entailed. In such time periods in Islam's history, especially during Islam's initial civilizational expansion, there was an immediate sense among the scholarly authorities and the righteous and saintly of Islam that something was going wrong with the practice of religion—that many Muslims had lost sincerity because they were so enamored of the luxuries gained by their victories, manifesting as the spread of Islam as a world religion. In this context of striving for sincerity in their religion with God, certain Muslims rejected the lower world (*dunyā*) and the ego's attachment to it. This need was fulfilled through embracing the inner-heart dimension of Islam in the form of Sufism. There was a kind of Christian or even Buddhist sensibility toward asceticism in this early period of the spiritual challenges that came with Islam's expansion as a world religion and civilization. In the context of such expansion, there were significant social, theological, and spiritual interactions among these three great world religions.

There are many well-known historical examples of theological interactions between Islam and other civilizations, such as with Christianity, Buddhism, and Judaism—interactions on the level of the mind. If we also examine the interaction between Muslims and the monks of other traditions that took place on the level of the heart in relation to cultivating spiritual virtues, there is much to be learned. To expound more fully on this would be to digress a bit from the topic of this chapter, but very briefly, one such influence came about through the way that the Christian and Buddhist monks were separating themselves from the world to focus entirely on God—or on their understanding of ultimate reality as revealed to or inspired in them. It is possible that some contemporary Muslims might have thought that that was akin to 'beautiful sincerity' and that they could learn in some way from it. Perhaps because of such interactions, certain Muslims began emphasizing purificatory or ascetic actions as expressions of their Islamic Sufism.

In this context, one of the inherent functions of Sufism was the purification of the human selfhood (*nafs*). *Tazkiyah al-nafs* was highlighted as a defining quality of Sufism. But Sufism is also—and has always been— primarily *taṣfiyah al-qalb*, the purification or washing of the heart. The refinement of the *nafs* and the purification of the heart are essential meanings of Sufism. Purification as a means of reaching God became a normative expression of Sufism, especially in the early or original period of its explicit unfolding as a form of Islam within the tradition. And yet in certain ways, Sufism was moving slowly and subtly away from its original expression in the early Prophetic period, which was actually focused on a combination of a direct knowledge of God and an intimate love of God, as the Prophet (s) taught the Companions. This is clear in the *ḥadīth qudsīs* that were transmitted by the Sufis, which emphasize the immediacy of divine love, which has everything to do with the divine presence, beyond one's effort to be more present, however important the doing of works is. More will be said about this later.

Divine Love, Purification, and Gratitude

An emphasis on knowing the unconditionally loving nature of God may seem to be a new development in Sufism, but as suggested, it is actually a return to the original Prophetic understanding, which in some way involves purification, without making that the starting point of the spiritual path *toward* God, or what Sufism often terms *sayr ilaLlāh*. This emphasis on divine love through intimate awareness (*ma'rifah*) of self and world as rooted in the blessings of God's presence is the way of *shukr*, gratitude. This way of gratitude, which is a perfect balance of the ways of knowledge and love, includes a recognition of the blessing of Islam as a divine mercy of the preserved Qur'ānic revelation and the finality of prophecy embodied by Muḥammad (s), of God's nearness, and then a quite natural thankfulness for this awareness as a concomitant of faith. The Sufi path in this context becomes a process of simply giving thanks to God for having sent a direct and authoritative means to arrive at a fully embodied God-consciousness, through connection with a teacher connected in some way directly to the sources of revelation—the first and foremost teacher being the Prophet (s) himself.

In this way of seeing things and approaching spirituality, the path of purification transforms into the path of recognizing the immediacy of the divine presence as a means of dissolving the egoic self (*nafs*) in order to embody more fully, on the relative plane of the human soul, the divine nearness. This transformation is a kind of awakening or shift from one path (that of purification) to another (that of gratitude), a transition from the journey toward God (*sayr ilaLlāh*) as a "distant" other, to the journey *in* God's presence of nearness, or *sayr fī Llāh*. The means of this purificatory dissolution of the lower self (*nafs*) is the remembrance of God (*dhikr Allāh*), which results in good character (*aḥsan al-akhlaq*). Through gratitude, purification—in and of itself—is often a natural corollary to this awakening to gratitude, but takes a secondary role.

Imām Abū al-Ḥasan al-Shādhilī—who is the founder of the Shādhilī School of Sufism/Islamic spirituality and is considered its most influential master and spiritual pole (*quṭb*)—specifically called his way of divine remembrance "the way of *shukr*," the way of gratitude, which implies a recognition or awakening to the immediacy of the divine presence through transmitted spiritual practices in connection with a realized saintly human soul. This is why the first tenth of the renowned Sufi text the *ḥikam* of Ibn 'Atā Allāh al-Iskandarī (2021), the third major master of the Shādhilī chain, focuses on how seekers should stop relying on their own works in reaching God, for God is already present. All one has to do as a practice is to move out of the way in order to be aligned with the way of gnosis and willful surrender through intimate knowing of God beyond one's sense of doership—or amidst doership. This is the message of the first ten aphorisms, which focus on the illusion of one's effort in reaching God. For we do not reach God at all; God reaches us. And in fact, God has already reached us, for He is ever-present, all-pervasive, vast and all-embracing by

His attributes and essence. This is one of the great meanings of the Qur'ānic verse,

"And if My servants ask you of Me, then verily I am near" (2:186).

To inquire unto God is to recognize His nearness. It is to discover our immediate—that is, non-mediated and direct—presence with God's nearness. This discovery of our immediacy is not because we are directly connected to God, but because God directly connects to us through His immediate presence of nearness.

This is the explicit teaching of Ibn 'Atā Allāh Iskandarī, who is a major early authority of Shādhilī Sufism, which he received from his teachers, Sayyid Abū al-Abbās al-Mursī and Shaykh Abū al-Hasan al-Shādhilī, the spiritual poles of the order. He taught that by attachment to a spiritual guide or *walī* of Allah, one receives the divine love immediately, because God loves those who love and connect themselves to those whom He loves. In this case, God loves those saints or Friends of God who are established in his following of the Prophet (s). God has befriended them out of love due to their sincere and loving following of the Prophet (s) for God's sake. And if you love the ones that God loves, then according to a Prophetic statement,

"You are with the ones you love," (*Sahīh al-Bukharī*).

The Qur'ānic verse that speaks most explicitly to this reality is,

"O you who have Faith, if you love God, follow me [the Prophet], and God will love you" (3:31).

By associating, accompanying, and being in the presence of the master who, as a follower of the Prophet Muhammad (s) and Friend of God, is loved by God, one is in a state of *suhbah*, initiatic companionship, with the master. Such companionship evokes the presence of Divine Love one is seeking. In other words, companionship with the spiritual teacher attracts divine love. This is reminiscent of the original *suhbah* of Islam: the companionship of the blessed Companions with the Prophet (s). Indeed, all Sufi companionship is modeled after this Prophetic paradigm. Such spiritual companionship is a direct path unto God's presence, as it "presences" divine love, which informs the adept's virtue embodiment.

To evoke something—such as divine love—means to more consciously recognize something that is already present. It is an unveiling of that which is apparently hidden, or *kashf al-mahjūb*. Something that is hidden is not necessarily absent—but it must be remembered and thereby invoked in order to be consciously actualized and embodied. This brings us back to the essential methodology of Sufism, the remembrance of God

15

(*dhikr Allāh*), which is the remembrance of a reality that is always present but that we had neglected, which is thereby rendered present as remembrance. It is for this reason of evoking God's presence that invoking the Name of God is the means *par excellence* to purifying the spiritual heart (*qalb*) from the effects of the lower self (*nafs*) that veils the heart from consciously abiding in God's nearness and thereby actualizing or embodying Prophetic virtue.

Differentiating the Way of Purification and the Way of Presence

What follows is a closer examination of these two ways—the way of purification and the way of gratitude. Imām al-Ghazālī, one of the most well-known scholars from Islamic tradition, is more known for speaking of the way of works or the way of purification. However, this kind of labeling can be misleading with regard to his own personal spiritual realization. Certain statements Imām al-Ghazālī made regarding his works on Sufi methods suggest he was aware of the second way of gratitude. Moreover, his own life story and his recognition by the spiritual traditions as one of the great saints (awliyā') and leaders (imāms) of the community, suggest that his path was that of a great opening through both gratitude and purification. He did emphasize in his works, such as the Iḥyā' 'ulūm al-dīn (The Revival of the Religious Sciences) (2017), the necessity of purification of the soul and of the recognition of the blameworthy traits one unconsciously embodies that veil one from God. But he also emphasized in this process embodying more fully or evoking the praiseworthy qualities as foundational in the Prophetic path to God. In this way, he could be said to be the first traditional spiritual psychologist of Islam because he speaks so explicitly about these dynamics of spiritual purification as a mode of immanent self-knowledge rooted in the intellect, and transcendent God-knowledge rooted in divine revelation. But it would be somewhat of a misunderstanding to think of Imām al-Ghazālī as an exclusive proponent of the way of works. When he speaks about the remembrance of God, it is clear he is not saying that we can arrive at God at some later time on the merit of our work of purifying the heart alone. God is already present; our work is the work of moving ourselves out of the way, emptying our minds, and simply being more consciously present in order to rediscover the grace (tawfīq) of God's present presence. This is, in fact, one of the meanings of remembrance in Arabic, as al-Rāghib al-Isfahānī reminds us: dhikr can also mean "rendering present." (Kazemi, 2006, pp. 137) What are those who perform or participate in dhikr rendering present? They are actually rendering themselves, their very being as a presence of heart, more present for that which is already present: God's presence.

This presence with God awakened through a conscious awareness of God's immediacy or nearness is the essence of the Sufi path. The seeker's presence with God emphasizes an intimate knowing of God and of embodying this knowledge on the level of body, mind, and soul. This understanding was already embedded in the tradition of Islamic spirituality even when a gradual approach to purification was taking shape. Purification is important and essential—but from the standpoint of the way of presence (or the way of gratitude), purification is not sufficient for arriving at an abiding awareness of God's nearness. Muslim seekers should start with God and not their own shortcomings: for *lā ilāha illā Llāh* (there is no god but God). This is the very purpose of starting with *dhikr Allāh*. Before our shortcomings, God is real and already present with us. So let us start there, or rather here, in the heart, with God, and then move into working with what is obstructing us from remaining with the awareness of God's ever-present Nearness to us. This is the way of gratitude, the way of presence—the original and essential way of Islam and Sufism.

Shaykh Abū al-Ḥasan al-Shādhilī's way is a return to the origin, which was always the Prophetic way. This is what was meant by "our beginning is their...end." (Hendricks et al., 2019 pp. 50) What seekers of other paths, and especially the path of striving and purification, believe they will receive or be opened to at the end of the journey ("arrival" at God's presence) is already the starting point of the Shādhilī path as a way of gratitude, a way of presence. But then he adds a nuance to the description of his way, something even more elliptical, but to the same point of reciprocity: he says, "and our end is their... beginning." (Hendricks et al., 2019, pp. 50) What the path of purification begins with—that is, the lower self (*nafs*) or purifying the heart from the effects of the separate or lower self—is what the way of gratitude works with toward the end of the path, in order to fully dissolve a sense of separation or distance through an awakened awareness of God's grace and presence of nearness. Such profound nondual perspectives on presence and its relation to the relative levels of the experience of the human soul as duality, which are becoming more in vogue today in contemporary spirituality, have already been present in the tradition as a way of knowledge and a way of love fully rooted within the framework of traditional Islam. Such a way, although present at the beginning of the Islamic revelation, was crystallized into a specific way in the 1200s (CE) (seventh century H), especially through the Shādhilīyah school of Islamic spirituality.

In an apocryphal story, the great Sufi 'Abd al-'Azīz Dabbāgh, an illiterate Shādhilī from Morocco, was once respectfully asked by Islamic scholars, "How do you have authority to say anything concerning religion when you are not formally learned in the religion and do not know how to read?" His followers transcribed his response in the *Ibrīz*: "I inherited the illiteracy of the Prophet and thereby follow only the Prophet (s)." That is to say, "My learning is directly from God. Your learning is from other than God or secondary sources, as your learning comes from books." And then he added a statement that paraphrases the great Sufi Abū Yazīd al-Bisṭāmī: "I learn from the Ever-Living (al-Ḥayy) God, and you learn from the dead and the dying." (Chittick, 2013, pp. 231) Such knowledge or intimate knowing by presence—one's presence with God—as embodied by this great Sufi of the Maghrib (Northwest Africa) is a profound case in point for how presence with God awakens the true seeker to a natural or spontaneous process of purification, character transformation, and virtue embodiment.

The Way of Works, the Way of Gratitude, and Divine Love

To summarize the difference between the two ways of presence and purification, or gratitude and striving, as they concern Sufism, and how they can work in complement, we turn again to the aforementioned great friend and knower of God, ʿAbd al-ʿAzīz al-Dabbāgh. He was asked the following: Another question concerns the difference between the Path of ... al-Shādhilī, and his followers on the one hand, and the path of al-Ghazzālī and his followers, on the other hand. As for the first path, it revolves entirely around thankfulness and joy to the divine Benefactor [that is, God] without hardship and trouble [that is, exerting ourselves or struggling in arriving at God]. As for the other path, it revolves around [self-striving] (*riyāḍa*), fatigue, hardship, sleeplessness, hunger, and suchlike. So ... are the two not in agreement about [self-striving/purification]? And then does al-Shādhilī [enjoin] gratitude after one has come close to reaching God or when reaching Him, or does he [enjoin] gratitude and joy in God from the first instant and the outset? [Finally,] is it possible for one man to travel both these paths or is it impossible to benefit from the one without turning away from the other [?] (Lamaṭī, 2007, pp. 622).

Al-Dabbāgh answered, "The path of thankfulness is the original path, and the one adhered to by the hearts of the prophets, the elect Companions and others as well. It entails worship of God the Sublime with sincerity in being God's bondsman (*ʿubūdiyya*) and disavowal of all allotments in acknowledgement of impotence, shortcoming, and failure to fulfill the rightful claims of Lordliness (*rubūbiyya*), while this [attitude] remains constant in the heart during the passage of hours and periods of time. When God—He is blessed and exalted—knew their truthfulness in this, He rewarded them with what His generosity requires in the way of illumination regarding knowledge of Him and attainment of the secrets of belief in Him—He is mighty and glorious! ..."

And from the start the emigration (*hijra*) on the path of thankfulness was to God and to His Apostle, not to illumination and the acquisition of unveilings. Emigration on the path of self-mortification, however, was aimed at illumination acquisition of spiritual ranks.

Journeying on the first path is a journey of hearts, while on the second path it's a journey of bodies. And illumination on the first path is a sudden onslaught that the bondsman hadn't been desiring. While the bondsman was in the station of seeking repentance and forgiveness of sins, behold clear illumination came over him (Lamaṭī, 2007, pp. 622–623).

While some in the way of striving are busy with burdensome yet at times rewarding practices, those in the way of gratitude are simply *busy with being present in their hearts with God*: sometimes asking for forgiveness, but all the time just trying to be with God in their hearts. Their outer modes of worship, he goes on to say, may not be especially valiant. They may even seem ordinary in their following of the religion and religious or sacred law. But their inner hearts are constantly with God. It is this constant inner attentiveness or vigilance of heart-presence with God, known in Sufism as *murāqabah*, that is their true yet subtle inner work. Hence this way is deemed to be a way (or walking) of hearts, in distinction to a way (or walking) of bodies, which describes a way more fixated on bodily acts that purify the body and mind to obtain the spiritual opening (*fatḥ*). In other words, the first group of seekers seek to directly awaken their presence of heart in their orientation to their religion with God by starting with the heart and not with that which obstructs it. This is none other than a very clear description of the spiritual orientation of *iḥsān* as a way of presence embodied as Prophetic gratitude. Al-Dabbāgh continues, "Both paths are correct but the path of thankfulness is more correct and more sincere. Both paths are in agreement about self-mortification but in the first there is self-mortification of hearts by means of their attachment to God—He is mighty and glorious—and their compulsory devotion to His door and taking refuge with God in what one does and omits to do, and avoiding the forgetfulness that occurs in between one's occasions of spiritual presence (*ḥuḍūr*). In short, self-mortification consists of attaching one's heart to God—He is sublime and exalted—and perseverance in this, even if the exterior isn't involved with immense worship. Therefore the one who adopts it fasts and breaks his fast, rises [at night] and sleeps, is intimate with women, and undertakes all the stipulations of the law contrary to mortification of the flesh (Lamaṭī, 2007, pp. 623)."

In this light, al-Dabbāgh describes the way of gratitude as "devotion to His door and taking refuge with God in what one does and omits to do," and abiding in such "occasions of spiritual presence." He specifically uses the Arabic word *ḥuḍūr* for what is rendered in English in the above statement as "spiritual presence." This is why the way of presence, as we have briefly alluded to here and more so elsewhere, can be said to be synonymous with how "the way of gratitude" is understood in traditional Sufism in general, and Shādhilī Sufism in particular. "Presence" is a good synonym for "gratitude" in this context as gratitude starts with recognizing and deepening our awareness of what is already present by way of divine bestowal, such as the great blessings of existence and simply being Muslim and guided to Islam—which is understood by faith and direct verification to be a path protected by grace, and the well-traveled Prophetic way, as the *sunnah* of Muḥammad (s). Such gratitude as one's spiritual orientation is a Prophetic expression of the awareness of one's impotence and of God's omnipresence and loving embrace. Spiritual works or practices of purification are then engaged with as a natural response to a heart-felt gratitude for God's immense blessings.

To be sure, both of these ways (presence/gratitude as well as purification/striving) are valid ways of spiritual realization, according to al-Dabbāgh. Everyone begins somewhere—often striving to find some kind of opening to God's grace. But at some point, according to al-Dabbāgh, a sign of sincerity and maturity on the specific way of purification is that the seeker recognizes that everything—including the spiritual opening (*fatḥ*)—is directly from God without the intermediary of the merit of one's doership, especially as it concerns gnosis of God. If it took a lot of effort—even years upon years of effort—to come to this realization by direct experience that, in our path to God, "there is no might or power except it be God's" (*lā ḥawla wa-lā quwwata illā biLlāh*) then such conscious effort of purification that somehow made one more available for such a realization was worth it. But at this moment, what is relied upon is not one's own doership but a sense of surrendering doership to abide more deeply in the knowing of God's immediacy, intimacy, and nearness as presence. Thus, we return to Imām al-Shādhilī's statement "Our beginning is their end."

All in all, this kind of spiritual awakening is nothing more than a shift in perspective in one's spiritual purification and journeying (*sulūk*) from the path of works and purification to a path of gratitude and presence. Each path complements the other. But the way of presence is a more direct and sincere path. It is also a more comprehensive or integral path that encompasses the way of purification, whereas the way of purification may, by grace, be opened unto the path of presence. In any case, the way of presence may integrate when necessary, and with whatever means within the Prophetic framework, the way of purification as a mode of embodying gratitude. Yet the underlying pivot and the central orientation of the way of presence is a way of humble yet celebratory gratitude to God, who is discovered to already be present through a surrendering faith, humbling gnosis, and celebratory spiritual love.

This complementarity is also noted by the following commentary upon al-Dabbāgh's statement by Habib Umar bin Hafiz, a contemporary Islamic and Sufi authority who is quoted by Shaykh Seraj Hendricks and Dr. H. A. Hellyer (2019), who identifies this complementarity and combination of both ways as a signature of the Ba'Alawī tradition. His commentary upon the above long reference to al-Dabbāgh is found in the book *A Sublime Way*, "Both the Ghazali and Shādhilī paths are founded upon spiritual striving (mujāhadah) but the Ghazalian method begins by focusing on the external aspect and then works towards the internal whereas the Shādhilī method begins internally. Both methods agree that obligatory actions must be performed, prohibited actions must be avoided and supererogatory actions should be performed in abundance, but the Shādhilī method does not place great emphasis on outward actions. Mujāhadah, according to the Shādhilī method, focuses on attaining constant presence of heart with Allāh, awareness of His bounty and showing gratitude to Him. The Ghazalian method emphasizes seeking knowledge and acting upon it thereby attaining constant presence and the station of gratitude."

It is possible to combine the two methodologies, and this is manifested in the Bā 'Alawī path. This is achieved by being aware of Allāh's blessings, showing gratitude to Him and seeking to be present with Him from the outset while at the same time seeking knowledge and performing outward actions. (Hendricks & Hellyer, 2019, p. 39)

This complementarity of the ways of gratitude and purification as the practice of presence is what Sufism offers. As Rūmī says regarding the spiritual opening, eventually seekers realize that they were never the real seekers; they were always the sought. God is seeking us. When we more fully recognize this, we are finally found and arrive at the placeless place that is the Presence of God's Nearness. This awareness then begins to inform one's spiritual traveling and facilitate a more selfless form of virtue embodiment. When this shift occurs, the heart awakens to an immediate presence with God. In this light, the heart awakens to the presence of divine love that is inherent in and as the very substance of the heart, prior to any love for God that comes from the seeker, as the separate and apparently distant self. In the words of Abū Yazīd al-Bisṭāmī found in many treatises: "At the beginning I was mistaken in four respects. I sought to remember God, to know Him, to love Him, and to seek Him. When I had come to the end, I saw that He had remembered me before I remembered Him, that His knowledge of me had preceded my knowledge of Him, His love toward me had existed before my love to Him, and He had sought me before I sought

Him." (Frager & Fadiman, 1997, pp. 200) That God, in our direct experience of our "self" is prior to our perception of what we are, is truly an awakening to the presence of God's loving nearness to us. This is true presence with God, and it facilitates profound character transformation and selfless virtue.

All paths ultimately converge upon divine love and are realized to be nothing but divine love—sometimes the tough love of spiritual hardship and sometimes the sweet love of graceful ease, but ultimately the pure oneness that is love. This recalls the well-known Qur'ānic verses:

"Verily with hardship comes ease. Indeed with every hardship there is ease" (94:5–6).

We come full circle to a fuller realization of the *ḥadīth qudsī* where God says,

"I was a hidden treasure and I loved to be known. And so I created the world."

In other words, God was this hidden treasure of love as divine essence, and that He loved to share as if there was something other than Him to share it with. And so He objectified Himself into apparent existence as an object of devotion. When that object of divine devotion is found to be the spiritual heart of the human being, that heart through purification and journeying comes to recognize God's Presence in and as its true self. This whole cosmogonic process begins with love; its means is love; and its end is love. That love is nothing other than the treasure of the divine presence hidden in everything, and especially in the heart of human subjectivity as a seed or spark of love: loving to be known; and knowing to be loved.

Purification and Presence as Modes of Realizing and Embodying Divine Love

"I was a hidden treasure and loved to be [known], so I created the world in order to be [known]" – Hadith Qudsi (Chittick, 2013, pp. 4)

In the deepest sense, whether it is the way of purification or gratitude that allows us to recognize and bear witness to divine love and to begin a process of Prophetic embodiment of this love as selfless virtue, it is all one and the same way of presence with God. In many ways, the spiritual path is nothing other than the divine presence within us that is loving to be known through the human journey manifested as the experience of the inner struggles pertaining to striving of purification and the grace of presence.

According to certain schools of Sufi spirituality, love is divine and human. When love is divine, it is unconditioned, and it unconditionally loves to be known as an apparent other and through an apparent other. To say "world" and "creation" is to say other. It is to say distance, and thereby separation. As an apparent other, it is a love that manifests in the yearning and aspiration of the human soul to come to know and return to its very source of longing and loving as love itself. Through an apparent other, it is the very reflection of itself as love that yearns to be loved in and as other. This process of love is understood in Sufi spirituality as attraction (*jadhbah*). It is where divine and human love meet in a pull of grace and as that very pull itself. When human aspiration appears to dominate this process, we find ourselves in a journey of longing and yearning for and aspiring toward God, the source of love. This *himmah* is the fuel of love that facilitates the process toward self-transcendence that involves the purification of detaching ourselves from all that we come to love selfishly and are attached to in a self-interested or particular manner, in order to find selfless love in a universal manner.

When *jadhbah*-love dominates from the divine side of love, this pulls the consciousness of human seekers into the source of their yearning in order to realize their true source of self as love. When *maḥabbah* (love) dominates from the divine and manifests on the human side, what is realized is that love was always present, is already present, and will forever be present, before, through, and after one's aspiration for love. Apparent longing ceases because love has found itself in and as the longing. Longing is then expressed as a celebration of a natural unfolding of all that is. The whole is already the part, and the part is already the whole. The journey was and is from divine love to divine love, within divine love, and with divine love, back to divine love, as divine love.

In Islamic spirituality it is said that God's love is attained through human *himmah* or aspiration in two essential ways: one is through striving with acts of obedience and devotion; the other is through simply living and performing all tasks of life with the intention of their being for God's sake and His love alone. The former path involves what is called "gaining nearness to God through acts of worshipful devotion" (*qurb al-nawāfil*). It is stated in a *ḥadīth qudsī* cited in al-Bukhārī and by Imām Nawawī,

> "My servant never ceases to draw near me through devotional worship.... And My servant continues to draw near me until I love him, and when I love him, I am the Hearing with which he hears, the Seeing with which he sees."

This way to divine love involves a progressive yearning and the progression of spiritual aspiration toward being loved by God through the merit of spiritual works and devotional acts toward God.

The second way of attaining divine love is more direct, yet it is subtle and even difficult, as it involves a vigilant selflessness for God's sake. The Prophet (s) states (as cited in Aḥmad's ṣaḥīḥ collection),

> "My love is certainly due toward those who love for My sake, who gather for My sake, who visit each other for My sake, and who spend for My sake" (Mālik, *Muwaṭṭa', sha'r* 16; Aḥmad, Vol. 5, 233, 247).

Here, love is an immediate consequence of one's intentions, before, within, and beyond the actions of devotion performed. There is a great grace here of the directness of divine love, whose fruits of blessings immediately bring the servant into God's presence of love. While this way is more direct, it involves the subtle work of checking inner intentions and remaining vigilantly open to a sense of love and gratitude for divine love. It is none other than the way of gratitude found in the *hadīth* cited above.

However, there is an even more direct or immediate way to divine love. It is to recognize that divine love is already and always present unconditionally. It is to recognize the immediacy and unconditionality of God's eternal love for His creation, especially for the human soul. When this is recognized truly for what it is, then love is rendered present by realizing it has already been present. When this insight and awareness is fixed in the mind and heart, life is then lived without end-gaining or striving toward a goal to reach something even as lofty as divine love—because it is already found as the beginning, middle, and end of our relative or temporal existence. Life is celebrated as divine love through such understanding. This is a most pure way of presence in which seekers discover the presence of God's nearness as their truest being, as love. This wisdom is found in the Prophetic tradition cited previously: "I was a hidden treasure, and loved to be known."

From the stance of this third perspective on divine love—the unconditionality and omnipresence of divine love—striving or struggling as well as simply doing things is no different because love is ever-present and is not conditioned upon striving up until a point is reached—as in "until I love him." Nor is it conditioned upon having vigilance with an intention—as in "My Love is certainly due for those who love for My sake." (Tijani, 2022) Since the one who is of this way is aware that love is already present and therefore already given and received, the means become an expression of a love already received but recognized or found in the contemplative "now" of our very being and living—not of a love "attained" through a doing of those same means.

The first kind of attainment of divine love is experienced as a *progression* toward gaining a sense of God's nearness, through *striving* with acts of devotion that then by grace reveal God's nearness to the servants seeking through the attributes of hearing, seeing, etc. This progressive spiritual path toward divine love realized as the intimacy of nearness is akin to what certain Sufis call the "journey toward God" (*sayr ilaLlāh*). This is a normative way or means of approach to God or His presence through spiritual purification (*tazkiyah*). It is the approach of a *nafs* (an ego-self/mind-body) that understands it is separated, distant, or far from God that needs to be purified of the conditioned effects of its conscious and unconscious ego-conditioning in order to be worthy of entering upon the nearness of the divine presence encountered as the divine grace of love. This journey as a spiritual practice may be termed *mujāhadah* (striving).

The second kind of attainment of divine love is experienced as an awakening to God's intimacy of nearness as love through a vigilance with one's inner orientation toward all acts of devotion, no matter how big, small, or consistent these acts appear to be. This more direct route of awakening is what the Sufis would identify as the "journey in God" (*sayr fi Llāh*). Here, one is awakened to an experience of God's direct nearness as love. It is the approach of an awakened *qalb* (spiritual heart) that knows more intuitively that all it has to do is subtly open itself and vigilantly remain open to the presence of God's nearness as divine love. This journey as a vigilant spiritual practice can be termed *murāqabah* (vigilance). It is the "devotion to His door" and "spiritual presence" that al-Dabbāgh (2007) speaks of with regard to the way gratitude (*shukr*).

The third kind of way is a way that *awakens* to and *expresses* the immediate love of God that is already present in an effortless and unconditional sense. This immediate way of simply embodying more consciously what already is, is what the Sufis would identify as the "journey with God" (*sayr bi Llāh*). In the language of spiritual wayfaring, it is the approach of one's *sirr* or secret with God that simply bears witness to the unfolding of God's secret as one's life. This journey is a return to witnessing everything in one's life or every part of one's direct experience as one's whole secret with God. It may be termed *mushāhadah* (witnessing).

While the three ways are not mutually exclusive, they each point to a particular way that God's love is either attained, realized, or recognized by a level or dimension of human selfhood, and as a specific kind of spiritual standing, rank, or conscious stance (*maqām*) with God. The first way as *spiritual progression* aligns with *the way of purification* of the lower self (*nafs*) and religious and spiritual works; whereas the second way of *attracting directly* the divine love aligns with *the way of gratitude* or the way of presence, which awakens the seeker to the verities of the spiritual heart (*qalb*). Finally, the third way of *immediate recognition* of the precedence of divine love as prior to and the cause of our existence opens us to the immediacy of our secret with God as an expression of love. This third way could be called *love's way*, rather than the way of love. It is what Ibn 'Arabī calls "the religion of love." Love's way aligns with what could be termed the divine secret of human consciousness and being and allows life and living to unfold as God's loving secret with the human heart. It is a secret because it is only the individual as subject that can experience his or her unique secret with God. No one can know that or do that for anyone else. Yet the secret is one and the same for all—however uniquely it is realized and manifested in life.

While the starting point of each way is particular and distinct, each can benefit or be complemented by the other, especially as it concerns spiritual transformation, the cultivation of Prophetic virtues, and even self-transcendence. The first way of seeking divine love procures a sufficient purification of all that which veils us from God, as *nafs*. The *nafs* must be purified to a sufficient degree of its constricting egoic hardness and selfishness in order to be more *sustainably* opened to the experience of the divine presence as a selfless vastness of our heart-center (*qalb*). The second way of being with the divine love procures a sufficient presence of heart with God in order to deeply awaken to the all-encompassing and all-embracing nature of divine love as the secret (*sirr*) between God and the human being. The third way of recognizing and surrendering the pre-eternal immediacy of divine love allows God's secret (*sirr*) with human beings to unfold as an effortless yet humbling and grateful moment-to-moment awareness of the divine love as the true witness, which is then embodied on the level of the heart and the *nafs* (mind-body) in one's life.

The more purified the *nafs* and soul are toward God, the more receptive they are to recognizing and abiding in the immediacy of divine love as discovered in the heart (*qalb*). The more receptive the heart is intellectually and spiritually to this same immediacy of divine love, the more seekers "purify" themselves, their thoughts, their emotions, and their acts for love's sake as their lives unfold. Such a process of unfolding cannot but bring about even more divine love. This mode of *iḥsān*, as the religion of love, can only be realized as, as the Qur'ān states,

"Light upon light," (24:35).

In the end, purification is an expression of gratitude for awakened love. And love purifies one of any sense of separateness or otherness that the lower self (*nafs*) thrives upon.

Divine Love as Humanity's Final Frontier: Sufism and the Third Spiritual Journey of Integration of the Human Soul

This leads to a final and brief reflection on models of spiritual transformation and the third and final spiritual journey of the human soul as experienced by a blessed few in this lifetime. The spiritual transformation along this third journey of the human soul already encompasses self-transcendence as an intimate gnosis of the divine presence. The virtues in this journey are less about "development" and more of a Prophetic *embodiment* of virtue, as well as the contemplative *participation* in the unfolding of divine qualities that the sanctified and more fully integrated soul in this journey bears witness to, by divine choosing. In order to better understand this third journey, it will be briefly compared to the first two journeys alluded to in the previous section. This will help bring into context how divine love as purification and divine love as presence serve to some degree the possibility of vertical or spiritual transcendence and horizontal or psychospiritual integration of the human soul.

Theoretically and practically, as we find in the living embodiment of the prophets of God, may peace be upon them all, and the greatest of saints (*awliyā'/ṣiddiqīn*), it is in the third journey that a fuller or more complete integration of the spiritual and psychological or vertical and horizontal aspects of human consciousness occur by the grace of God, manifested as the fulfillment of divine love, "loving to be known," in its human fullness. At its full degree of development or divine self-disclosure, we have the manifestation of divine guidance through the soul of the Prophet Muḥammad (s), as found in the form of the sacred law (*sharī'ah*) of Islam. While the sacred law is the divine product of the third journey of the greatest of human souls (s), this law applies to all souls upon each and every journey. How one relates to this sacred law (whether from one's ego-self, spiritual heart, or inmost secret) depends on that person's footing in the first, second, or third journey (respectively). On each level or stage of the journey, the sacred law serves as an indispensable support for spiritual transformation and virtue embodiment.

The first journey of the human soul is the soul that believes and feels a great separation from God, amidst its own awe of God's presence and its own tendency to forget God, and even its tendency to reject God. It is here, in this human atmosphere or perspective of its place in reality, that purification is required. Purification is primarily from the accrued effects of the tendencies to act out our sense of separation from things and also a purification from reinforcing selfish tendencies of the ego-self (*nafs*). The way of purification is a way of striving and of religious, spiritual, and ethico-moral works. Those works are determined by the degree of one's adherence to the sacred law.

The second journey is that of the soul that has been more deeply awakened to the presence of God's nearness, manifested as grace, penetrating spiritual insight, discernment, humility, and gratitude. It is truly the journey of an awakened heart, whose spiritual vision is clearer and more direct with regard to its "object" of contemplation: God's presence. It is this heart (*qalb*) that more fully embodies the degree of *iḥsān* as communicated by Prophet Muḥammad (s) as the third dimension or level of religious practice:

"*Iḥsān* is to worship God as if you see Him."

Once one is sufficiently stabilized and abides as the awareness of divine nearness, or intimacy of divine presence, self-transcendence has effectively occurred in a manner that procures some degree of sufficient spiritual transformation. It is here that virtue development reaches a peak of "attainment" as one's sense of doership is genuinely surrendered and relinquished to its true source in God. Virtue is no longer being "done"; it is being participated in as an unfolding of existence rooted in the divine qualities. The definition of Sufism as "acquiring the character traits of God" is most apt and more fully realized at the peak of the second journey. It is for this reason that this second journey corresponds to the inner contemplative dimension of the sacred law, as the spiritual path (*ṭarīqah*).

It is perhaps in the third journey alone that the true meaning and reality of the definition of Sufism, "Sufism is *adab*" (spiritual courtesy), is borne witness to. At the heart of virtue as Prophetic virtue, God is found bearing witness to His own beautiful qualities. In this is to be found the meaning of the Prophetic *ḥadīth,*

"God taught me *adab* directly."

The directness of the "learning" of courtesy is the directness of Prophetic presence with God: God's sacred presence and humanity's gracious absence as Prophetic embodiment. This realized oneness of presence as courtesy is nothing other than pure and selfless divine love realized in the mirror of its self-reflection on the more relative plane of the human soul. If the early Sufis focused so much on Prophetic virtues and character development, it is for the reason that, under the care of a guide, through embodying such virtues more sincerely, devotedly, and selflessly, one passes quite profoundly, more directly, and most abidingly through the first and second journeys to arrive at the third great journey. When one arrives at the third journey, one has already been found with God, and any "subsequent" purifications with regard to the more relative aspects of our existence manifesting as our soul, relationships, and roles and interactions in life are simply modes of living Prophetic presence with God. The love that guides and heals our relationships with others in this journey is akin to the love of grandparents for their grandchildren and the sheer joy of gratitude for simply being present for it all. When one lives fully as this transparency of grateful love with all things in God, one lives the completeness of the third journey. This calls to mind the Prophetic statement mentioned at the beginning of this essay: "I was only sent to perfect noble character traits (*makārim al-akhlaq*)"—as well as the beautiful Prophetic prayer that is meant for the followers of Muḥammad (s), and truly any sincere seeker of God: "Oh God, you have made my physical creation beautiful, so make my character beautiful as well!"

Thus, to the question of whether it is purification, gratitude, or love that wins the day as the most apt model of spiritual transformation and virtue development, it depends entirely upon whether the human soul who makes this inquiry in order to "beautify character" is upon the first, second, or third spiritual journey. On the first journey, more of the way of personal purification is needed in order to receive glimmers of self-transcendence. Spiritual transformation transitions from a transient state (*ḥāl/aḥwāl*) to an abiding station (*maqām*) as a soul enters upon the second spiritual journey, which aligns more to the way of gratitude. Some degree of integration of the human soul with one's discovery of presence or self-transcendence occurs. A fuller psycho-spiritual integration of the human soul and personality occurs as divine love manifests itself in a more abiding way as the expression of a selfless and transparent, yet discerning and devoted, Prophetic living. We bear witness to God's with-ness. Life has always been and always is God "loving to be known." True and abiding spiritual transformation reveals God's oneness (*tawḥīd*) as a transparently transcendent inter-connectedness that is life. There is and can be no other, when it is realized that there is only the divine presence of Self in all.

References

Chittick, W. C. (2013). *Divine Love: Islamic Literature and the Path to God.* Yale University Press.

Frager, R. & Fadiman, J. (1997). *Essential Sufism.* Castle Books.

Al-Ghazālī, A. Ḥ. (2017). *Al-Ghazālī on Discipling the Soul (Kitāb Riyāḍat al-Nafs) and on Breaking the Two Desires (Kitāb Kasr al-shahwatayn): Books XXII and XXIII of the Revival of the Religious Sciences (Iḥyā' 'Ulūm al-Dīn)* (T. J. Winters, Trans.) Fons Vitae. (Original work written 12th century).

Hendricks, Shaykh Seraj, & Hellyer, H. A. (2019). *A sublime way: The Sufi path of the sages of Makka.* Fons Vitae.

Ibn 'Ajībah, A. (2021). *Four gems of Tasawwuf.* (Aisha Abdurrahman Bewley, Trans.). Diwan Press Ltd.

Al-Iskandarī, I. & Gangōhī, A. (2014) *The book of wisdoms: Kitāb al-Ḥikam: A collection of Sufi aphorisms.* (Victor Danner, Trans.). White Thread Press.

Kazemi, R. (2006). *Justice and remembrance: introducing the spirituality of Imam 'Alī.* Islamic Publications, Ltd.

Lamaṭī, Aḥmad b. al-Mubarak al-. (2007). *Pure gold from the words of Sayyidī 'Abd al-'Azīz al-Dabbāgh (Al-Dhabab al-Ibrīz min Kalām Sayyidī 'Abd al-'Azīz al-Dabbāgh)* (J. O'Kane and B. Radtke, Trans.). Brill.

Schimmel, Annemarie. (1975). *Mystical Dimensions of Islam.* University of North Carolina Press.

CHAPTER 2

Acquiring the Character Traits of God
(Takhalluq bi Akhlāq Allah) and
Character Development Through Cognitive Reappraisal

Haseena Sahib & Maneeza Dawood, PhD

Abstract

Acquiring and embodying the character traits of God (His names and attributes) is a fundamental component of Islamic spirituality. This process of *Takhalluq bi Akhlāq Allah* involves developing one's character and behavior to mirror the attributes of God such as mercy, forbearance, wisdom, and justice. In this chapter, we explore the concept of *Takhalluq bi Akhlāq Allah* and how it can be achieved through cognitive reappraisal, a psychological technique that involves changing, or reframing, one's thoughts and perceptions about a situation. We contend that challenging life experiences are opportunities for people to examine the spectrum of divine names and imbibe those that speak most to those unique circumstances. We examine the research on cognitive reappraisal and its effectiveness in promoting positive emotions and behavior change and discuss its application in the context of developing godly character traits with examples from the life of Prophet Muḥammad. We conclude the chapter with a discussion and recommendations for the future use of cognitive reappraisal as a technique for character development and embodying the divine names.

THE WAY OF LOVE

وَإِنَّكَ لَعَلَى خُلُقٍ عَظِيمٍ

"You [Muḥammad] are upon an exalted character." (Qur'ān, 68:4)

Acquiring the character traits of God (*Takhalluq bi Akhlāq Allah*), or embodying God's divine names and attributes, is a core concept in Islam in general and in Sufism (*Taṣawwuf*) more explicitly. In fact, the great Islamic scholar, philosopher, and mystic, Ibn al-Arabī (d. 638/1240) stated in his longest work and comprehensive *Futūḥāt* - in which he expounds on the Qur'ān and the spiritual journey - that the whole path of Sufism is acquiring the character traits of God (Chittick, 1989). Ibn al-'Arabī also stated that "God did not name Himself by any name without appointing for man a share in assuming the trait of that name" (Chittick, 1989, p. 283). Unfortunately, this realm of knowledge and practice (acquiring the divine names) has been underrepresented in contemporary Islamic education and psychological literature. The current emphasis is on purification of the soul/self (*tazkiyat al-nafs*), which is as equally important, but is usually a precursor to the greater spiritual stations (*maqāmāt*) of embodying the divine names. The first path - purification of the soul - aims to remove the blameworthy and unpleasant characteristics of the soul, such as jealousy, pride, anger, and lust. The second path - acquiring the divine names - aims for the human soul to embody the beautiful attributes of God, such as mercy, justice, forbearance, and generosity. In fact, the primary meaning of the root letters in *tazkiyat* mean to grow and thrive, and *not* purification as contemporary Islamic literature tends to emphasize. The prominent Islamic scholar and mystic Imam al-Ghazālī (d. 505/1111) attempted to join the two realms of purification and virtue development when he described *tazkiyat al-nafs* as a process of perfecting one's soul by means of both cutting down its desires and allowing its noble characteristics to evolve (Winter, 1997).

The path of developing virtues or acquiring the character traits of God views the soul as a neutral entity that has the potential to receive and manifest the beautiful attributes of God, rather than an egoistic entity that succumbs to carnal desires. This is a powerful cognitive shift that has the potential to decrease anxiety, depression, and stress in humans, and increase aspiration, excitement, and will-power. Acquiring the divine names shifts the focus from the limitations and removal of the lower tendencies of the human ego to a practice of conscious awareness, acquisition, and manifestation of the divine names.

In this chapter we begin by exploring Ibn al-'Arabī's and Qur'ānic thought in the acquisition of the divine names and character traits of God. We will then examine how using the psychological concept of cognitive reappraisal can be a useful tool in acquiring the traits of God, and analyze various examples from the life of Prophet Muḥammad that demonstrate the use of cognitive reappraisal and the embodiment of divine attributes. The chapter will conclude with a discussion and some recommendations for potential ways to move forward with this path of inquiry.

Ibn al-ʿArabī's Thought on Acquiring the Traits of God

The names of God are considered to be a source of inspiration and guidance for Muslims seeking to develop their character and cultivate a deeper relationship with God. The process of *Takhalluq bi Akhlāq Allah* involves reflecting on the names of God and striving to embody the qualities they represent in one's own life. For example, the name *Al-Raḥmān* (the Most Merciful) represents God's attribute of universal mercy, and Muslims are encouraged to manifest mercy and compassion towards others and their own selves throughout their lives. Similarly, the name *Al-Ḥakīm* (the Wise) represents God's attribute of wisdom, and Muslims are encouraged to contemplate knowledge and apply it judiciously in new circumstances as they arise. Reflecting on the name *Al-Wadūd* (the Most Loving) allows Muslims to better express love, especially during times of service to oneself and others. Reflecting on the names *Al-Mālik* (the King) and *Al-ʿAdl* (the Just) can cultivate a sense of humility before God's just sovereignty, in addition to cultivating a sense of just leadership towards other humans on earth. After sincere human effort, Sufi scholars advise that God Himself will make it easy for His servants to embody His names and will facilitate the process with ease. Each of these names represents a different aspect of God's character, and reflecting on and embodying these names allow Muslims to cultivate a deeper sense of spirituality and connection with Him. The number of the names of God are popularly described as 99, however the actual number is infinite since God is beyond limitation and demarcation. The names presented in the Qurʾān and ḥadīth provide the initial framework for developing a holistic understanding of God's nature and character, and thereby for developing human character.

Ibn al-ʿArabī expressed that *Takhalluq bi Akhlāq Allah* was essential for spiritual growth and enlightenment. By cultivating the qualities of God within oneself, one could attain a deeper understanding of both divine and human nature, and thereby draw closer to God. The following passage from Ibn al-ʿArabī confirms that knowledge of the divine names is a duty upon man, exclusive of other creations, "No existent thing is named by all the divine names except man, who has been charged to assume the names as his own traits. That is why he was given the vicegerency and the deputyship, and the knowledge of all the names. He was the last configuration within the cosmos, bringing together all the realities of the cosmos," (Futūḥāt II 603.4, found in Chittick, 1989, p. 286).

Only humans can "bring together all the realities" because they are the only creation with the capacity to manifest the full spectrum of the divine names. In fact, all of the divine names are already within the human's original constitution or primordial nature. Ibn al-'Arabī states, "All of the divine character traits are found in man's innate disposition," and, "God is generous without delimitation, and so also man is generous without delimitation" (Chittick, 1989, p. 287). The human is the goal and fruit of existence and has been entrusted with taking care of the earth and manifesting the names of God in it.

In addition to human effort and contemplation, acquiring the divine names is also a process of God bestowing them onto His servants. Ibn al-'Arabī believed that true understanding of God's character and qualities cannot be attained through intellectual analysis alone, but also through direct experience via spiritual tasting and unveiling, whereby God discloses the secrets of His names directly to His servants. Ibn al-'Arabī stated, "God is the Necessary Being through Himself, while man exists through His Lord, so he acquired existence and character traits from Him" (Chittick, 1989, p. 287) and "God discloses Himself to the lover in the names of engendered existence and in His Most Beautiful Names" (Chittick, 1989, p. 43).

Acquiring the character traits of God is also a sign of sincerity in love and a means of deepening one's love for God. The following passage from Ibn al-'Arabī elucidates this. He explains that those more in love with God will become qualified by His traits, since the lover always takes on the traits of their beloved:

Sincerity in love makes the lover become qualified by the attributes of the beloved. The same is true in the sincere servant's love of his Lord. He assumes the traits of His names. So he becomes qualified by "independence" from anything other than God, "exaltation" through God, "giving" through the hand of God, and "preservation" by the eye of God. The learned masters know about assuming the traits of God's names and have written many books about it. Since they loved God, they became qualified by His attributes to the degree appropriate for them (Futūḥāt III 398.21, as cited in Chittick, 1989, p. 284).

Love for God is exemplified through the embodiment and acquisition of His divine names. Thus, using every experience and encounter in life as a means to acquire the divine names is also essentially a means of increasing and developing one's love for God.

Emphasis on Character Development in the Qur'ān and Ḥadīth

The Qur'ān highlights both the ethical and ontological connotation of the term "character" (*khuluq*) when it speaks directly to Prophet Muḥammad and states

"Truly you are of a *khuluq 'adthīm*" (Qur'ān, 68:4).

Pickthall translates this description as "tremendous nature"; Arberry translates it as "mighty morality"; and Nasr translates it as "exalted character" (Chittick, 1989, p.21). These various translations indicate that the Prophet's character was not only described by his interactions and dealings with people (ethics), but was a manifestation of his innate, primordial nature (ontology). The qualities and character traits of generosity, justice, benevolence, patience, and all other virtues are not extraneous to his natural human state. Rather, they define what it means to be "Muḥammadan." Since all humans are advised by the Qur'ān to follow the example of Prophet Muḥammad, his character traits are also the definition of being "human," and in the Islamic tradition he is considered to be the perfected human being (*al-insān al-kāmil*). He was able to actualize the full spectrum of the divine names and reach the fullness of existence. Chittick (1989), in his discussion of character in the Qur'ān, writes, "Only by actualizing such qualities [virtues] does one participate in the fullness of existence" (p. 21).

This fullness and apex of existence was reached by all the prophets and many saints (close friends of God). However, the character of Prophet Muhammad is consistently highlighted throughout the main sources of classical Islamic religious literature as the fountainhead of beautiful human character. The Prophet himself stated,

"I was sent [as a prophet] to complete the beautiful character traits (al-Muwaṭṭa', 1614)."

The Prophet's last wife 'Ā'isha stated that the Prophet's character was the Qur'ān (Ḥadīth in Muslim), equating the nobility and beauty in the sacred text with his character. The Prophet also advised his followers to cultivate good character when he stated,

"Among the best of you is the one most beautiful in character traits" (Ḥadīth in Bukhārī, Muslim & Tirmidhī).

"The most perfect of the faithful in faith is the most beautiful of them in character" (Ḥadīth in Bukhārī, Muslim & Tirmidhī)

"The best thing in the scale on the Day of Judgment will be a beautiful character" (Ḥadīth in Bukhārī, Muslim & Tirmidhī)

and,

> "Oh God, as you have beautified me, beautify my character" (Ḥadīth in Aḥmad).

It is evident that the Prophet's focus and recommendation for his followers was to cultivate beautiful character traits, which originate from and are derived from the divine names of God. Ibn al-ʿArabī writes, "To God belong the Most Beautiful Names, and to the cosmos belongs manifestation through the names by assuming their traits" (Futūḥāt II 438.23, as cited in Chittick, 1989). One of the main roles of the prophets and friends of God is to help bring out these beautiful character traits in humans that are intrinsic to their nature.

The creation story of Adam in the Qurʾān is another testament to the role of the human being and his/her connection to the divine names. After Adam was created, God states in the Qurʾān,

> "And He taught Adam all of the names" (2:31).

God then asked the angels to describe the names, but they were incapable of doing so, proclaiming:

> "We have no knowledge except what You have taught us" (Qurʾān, 2:31).

God then instructed Adam to explain the names to the angels. This story exemplifies that humans can reach a station above the angels in their knowledge, understanding, and embodiment of the divine names. This knowledge is a duty upon humans and the means of becoming a perfect human being (*al-insān al-kāmil*). In fact, Prophet Muḥammad narrated that,

> "God created Adam upon His own form/image" (Ḥadīth in Bukhārī & Muslim).

According to Chittick (1989), this means that God placed within man every one of His own attributes, just as He placed all of His attributes within the cosmos). These attributes are dispersed and scattered in the cosmos, but are gathered together and concentrated in the human.

Cognitive Reappraisal and Acquiring the Divine Attributes

Cognitive reappraisal is defined as changing one's perception of the meaning or self-relevance of a situation to change its emotional impact (Gross, 2015). It is a technique used within contemporary psychology that involves reevaluating and changing the way we perceive and interpret a situation to regulate our emotions and behaviors. Cognitive reappraisal involves reframing the problem or thinking about it in a different way. It has been explored in various ways including asking individuals to imagine a context in which an emotional event or experience would be neutral (Ochsner et al., 2002), in which it retreats into the distance (Davis & Levine, 2013), and in which the individual acts as an objective, scientific observer without being emotionally involved (Goldin et al., 2008). Extensive research has highlighted cognitive reappraisal as an adaptive emotion regulation strategy (Augustine & Hemenover, 2009; Gross, 2013). Among adults, frequent use of reappraisal is linked to indicators of psychological health and wellbeing, including positive shifts in affect, greater life satisfaction, better interpersonal relationships, and fewer symptoms of psychopathology (Gross & John, 2003; Haga et al., 2009; Aldao et al., 2010).

Within contemporary psychology, character development is often situated within the concept of emotion regulation. Emotion regulation within psychological literature refers to "the processes by which individuals influence which emotions they have, when they have them, and how they experience and express these emotions" (Gross, 2015). It also refers to the application of strategies that increase, maintain, or decrease the intensity, duration, and/or quality of an emotion (Gross, 2013). Emotions serve to motivate behavior, and being able to regulate one's emotions allows for engagement in behaviors that provide long-term reward. Deficits in emotion regulation have been shown to be associated with poorer psychological health, increased anxiety, and decreased social functioning. Cognitive reappraisal is often studied as a type of emotion regulation strategy.

We suggest that the process of developing noble virtues as character traits can be seen as a form of cognitive reappraisal, which has been extensively researched in contemporary psychology. This process encourages individuals to reframe difficult experiences in a way that enables them to embody the divine attributes. When confronted with a challenging situation, one can choose to reframe it in a way that allows them to manifest the character traits of God. For example, if one feels that their property has been taken advantage of, they can choose to view the situation as an opportunity to exhibit divine generosity and/or just leadership instead of seeking revenge or holding resentment. This reframing of experiences requires significant shift in perspective. This practice can be particularly helpful in cultivating resilience, empathy, and justice in the face of adversity. Therefore, we argue that *Takhalluq bi Akhlāq Allah* can be an effective means of character development, as long as it is applied judiciously and with consideration for the nuances of a person's unique situation.

Cognitive Reappraisal That Prophet Muḥammad Exemplified in His Lifetime

The Qur'ān enjoins Muslims to follow the path and character of the Prophet,

> "If you love God, follow me [Prophet Muḥammad], and God will love you," (3:31).

Hence, it is conducive for Muslims to examine the Prophet's life and actions on how to appropriately tread the path of *Takhalluq bi Akhlāq Allah.* Every encounter and experience that Prophet Muḥammad had during his lifetime was an opportunity to manifest the character traits of God, and many of these occasions can be observed through the lens of cognitive reappraisal.

An example of cognitive reappraisal during Prophet Muḥammad's life is his reaction to the assassination attempt on his life during the early days of Islam. A group of his antagonists had conspired to kill him as he slept, but according to Islamic tradition, God protected him by revealing to him their plot in a dream. Instead of responding with anger and revenge, the Prophet chose to reframe the situation and respond with forgiveness and mercy. When he had the opportunity to punish the would-be assassins after they had been captured, he chose to exemplify forgiveness and ultimately decided to release them, stating,

> "There shall be no retribution today. You are free to go" (Ḥadīth in Bukhārī & Muslim).

He reframed this situation and focused on the potential outcome of these current assassins becoming faithful believers in the future.

This cognitive reframing was rampant throughout his lifetime, because he later chose to respond to the insults and mockery that he received from his enemies (especially from some prominent members of the Quraysh tribe) with clemency and forbearance. Instead of responding with anger and retaliation, the Prophet chose to reframe these situations in the hopes that these current enemies would one day grow in understanding of his mission and message. During this time the Prophet would state,

> "Oh God, guide my people, for they do not know" (Ḥadīth in Muslim).

Another example can be found in the Prophet's response to the Treaty of Ḥudaybiyya, which was a compromise in which the Makkans recognized the growing Muslim population of Madinah. Although some components of the treaty were unfavorable to the Muslims, the Prophet reframed this situation and viewed it as another opportunity to spread his message peacefully. He encouraged his companions to shave their heads and perform the *'Umrah* pilgrimage despite the unfavorable terms of the treaty. This act of cognitive reappraisal allowed the early Muslims to achieve their goal of spreading the message of Islam through their pilgrimage, and especially while avoiding bloodshed.

The Prophet also displayed cognitive reappraisal in the realm of charity, asceticism, and moderation. According to a narration from ʿĀʾisha, the Prophet had asked her how much was remaining of a sheep that they had recently slaughtered. When she responded that nothing remained of the sheep except for its shoulder, the Prophet responded:

"All of it remains except its shoulder" (Ḥadīth in Tirmidhī).

Ḥadīth commentators have stated that the "remaining" portion that the Prophet referred to here was given away as gifts and charity to their friends and family, hence that portion was being multiplied in *barakah* (spiritual blessings) and reward, while the portion that stayed with the Prophet and ʿĀʾisha (the sheep's shoulder) did not reap the same spiritual status. The Prophet completely reframed and reinterpreted this situation to transition the focus from the portion of the sheep that they did not have to the spiritual reward that was connected to the sharing of this portion with others.

One of the most devastating moments during the Prophet's life, when he was stoned by children at the city of Ṭāʾif, allowed him to manifest the divine names of forgiveness, forbearance, foresight, mercy, and more. He and one of his companions were bleeding and exhausted after having finally sought safety from the storm of stones and rocks being thrown their way by the youth of the town. Angel Gabriel descended during this moment and asked the Prophet if he would be open to the idea of the angel "crushing" the town and thus putting an immediate stop to their violent antagonism. However, the Prophet reframed and reinterpreted this event as a precursor to something beneficial in the long-term, and told the angel that there may come a time when these same children will have a deeper understanding of his teachings, and to let the town be:

I looked up and saw Gabriel. He called me saying: "God has heard your people saying to you and how they have replied, and God has sent the Angel of the Mountains to you that you may order him to do whatever you wish to these people." The Angel of the Mountains greeted me and he said: "O Muḥammad, order what you wish, and if you like, I will let the mountains fall on them." The Prophet said, "No, rather I hope that God will bring from their descendants people who will worship God alone without associating partners with him." (Ḥadīth in Ṣaḥīḥ al-Bukhārī 3231 and Ṣaḥīḥ Muslim 1759).

Another important and testing event during the life of the Prophet was when his wife ʿĀʾisha was falsely accused of being disloyal to him. She had fallen behind the rest of a caravan that was heading to Madinah while looking for one of her most prized possessions and wedding gifts – an onyx necklace from her mother. When she had retrieved it and returned to the campsite of the caravan, the group had already left without her. During her moment of panic, another male companion of the Prophet who had also been left behind recognized her and offered to guide her back to Madinah. When both of them returned to the city, the spectacle of seeing them arrive alone together was an opportunity for the hypocrites of the town to misalign the name and loyalty of ʿĀʾisha to the Prophet Muḥammad.

During this time the Prophet did not take seriously the scandalous information that was being spread about her throughout the city. He chose instead to wait for revelation. During that time, he also asked about the character of ʿĀʾisha from her close relatives and companions. Although the Prophet already knew the stellar character of his wife, he knew that these references would help appease the people of Madinah who were being affected by the rumors of his wife's disloyalty. These references would be helpful in defending her against the misinformation being spread by the hypocrites of the town. In fact, after receiving her character references, he went to the pulpit himself and proclaimed,

> "Oh people, what say ye of men who injure me with regard to my family, reporting of them what is not true? By God, I know naught but good of my household, and naught but good of the man they speak of, who never enters a house of mine but I am with him" (Lings, 1983, p. 244).

His own character testimony for his wife was sufficient to please many people. The Prophet reinterpreted this vastly uncomfortable situation to set a precedent for his followers: the importance of relying on revelation (direct guidance from God) and character references in many matters of injustice and domestic disharmony. During this time, he exerted the divine names of the Just, the Guide, and the Forbearing. He used this opportunity as a means of manifesting virtues that would ultimately inform his followers of the guidelines for dealing with scandals of this nature.

Prophet Muḥammad's use of cognitive reappraisal in these situations and throughout his life demonstrates the importance of emotional regulation and the power of reframing situations in a positive light. By choosing to respond with forgiveness, mercy, forbearance, justice, and wisdom, he exemplified *Takhalluq bi Akhlāq Allah* and set an example for Muslims to follow.

Discussion

Prominent scholars within the Islamic tradition, such as Ibn al-ʿArabī and al-Ghazālī, emphasized the importance of *Takhalluq bi Akhlāq Allah* as a means for personal transformation, spiritual growth, and developing close proximity to God. Cognitive reappraisal also emphasizes the importance of personal transformation and character development as a means of attaining a deeper connection to oneself and the divine. While Ibn al-ʿArabī 's approach focuses on contemplation and spiritual insight/tasting as a means of embodying the divine names, cognitive reappraisal is a psychological technique that encourages individuals to reinterpret and reframe their thoughts and beliefs in a positive and productive way. Both approaches recognize the importance of cultivating positive character traits and embodying the divine qualities of beauty, goodness, and justice.

In addition to demonstrating the practice of cognitive reappraisal, the Prophet also emphasized the importance of self-awareness and mindfulness in regulating emotions and behaviors. He encouraged his companions to reflect on their actions and intentions, and to strive for self-improvement. He said,

"He who knows himself knows his Lord" (Ḥadīth in Muslim),

and,

"Actions are based on intentions" (Ḥadīth in Bukhārī and Muslim).

These statements clearly exemplify the connection between knowledge of one's character to the knowledge of God's character, and that intentions are what animate and affect human actions. Humans thus must become aware of their automatic thought patterns and emotional responses to situations and learn to identify when they are not aligned with God's character traits. As such, *Takhalluq bi Akhlāq Allah* is one aspect of a broader, life-long pursuit of character development which encompasses many components (e.g., see Rothman & Coyle, 2018).

The Prophet Muḥammad's teachings and examples provide valuable insights into the practice of cognitive reappraisal and emotional regulation from an Islamic perspective. By cultivating self-awareness, reframing situations in a positive light, and responding with compassion, forgiveness, and justice, Muslims can develop the emotional intelligence and character traits necessary to live a fulfilling and meaningful life. The following steps are helpful in this regard:

1. Examine and observe a stressful situation in one's life.

2. Reframe the situation to develop alternative paths that lead to healthier emotional outcomes.

3. Reflect on the divine names and attributes that this situation is asking one or allowing one to nurture and embody.

4. Meditate upon and bring to life the divine names that one has resolved that this situation is asking for.

Takhalluq bi Akhlāq Allah is a process of character development that encourages individuals to embody and mirror the divine attributes of God in their thoughts, feelings, and actions. It involves internalizing God's names and attributes, such as His mercy, forbearance, wisdom, and justice, and using them as a framework for personal growth and transformation. This entails discovering whether God's attributes of justice and majesty or His attributes of mercy and immanence should prevail in a given situation.

In cases where assertiveness and boundary setting are necessary, one may need to manifest justice and speak up against mistreatment and injustices. Individuals can use the divine name *Al-'Adl* (The Most Just) to guide their response and work towards creating a more equitable society. Relying on this name can help individuals to feel empowered to take action towards rectifying the situation. They can choose to respond with measured and fair action rather than reacting impulsively or seeking revenge. *Takhalluq bi Akhlāq Allah* thus becomes a powerful tool in developing courage and resilience, and maintaining a positive outlook in the face of adversity.

Recommendations for Future Directions

The concept of *Takhalluq bi Akhlāq Allah* and its connection to cognitive reappraisal presents a promising avenue for further research in the field of Islamic psychology. While current literature in contemporary psychology suggests that cognitive reappraisal can be an effective technique for character development, there is still much to explore in terms of its application in specific contexts, and in particular, for the development of divine attributes.

One area for further research can be examining the impact of *Takhalluq bi Akhlāq Allah* and cognitive reappraisal on mental health and well-being among Muslim populations and possibly even members of other faith groups. For example, does practicing *Takhalluq bi Akhlāq Allah* and cognitive reappraisal lead to lower levels of anxiety, depression, and stress? Additionally, further research can explore the role of *Takhalluq bi Akhlāq Allah* and cognitive reappraisal in promoting forgiveness and compassion, as well as its potential for reducing prejudice and discrimination. Given the current global political climate and rising polarization, understanding how to foster empathy, compassion, and understanding across diverse groups is crucial for promoting social harmony and addressing issues of injustice.

Studies can explore how *Takhalluq bi Akhlāq Allah* can be used to promote intergroup and interfaith reconciliation, harmony and constructive dialogue.

Another area of potential research can be the role of *Takhalluq bi Akhlāq Allah* in trauma and abuse recovery. While reframing challenging experiences can be a powerful tool for developing resilience and growth, it is important to ensure that the approach does not inadvertently perpetuate harmful power dynamics or minimize the experiences of survivors. Future studies could explore how to integrate cognitive reappraisal techniques with trauma-informed care practices to support individuals in developing divine character traits while also prioritizing their safety and well-being. Preliminary research questions may include: how can *Takhalluq bi Akhlāq Allah* and cognitive reappraisal be integrated into existing psychotherapeutic interventions for Muslim clients? Would a group-based approach or an individual-based approach be more effective in promoting *Takhalluq bi Akhlāq Allah* and cognitive reappraisal? We suggest that studies could examine such questions in both Muslim and non-Muslim populations.

Overall, while there is existing research *on Takhalluq bi Akhlāq Allah* and cognitive reappraisal, there is still much to be explored and discovered within the context of Islamic psychology. This chapter suggests some preliminary research directions and applications, but the potential for promoting character development, mental health, and well-being through these practices is vast and warrants further exploration.

References

Aldao, A., Nolen-Hoeksema, S., & Schweizer, S. (2010). Emotion-regulation strategies across psychopathology: A meta-analytic review. *Clinical Psychology Review, 30*(2), 217-237.

Augustine, A. A., & Hemenover, S. H. (2009). On the relative effectiveness of affect regulation strategies: A meta-analysis. *Cognition and Emotion, 23*(6), 1181-1220.

Chittick, W. C. (1989). *Ibn al-'Arabī's metaphysics of knowledge: The Sufi path of knowledge.* State University of New York Press.

Davis, E. L., & Levine, L. J. (2013). Emotion regulation strategies that promote learning: Reappraisal enhances children's memory for educational information. *Child Development, 84*(1), 361-374.

Goldin, P. R., McRae, K., Ramel, W., & Gross, J. J. (2008). The neural bases of emotion regulation: reappraisal and suppression of negative emotion. *Biological Psychiatry, 63*(6), 577-586.

Gross, J. J., & John, O. P. (2003). Individual differences in two emotion regulation processes: implications for affect, relationships, and well-being. *Journal of Personality and Social Psychology, 85*(2), 348.

Gross, J. J. (2013). Emotion regulation: conceptual and empirical foundations. *Journal of Cognitive Neuroscience*, 16.

Gross, J. J. (2015). Emotion regulation: Current status and future prospects. *Psychological Inquiry, 26*(1), 1-26.

Haga, S. M., Kraft, P., & Corby, E. K. (2009). Emotion regulation: Antecedents and well-being outcomes of cognitive reappraisal and expressive suppression in cross-cultural samples. *Journal of Happiness Studies, 10*, 271-291.

Lings, M. (1983). *Muhammad: His life based on the earliest sources.* Inner Traditions International, Ltd.

Ochsner, K. N., Bunge, S. A., Gross, J. J., & Gabrieli, J. D. (2002). Rethinking feelings: an FMRI study of the cognitive regulation of emotion. *Journal of Cognitive Neuroscience, 14*(8), 1215-1229.

Quran. (n.d.). The Noble Quran.

Rothman, A., & Coyle, A. (2018). Toward a framework for Islamic psychology and psychotherapy: An Islamic model of the soul. *Journal of Religion and Health, 57*, 1731-1744.

Winter, T. J. (1997). *Al Ghazālī on disciplining the soul and breaking the two desires.* Islamic Texts Society.

CHAPTER 3

————— ◆◆◆ —————

Extreme Altruism
as a Manifestation of Islamic Virtues

Anisah Bagasra, PhD

Abstract

The goal of this chapter is to examine the role of Islamic virtues in the lives and actions of individuals who have engaged in extreme altruism. In this chapter we discuss extreme altruism in the lives of historical and contemporary Muslims and discuss the place of altruistic behavior in the Islamic context. Altruism is considered a distinct form of prosocial behavior that involves helping with no benefit to the helper, and in some cases, helping may actually be detrimental to the helper. Extreme altruism are altruistic acts that meet the previously outlined qualifications but also involve great risk or self-sacrifice on the part of the altruist. Little research has sought to examine altruism from the perspective of religion and spirituality, especially within the Islamic tradition. This chapter will highlight the qualities found in individuals who have engaged in altruism and how others can foster these virtues in their own lives.

There are many behaviors that Muslims are expected to engage in as part of moral, religious, and societal obligations. These range from giving charity, engaging in prescribed worship, visiting the sick, to basic *adab* or manners (Baqutayan et al., 2018). Most of these behaviors serve prosocial purposes, contributing to the maintenance of order and harmony in society. Other behaviors emerge over time as part of an individual's spiritual development and may go beyond adhering to social norms or fulfilling what is viewed as obligatory (*fard*) behaviors. This chapter focuses on a specific form of prosocial behavior that researchers have concluded is only demonstrated by a small percentage of people (Rhoads et al., 2023) called extreme or extraordinary altruism, which goes beyond ordinary helping acts or charity. Though this path is trodden by only a few, there are many lessons that we can learn from studying the lives and actions of extreme altruists.

Altruism and Extreme Altruism

Altruism refers to a type of prosocial behavior that not only helps another person, animal, or the greater community, but actually can come at a cost to the person engaging in the altruistic act (Dibou, 2012; Batson, 2011; Batson, 1995; Weiler, 2003). The main qualification for altruism is that a) the act must involve the intention to help another person and, b) there must be no expectation of reward or direct benefit for helping (Post, 2005). Motivations for altruism are not always clear. Research on extreme altruists (sometimes referred to as extraordinary or super altruists) usually focuses on the motivations behind living kidney donation and not any other form of extreme altruism. For example, kidney donation is considered one of the most common forms of extreme altruism. Of the more than 17,000 kidney donations made in the United States annually, only about thirty three percent are from living donors. Of these, the majority are donations to family members or people the individual knows. A much smaller number of living kidney donations are to strangers. One study found that a desire to do good and save lives was the main motivator for living organ donation (Kurleto, et al., 2020).

Extreme altruism appears to originate from moral foundations surrounding the idea of relieving suffering (Amormino, et al., 2022b). Unlike other prosocial behavior such as charitable acts that pose no danger to the benefactor, factors such as reciprocity, kinship, and socio-cultural or religious norms cannot easily explain willingness to engage in acts of altruism (Piliavin, 2003; Whatley et al., 1999). Some researchers suggest that altruism is a behavior unique to humans and may be tied to personality factors (Hilbig, et al., 2014) or empathy for the other person (Graziano et al., 2007). Attempts to study altruism experimentally fail to capture significant 'cost' to the altruist in experimental design (Aknin et al., 2015). A lack of empirical research on altruism creates a significant gap in understanding the internal and external forces that motivate altruism in people. We do not know if altruistic behavior varies across cultural or religious groups or if one gender or age group is more altruistic than another. Historical case studies provide some of the best options for studying altruism.

There are significant differences between altruism and extreme altruism. Giving away food that you were going to eat and going hungry yourself is an act of altruism that costs the giver something but is not likely to lead to the person risking the loss of their own life. Extreme altruism, on the other hand, represents actions or behaviors that have greater risk attached to them. Extreme altruism is actions such as rushing into a burning building to save others or jumping into a body of water to help someone who is drowning, at risk of drowning yourself. The possibility of death or severe injury are much higher and possibly imminent. Confronting an active shooter or someone who holds a position of power that can lead to violence or death are other examples of extreme altruism. We will examine many examples such as these described in this chapter, that illustrate Islamic virtues though selfless acts that benefit individuals or communities.

In this chapter the focus is on the manifestation of extreme altruism as an Islamic virtue that has been seen in the character of both Prophet Muhammad (pbuh) and his companions and has been developed as a unique characteristic of individuals whose Islamic worldview focuses on love for all humanity, justice, and equality. In the next section this Islamic worldview will be outlined and connected to acts of altruism and extreme altruism.

Manifestations of Altruism in Islamic Discourse

According to one researcher, at the core of altruistic behavior is a belief that others deserve to be helped (Amormimo et al., 2022b). Some have found that altruists possess a strong sense of moral and social responsibility (Lee, et al., 2005; Amormino et al., 2022a). Lee & Chung (2008) found that people who they term exemplary altruists have a higher positive illusion than non-exemplary altruists. This means they have a more positive view of others and a positive outlook on the future. This research suggests a greater love for others (humanity) than the average person. Within the Islamic tradition, love for God, love for the Prophet (pbuh), and love for humanity are all emphasized (Murata & Chittick, 1994). As will be seen in the case studies of extreme altruists, many of these individuals often exhibit a love for humanity that is the driver behind their willingness to sacrifice oneself for others. Within the Islamic tradition, selflessness and wanting for others what you want for yourself is expressed through the hadith,

"None of you truly believes until he loves for his brother what he loves for himself" (Sumer, 2012, p.154)

This love is not a conditional love based on getting something in return (reciprocity), close relations (kinship), or other worldly benefits. From this type of love, characteristics such as generosity, compassion, and a desire for justice can emerge. The actions of extreme altruists typically demonstrate these characteristics.

In Islam, selflessly helping others is highly encouraged. The Quranic verse that is often associated with altruism is chapter 3 verse 92,

> "You shall never come to piety unless you spend of things you love; and whatever you spend is known to God" (Ali, 1988, p. 60).

The Quran emphasizes that giving and helping should involve sacrifice on the part of the giver. One *hadith* records Prophet Muhammad (pbuh) as saying,

> "He who endeavors to relieve the needy, the desolate, and the poor, is as one who endeavors in the service of God, is as one who stands up to pray all night and does not relax and rest, and as one who fasts and breaks it not" (Sumer, 2012, p.27)).

Serving others is viewed as an act equivalent to forms of worship. In another, more specific *hadith* recorded by Bukhari the Prophet emphasizes helping behaviors:

> "What actions are most excellent? To gladden the heart of human beings, to feed the hungry, to help the afflicted, to lighten the sorrow of the sorrowful, and to remove the sufferings of the injured" (Sumer, 2012, p.148).

Though not specified that such actions should come at a cost to the giver, there are many examples from the life of the Prophet (pbuh) and his companions that illustrate elements of self-sacrifice in fulfilling this call to action.

Persecution of the Prophet (pbuh) and his early followers established the foundation for Muslims to persist in the face of a threat of injury or death. These examples provide insight into the amazing amount of self-sacrifice we see on the part of historical Muslims, not only in the face of threats to their faith, but also in the face of injustice and oppression. In one biography of the Prophet (pbuh) the real threat to life and livelihood is highlighted: As the number of Muhammad's followers increased so did the malice and the cruelty of their persecutors. They would drag a victim out into the scorching heat of the mid-day sun, lay him down on the burning sand and then pile heavy stones on his chest or back and keep him prostrate. They would sew up a man inside the raw skin of a new-killed animal and throw him out to rot in the sun. Or they would put chains or ropes around the neck and feet of others and drag them through the streets. But all of these atrocities proved of no avail. None of the believers either renounced his creed or foreswore his oath; not one of them wavered or faltered (Waheed ud-Din, 1995, p.14).

Examples of altruistic behaviors are numerous from the life of Prophet Muhammad (pbuh) and his companions, from giving away food and remaining hungry themselves, to continuing to call people to Islam in the face of Meccan persecution. Helping behaviors emphasized in historical biographies of the Prophet's companions focus on the giving away of personal wealth, cooking and cleaning for the elderly who could not do so for themselves, setting themselves between the Prophet and potential danger (as outlined in the accounts of the flight from Mecca to Medina by the Prophet and Abu Bakr for example), and actions to help others during numerous battles. As the Prophet's life is an example of the way of love, a clearer picture can form for those who study the life of the Prophet regarding the role of altruism in the development of the way of love. For those seeking to emulate this path, altruism is an important characteristic to cultivate. Extreme altruism is much harder and often not necessary in the everyday life of average individuals. When situations arise that require acts of extreme altruism, it is beneficial to look at the overall lives and traits displayed by the extreme altruist.

Extreme Altruism Among Muslims: Past and Present

In the following section we will discuss examples of extreme altruism, primarily over the past century among Muslims residing throughout the world, that highlight both the different types of altruistic acts and in some cases the potential religious and moral motivations behind them. Advancements in media and social media over the past century have increased the documentation of altruism in societies, which can contribute to a greater understanding and deeper analysis of the context and characteristics of altruists. In this section, the acts and circumstances that led to the extreme altruistic act will be described and wherever possible anecdotes about the person and their motivations, or interviews with explanations from the person are included. These case studies include secondhand accounts, news reports, interviews, biographical, and autobiographical data.

Case Study One: Muslims Who Saved Jews During World War II

One well-documented historical example of extreme altruists occurred during the Nazi persecution of the Jewish people. There were individuals and families who risked their own lives to hide or help Jewish families escape during World War II. This included diplomats and ambassadors such as Behec Erkin, the Turkish ambassador to France, Necdet Kent, another Turkish consul serving in France, Abdul Hossein Sardari, an Iranian diplomat, and Selahattin Ülkümen, a Turkish consul serving on the island of Rhodes. All of these individuals used their positions to issue passports or otherwise prevent the deportation of Jews to concentration camps. Necdet Kent boarded the train himself that was bound for Germany to prevent Jewish Turkish citizens from being deported. Selahattin Ülkümen stood up to the Gestapo. In a contemporary article where he spoke about his actions of the past, he said, "Under Turkish law all citizens were equal. We didn't differentiate between citizens who were Jewish, Christian, or Muslim" (Daily Sabah, 2018).

As a result of his actions, the consul in Rhodes was bombed by the Nazis, his wife was killed, and he was placed in detention for the rest of the war. Historical evidence suggests that for these individuals engaging in one-time acts of extreme altruism, they were aware of the imminent dangers of engaging in acts defying Gestapo deportation orders. Though little is known about the spiritual or religious motivations behind these actions, each man demonstrated a moral obligation to protect ordinary people from unjust persecution, even when those individuals were not of their same ethnic or religious background.

The Pilkus family in Albania was one of many Muslim families who hid Jewish people during World War II. Joanna Neumann, one of the survivors who was hidden by the family said, "They put their lives on the line to save us," (Chan, 2017, para. 2) Neumann, now 86, told TIME. "If it had come out that we were Jews, the whole family would have been killed." (Chan, 2017, para. 2). Clear and unequivocal decisions to save the lives of others despite danger to themselves is seen in all of these examples.

In an interview with Esmond Rosen, one of the authors of a booklet on the role of righteous Muslims, Rosen reiterates the role of belief in the actions of Muslim who have been recognized for saving the lives of Jews during the Holocaust; "And I think also these were just ordinary people, guided by their faith in Islam and their personal desire to do what was right, and they saved Jews' lives during the Shoah, during the Holocaust, and I think they were also very noble and brave Muslims that saw what was occurring around them and hid and protected Jewish people from the sheer brutality and injustice of the Nazi war machine. So they illustrate the social justice that exists within Islam, and I think that's the importance. Which shaped their actions – of many Muslims during this period and they served as a sense of – the stories served as a sense of pride for Islamic communities throughout the world (Holocaust Memorial Day Trust, 2023)."

The concept that to save one life is like saving all of humanity is also found within the Islamic tradition. Unjust killing is strictly forbidden, and protection of life is viewed as an important action. Thus, it is not surprising to see individuals who embody these virtues following them in extreme situations as developed during World War II and the Nazi persecution of the Jewish people living in both Germany and Nazi occupied countries.

Case Study Two: Muslims Stopping Acts of Terrorism

Muslims who have lost their lives engaging in the ultimate form of extreme altruism by stopping acts of terrorism include Adel Termos, who tackled a second suicide bomber in Beirut, Lebanon in 2015, preventing him from detonating in a crowded market; Aitzaz Hasan, a 9th grader in Pakistan who stopped a suicide bomber from entering his school in 2014; and Lassana Bathily, who saved lives during the Charlie Hebdo attack in France.

Witnesses in a market in Lebanon saw Adel Termos tackle a man who was running and shouting Allahu Akbar as he was approaching a crowded area. This forced the suicide bomber to detonate where he was, which witnesses said saved the lives of many more people, but cost the life of Adel, a father of two. In an interview, Adel Termos's brother-in-law emphasized the approach to Islam that may have motivated the actions of Adel; "The problem is these people think that by blowing themselves up they are going to join the prophet in heaven. Our prophet is a prophet of mercy, our Islam is a religion of forgiveness, kindness, compassion, not a religion of killings and swords and slaughter," (Shaheen, 2015, para. 12).

In this interview we see the way of love articulated by the family of the extreme altruist, and the opposition to other worldviews that fail to view life as sacred and Islam as a religion of compassion and mercy.

Similarly, 15-year-old Aitzaz Hasan stopped a suicide bomber from entering his school in Northwest Pakistan in 2014. According to his friends they were outside of their school when they saw a man approach the school wearing a suicide vest. Despite pleas from his friends, he decided to confront the man, "So he told them 'I'm going to stop him. He is going to school to kill my friends'. He wanted to capture this suicide bomber. He wanted to stop [him]. Meanwhile the suicide bomber blasted himself which resulted in the death of my cousin," (BBC News, 2014). It was Aitzaz Hasan's determination to protect his school and classmates that resulted in his own death. Once again, a desire to save others emerges as a primary motivator for the ultimate act of extreme altruism.

Lassana Bathily is a Muslim immigrant from Mali living in France who saved the lives of over a dozen people during a hostage situation at the kosher market where he worked. He risked his life to hide customers in the storage freezer and then climbed out a window to police when everyone else was too scared to do so, in order to provide them information about the location of the hostages, and how to enter the market without endangering the lives of those inside. When questioned in an interview about why he risked his life to help Jews, he said, "Yes, I aided Jews. We're brothers. It's not a question of Jews, Christians, or Muslims. We're all in the same boat. We need to help each other to get out of this crisis," (Oh, 2015, para. 4).

The idea of brotherhood and shared humanity is a reoccurring theme when examining the actions of extreme altruists. Bathily faced the danger of the gunman and then chose to climb out and risk being killed by police. It took him a while to convince police that he was an escaped hostage and not affiliated with the terrorist in this case. Enduring this situation required both patience and determination with a complete focus on the victims of the hostage situation.

Case Study Three: Running Into Burning Buildings and Jumping in to Save the Drowning

Similarly, we see individuals who engage in extraordinary acts of bravery and determination during sudden emergency situations. Mohammad Salman Hamdani was a Pakistani-American emergency medical technician and New York city policy cadet who entered Tower two on September 11th to offer assistance. His remains were later found under the rubble. Initially viewed as a possible suspect, his name was later cleared, but he was not recognized as a first responder in 9/11 memorials, despite his body being found near other first responders. His mother described him as a helpful, caring person who wanted to go to medical school (Davis & Anwar, 2017).

More recently many Muslims who lived in Grenfell tower in London were praised for being awake during Ramadan, preparing the pre-dawn (*Suhur*) meal and alerting their neighbors of the fire that was consuming the building. One person interviewed said, "If it wasn't for all these young Muslim boys round here helping us, coming from mosques, 'nuff more people would have been dead." (Harris et al., 2017, para. 5).

Other recent news media reports focus on the actions of Muslims saving drowning victims in India. In October of 2022, during a festival that both Muslims and Hindus were attending, a flash flood washed away dozens of people into the river. Several young men jumped in to save those who were drowning. When asked why, twenty-year-old Toriful Islam said, "See, I only have one life. What I saved was 10 lives. Ten is greater than one. Isn't it?" (The Wire India, 2022).

He also responded to inquiries about helping Hindus, "If I, as a Muslim, had stood there and looked at Hindus being washed away, it would have been a sin. We are humans. We should become humans before becoming Hindus and Muslims" (The Wire India, 2022, para. 6).

In India, these acts are frequently highlighted because of ongoing tensions between Muslim and Hindu populations and given as examples of the potential for more harmonious relationships between the two communities. When the sacredness of life and shared humanity are seen as virtuous traits within a community, the occurrence of divisiveness and violence may start to dissipate.

Case Study Four: Humanitarianism in the Face of Violence

There are other Muslims who risked their lives to maintain humanitarian missions in the face of war or sectarian violence. Examples of such individuals include Dr. Hawa Abdi of Somalia and Abdul Sattar Edhi of Pakistan. Both of these individuals focused on human welfare, risking their own lives to provide medical services to those in need during conflict situations.

Dr. Hawa Abdi was a Somali doctor who built a hospital and refuge on her land and spent decades treating Somali patients during famine and war. She risked her life to do so, was constantly threatened (often at gunpoint), and chose to stay in Somalia to run her hospital rather than practice medicine or raise her family in another country (Dahir, 2020). When members of an insurgent group threatened her at gunpoint to turn hospital management over to them, she refused. In reflecting upon this incident in her autobiography she stated, "I remember so clearly my walk back to the hospital that day, to the sixty patients waiting in the outpatient clinic – and the additional hundred who had been admitted. I knew these invaders, with their guns and their religion, were motivated solely by owning and taking, but in my anger, I would stand firm. My Islam sees women as valued members of society – as equals - so I never showed my despair" (Abdi & Robbins, 2013, p. xv).

This passage demonstrates once again an Islamic worldview that values life, justice, and equality and served to motivate Dr. Abdi to face death in order to continue to maintain her hospital and take care of people in her community.

Abdul Sattar Edhi was considered the Mother Theresa of Pakistan and demonstrated extreme altruism. He dedicated more than half a century of his life to creating a humanitarian agency that operates across Pakistan and internationally. His work included the creation of the first ambulance service in Pakistan, homes for orphans and the disabled, and medical dispensaries and other emergency services. For decades he was the first on hand when a natural disaster occurred in Pakistan and neighboring countries. His cradle program, allowing people to drop off unwanted babies, and his nurse training programs for women, earned him death threats and negative propaganda against his foundation for many years. Eventually he earned the respect and even reverence of his fellow countrymen for his life of selflessness. Abdul Sattar Edhi dedicated his life to the concept of social welfare and identified his commitment to helping others as religiously motivated. He states in his autobiography, "The five basic tenets of Islam continue into the sixth for me. Huquq-ul-Ibaad, or humanitarianism. That it is not proclaimed as obligatory has deeper meaning; as right and wrong are left to human initiatives its importance would be lost if forced. Within this tenet lies the essence of all religions and the test of all mankind. A universal unity is evident from it. All religions move in the same direction and towards the same goal - humanitarianism. All holy books hold the same meaning. No religion declares humanitarianism as obligatory, yet all stress upon it as the only acceptable way of life. In fact we are different only by rituals formulated according to the terrain and temperament of people that prophets were sent to direct," (Edhi & Durrani, 1996, p. 52).

Edhi emphasizes that engaging in humanitarian activities is a unifying force for people regardless of background. Though he acknowledges that the work he does is not obligatory on Muslims, for him it serves as a "6th pillar".

Case Study Five: Individuals Risking Their Lives for Social Causes

There are dozens of examples of contemporary Muslims who have risked (or lost) their lives to fight against social injustices and oppression. This includes Meena (Chavis, 2003), the founder of the Revolutionary Association of Women of Afghanistan (RAWA); Badshah Khan, who joined Gandhi in peacefully resisting the British occupation of India (Easwaran, 1984); Noor Inayat Khan, who served as a Morse code operator during World War II to fight against Nazi oppression (Basu, 2007); Malala Yusufzai, who risked her life to speak out for girls' rights to education; Abdel Khader Haidara, who works to protect the cultural heritage of Mali; and Linda Sarsour, a Palestinian American activist who continues to receive threats, but works to bring attention to social injustices and oppression, particularly the Black Lives Matter and Women's Rights movements in the United States. All of these individuals' lives are worthy of study to delve deeper into the role Islamic virtues play in their decisions to engage in actions to fight societal injustices. As noted earlier, the specific spiritual and moral worldview of each individual shaped their life mission and has been documented in biographies or autobiographies. In this section I will focus on two of these individuals in depth, highlighting the work of Abdel Khader Haidara and Linda Sarsour as unique examples of how their identity as Muslims has shaped their activism.

Abdel Khader Haidara's life and mission to protect manuscripts in

Mali has been chronicled in the book *The Bad-ass Librarians of Timbuktu* by Joshua Hammer (2016). Haidara worked to protect Mali's historical manuscripts during years of civil unrest when the manuscripts were under threat of destruction. Many precious historical records were destroyed, but hundreds were saved by Haidara and his team. During their actions to remove the books, many of which were hundreds of years old, Haidara persevered in his mission despite the risks: But the face-offs with the jihadists kept coming. AQIM [Al Qaeda of the Islamic Maghreb] operatives stopped, searched, and arrested Haidara's couriers. Bandits captured a boat full of books on the Niger River and held it for ransom. Malian government soldiers often broke open trunks full of manuscripts in search of weapons, roughly pawing through the fragile volumes (Hammer, 2014, para.11).

Haidara viewed his mission of protecting manuscripts from destruction as preservation of the intellectual legacy of Mali and greater Africa. The extreme risk that Haidara and his team took to save the manuscripts from destruction included being confronted by jihadists who took over Timbuktu and accused them of stealing, and French military mistaking their boat convoys for arms dealers and almost bombing them. Haidara argued that protecting the manuscripts was part of protecting the history of his religion: "The manuscripts show that Islam is a religion of tolerance,"....arguing that his collection would go a long way toward breaking negative perceptions in the West (Hammer, 2014, para.18). It may seem odd to include this as an example of altruism without understanding the significance of the manuscripts for understanding the rich spiritual and intellectual legacy that they provide in countering misinformation about Africa. Knowledge and seeking knowledge is so important in Islam that the Prophet told people that,

> "Seeking knowledge is mandatory for every Muslim (male and female)" (Sumer, 2012, p.150).

Linda Sarsour is a Palestinian American civil rights and racial justice activist and organizer of several women's marches. As an activist involved in many Black Lives Matter protests, she has been arrested numerous times and faced death threats for her activism. She helps to train grass roots activists, has protested police brutality, the condition of prisons, surveillance of the Muslim community, and many other issues. As a result of her intersectional approach to social justice issues and unapologetic discourse, she has faced a lot of criticism from various communities (Gharib, 2016). Following the Women's March on Washington (2017), Sarsour gained national recognition which came with death threats. In her autobiography she notes, "Meanwhile, on social media, people wrote the most despicable things. 'A good Arab is a dead Arab. You're getting two bullets in the head. Your time is coming'," (Sarsour, 2020, p.214).

Despite ongoing threats to her life and threats against her family, Sarsour continues to rally against police brutality, engage in work to reform at the legislative level, and speak out against social injustices facing oppressed communities. Both of these examples demonstrate that sometimes altruism does not take the form of helping a person or a community in the literal meaning, but can also take on a more abstract definition of helping others through a cause or long-term processes that will benefit people in the (near) future.

Common Characteristics of Extreme Altruism

In an analysis of the diverse types of extreme altruism documented among Muslims, several clear characteristics emerge. The first common trait is a disregard for personal safety. We see this in almost all of the instances. Despite clear awareness of the danger, each individual chose to take action to help others. Second is a high value on the sanctity of life. Altruists view life as sacred and in need of preserving. This leads to the third trait which is viewing all humans as equal regardless of gender, age, religion, ethnicity, or other status. Thus, extreme altruists are willing to risk their own life to preserve the lives of others regardless of whether the person(s) is Muslim, going beyond both kinship and fictive kinship. This aligns with Seglow's (2004) criteria which notes an absence of concern for one's own safety and wellbeing, and willingness to help everyone regardless of gender, race, ethnicity, religion, and nationality. Similar findings regarding selflessness as a major characteristic of extreme altruists have been reported in other research (Crockett & Lockwood, 2018). It can also be noted from the case studies that most extreme altruists engage in multiple acts of extreme altruism over time (as seen with Hawa Abdi and Abdul Sattar Edhi) unless their act results in their own death (such as the case for Adel Termos, Salman Hamdani, and Aitzaz Hasan) or the situation that has prompted their act of extreme altruism changes (such as the end of World War II). Perseverance in the face of danger, and a sense that their purpose in choosing action is greater than themselves is commonly seen amongst extreme altruists. The sanctity of all life, a sense of universal brotherhood or sisterhood, and a desire to improve one's community especially through humanitarian and social justice efforts, are common elements found in these case studies.

What Can Be Learned from Extreme Altruists?

Most people are not going to become extreme altruists or even engage in repeated acts of extreme altruism in their lifetime. However, much can be learned from those who engage in extreme altruism both historically in the early days of Islam and recent instances of extreme altruism. In fact, contemporary extreme altruists, because of documentation and often existing interviews that give insight into their potential motivations, provide a great deal of information on steps one can take to incorporate the qualities found in extreme altruists into one's own life. A great deal can also be learned about how Muslims specifically navigate modern society by the types of altruism and response to such altruism.

Muslim altruists are viewed as a rarity in Western media, and news reports often act surprised when associating the altruist with their religious identity. This skewed lens can impact how Muslims see themselves. Dehumanization of Muslims as a result of Islamophobia has drawn attention to negative traits, associating Muslims with acts of terrorism, when in fact Muslims are the largest population who are victims of terrorism and are also the ones most actively battling terrorism and extremist mindsets within their communities. Extreme altruists defy stereotypes and are viewed as anomalies in contemporary society, when in fact such level of self-sacrifice and love for humanity has existed within Muslim communities since the start of Islam.

A careful study of Islamic discourse and the biographies of both the Prophet Muhammad (pbuh) and his companions demonstrate that altruism is a behavior based on traits of piety, humility, and love that can be cultivated by all followers. Similar traits can be found when examining the lives of contemporary Muslims who have engaged in acts of extreme altruism. Those of us who observe carefully can strive to incorporate elements of such traits within our own lives for the betterment of ourselves and those around us.

Within the field of psychology, research on extreme altruism is in its infancy. Very few empirical studies have been conducted to examine factors that lead to extreme altruism, let alone predictors of altruism in various situations. Experimental field studies may yield important data that can be applied to real life scenarios. Surveys are another potential methodology that can yield large sample sizes. These could, for example, measure willingness to be a living organ donor while also examining personality and moral characteristics, personal spirituality, and other related measures to see what internal factors produce extreme altruism.

As work on human character and virtue development continues within the field of Islamic psychology, alongside similar work in the areas of psychology of religion and positive psychology (Pasha-Zaidi, 2021), understanding extreme altruism can contribute to human flourishing. Research in this area can help us gain greater insight on resiliency, social justice work, and overall health and well-being. For Muslims, integrating virtues such as altruism from an Islamic psychological and moral development perspective can be particularly beneficial to help counteract distress arising from contemporary struggles that include negative perceptions of Islam and Muslims, that impact identity development, societal marginalization, and international conflict. Extreme altruism as a model of outstanding human virtue can contribute to personal growth and community development.

References

Abdi, H., & Robbins, S. (2013). *Keeping hope alive.* Grand Central Publishing.

Aknin, L. B., Broesch, T., Hamlin, J. K., & Van de Vondervoort, J. W. (2015). Prosocial behavior leads to happiness in a small-scale rural society. *Journal of Experimental Psychology: General.* http://dx.doi.org/10.1037/xge0000082

Ali, A. (1988). *Al-Quran; A Contemporary Translation.* Princeton University Press.

Amormino, P., Ploe, M. L., & Marsh, A. A. (2022a). Moral foundations, values, and judgments in extraordinary altruists. *Scientific Reports, 12*(1), 1–11. https://doi.org/10.1038/s41598-022-26418-1

Amormino, P., O'Connell, K., Vekaria, K. M., Robertson, E. L., Meena, L. B., & Marsh, A. A.

(2022b). Beliefs about humanity, not higher power, predict extraordinary altruism. *Journal of Research in Personality,* 101, N.PAG. https://doi.org/10.1016/j.jrp.2022.104313

Baqutayan S.M.S., Mohsin M.I.A., Mahdzir AM., & Ariffin, A.S. . (2018). The psychology of giving behavior in Islam. *Sociol Int J. 2*(2):88-92. DOI: 10.15406/sij.2018.02.00037

Basu, S. (2007). *Spy princess: The life of Noor Inayat Khan.* Omega Publications.

Batson, C. (2011). *Altruism in humans.* Oxford University Press.

Batson, C. (1995). Prosocial motivation: Why do we help others? In Tesser, A. (Ed.). *Advanced Social Psychology.* McGraw Hill.

BBC News. (2014). *Aitzaz Hasan: Tributes to Pakistan teenager killed when he stopped a bomber.* BBC. https://www.bbc.com/news/world-asia-25663992

Chan, E. (2017). *The Forgotten Stories of Muslims Who Saved Jewish People During the*

Holocaust. Time. https://time.com/4651298/holocaust-memorial-day-muslims-jews/

Chavis, M. E. (2003). *Meena Heroine of Afghanistan: The martyr who founded RAWA The revolutionary association of women of Afghanistan.* St. Martin's Press.

Crockett, M. J., & Lockwood, P. L. (2018). Extraordinary altruism and transcending the self. *Trends in Cognitive Sciences*, *22*(12), 1071–1073. https://doi.org/10.1016/j.tics.2018.09.003

Dahir, A. L. (2020). *Hawa Abdi, doctor who aided thousands in Somalia, dies at 73*. The New York Times. https://www.nytimes.com/2020/08/06/obituaries/hawa-abdi-dead.html

Davis, W., & Anwar, L. (2017). *A mother remembers her son, a Muslim-American first responder who died on Sept. 11*. NPR. https://www.npr.org/2017/09/08/549251929/a-mother-remembers-her-son-a-muslim-american-first-responder-who-died-on-sept-11

Dibou, T. (2012). Thinking about altruism. *Study of Changing Societies: Comparative and Interdisciplinary Focus, 2*(4), 4-28.

Easwaran, E. (1984). *A man to match his mountains: Badshah Khan, nonviolent soldiers of Islam*. Nilgiri Press.

Edhi, A., & Durrani, T. (1996). *Abdul Sattar Edhi – A mirror to the blind: an autobiography*. Ferozsons.

Gharib, A. (2016). *Muslim, American, & intersectional: The activism of Linda Sarsour*. ACLU. https://www.aclu.org/news/immigrants-rights/muslim-american-intersectional-activism-linda-sarsour

Graziano, W. G., Habashi, M. M., Sheese, B. E., & Tobin, R. M. (2007). Agreeableness, Empathy, and Helping: A Person x Situation Perspective. *Journal of Personality & Social Psychology*, 93(4), 583-599

Hammer, J. (2016). *The Badass Librarians of Timbuktu*. Simon & Schuster

Hammer, J. (2014). *The brave sage of Timbuktu: Abdel Kader Haidara*. National Geographic.https://www.nationalgeographic.com/culture/article/140421-haidara-timbuktu-manuscripts-mali-library-conservation

Harris, S., Sherif, L., & Anselmi, P. (2017). *London fire: Locals praise Muslims for helping save lives in Grenfell Tower*. Huffpost. https://www.huffingtonpost.co.uk/entry/london-fire-local-praise-muslims-for-helping-save-lives-in-grenfell-tower_uk_59413dffe4b003d5948c69aa

Hilbig, B. E., Glöckner, A., & Zettler, I. (2014). Personality and prosocial behavior: Linking basic traits and social value orientations. *Journal of Personality & Social Psychology, 107*(3), 529-539. doi:10.1037/a0036074

India: 'Humans Before Hindus or Muslims,' say Men Who Saved Lives During Durga Idol Immersion in Bengal. (2022). *South Asia Journal.* https://southasiajournal.net/india-humans-before-hindus-or-muslims-say-men-who-saved-lives-during-durga-idol-immersion-in-bengal/

Kurleto, P., Skorupska-Krol, A., Broniatowska, E., & Bramstedt, K. A. (2020). Exploring the motives of Israeli Jews who were living kidney donors to strangers. *Clinical Transplantation, 34*(10). https://doi.org/10.1111/ctr.14034

Lee, J. Y., & Chung, H. Y. (2008). Positive Illusion of Exemplary Altruists. *Asia Pacific Education Review, 9*(2), 94–100.

Lee, D. Y., Kang, C. H., Lee, J. Y., & Park, S. H. (2005). Characteristics of exemplary altruists. *Journal of Humanistic Psychology, 45*(2), 146-155. https://doi.org/10.1177/0022167805274954

Murata, S. and Chittick, W. (1994). *The Vision of Islam.* Paragon House.

National Kidney Foundation (2023). Organ Donation and Transplantation Statistics:https://www.kidney.org/news/newsroom/factsheets/Organ-Donation-and-Transplantation-Stats

Oh, I. (2015). *The Muslim Hero Who Saved Lives at a Paris Kosher Market Is Being Awarded French Citizenship.* Mother Jones. https://www.motherjones.com/politics/2015/01/lassana-bathily-citizenship/

Pasha-Zaidi, N (Ed.). (2021). *Toward a Positive psychology of Islam and Muslims: Spirituality, struggle and social justice.* Springer. 10.1007/978-3-030-72606-5

Piliavin, J. A. (2003). Doing well by doing good: Benefits for the benefactor. In C.L.M. Keyes & J. Haidt (Eds.), *Flourishing: Positive psychology and the life well-lived* (p.227-247). Washington, DC: American Psychological Association

Post S. G. (2005). Altruism, happiness, and health: it's good to be good. *International journal of behavioral medicine, 12*(2), 66–77. https://doi.org/10.1207/s15327558ijbm1202_4

Rhoads, S., Vekaria, K., O'Connell, K., Elizabeth, H., Rand, D. Williams, M. & Marsh, A.

(2023). Unselfish traits and social decision-making patterns characterize six populations of real-world extraordinary altruists. *Nature*

Communications, 14(1), 1–15. https://doi.org/10.1038/s41467-023-37283-5

The Muslims who saved Jews during the Holocaust. (2018). Daily Sabah.https://www.dailysabah.com/history/2018/08/07/the-muslims-who-saved-jews-during-the-holocaust

The Role of the Righteous Muslims. (2023). Holocaust Memorial Day Trust https://www.hmd.org.uk/resource/the-role-of-the-righteous-muslims/

Shaheen, K. (2015). *Dad is a martyr': How Adel Termos became a saviour in Beirut bombings.* The Guardian. https://www.theguardian.com/world/2015/nov/17/adel-termos-martyr-father-became-saviour-beirut-bombings

Sarsour, L. (2020). *We are not here to be bystanders*. Simon & Schuster.

Seglow, J. (2004). *The ethics of altruism*. Frank Cass.

Sumer, S. (2012). *The Basic Values of Islam*. A.S. Noordeen.

Waheed ud-Din, F. (1995). *The Benefactor and the Rightly-Guided*. Chicago: Kazi Publications

Whatley, M.A., Webster, J.M. Smith, R.H. & others. (1999). The effect of favor on public and private compliance. How internalized is the norm of reciprocity? *Basic and Applied Social Psychology*, 21, 251-261.

Weiler, E. (2003). *Altruism, volunteerism, and personality*. St. Mary's College of Maryland.

CHAPTER 4

Sufi Ethical Discourse: The Relationship Between Self-Transcendence, Compassion, and a Beatific Vision

Ghena Ismail, PhD

Abstract

Sufism, the inner mystic tradition in Islam, may be partly known through its exposition of metaphysical doctrines central to tawhid. It is also known for its description of the states and stations that led to realizing tawhid. While the order and precise nature of these states varies across different Sufi schools, the constitutive link between Sufism and ethics is denoted in the definition of Sufism as residing "entirely in *adab* [spiritual decorum]" (Mayeur-Jaouen & Patrizi, 2017, p.1). Central to Sufi ethical discourse is the theme of self-transcendence (Orfali, Khalil & Rustom, 2021). In this chapter, I discuss this theme in the context of a beatific vision that entertain the possibility of an encounter with God or essence within. After discussing the motive force of Sufism being love and realization of one's authentic self, I discuss the psychospiritual role of ascetic practices and how they may inadvertently feed the ego. I also discuss different (hidden) forms of egoism as detected in Sufi literature. Self-compassion is presented as an antidote to egoism. The centering function of the heart and its connection to making clear one's intention is highlighted. I conclude with a section on the importance of being mindful of one's intentions, motives and values. Primary and secondary Sufi sources are consulted in conjunction with contemporary psychological discourse and ancient sources that may not be known to the contemporary reader of psychology. Implications on the contemporary practice of psychotherapy and our understanding of what it means to be human will be discussed.

Over the past few decades, writings on the relationship between psychology and monotheistic religions has proliferated. The impact of such writings has remained limited, however, to scholarship within the field of Psychology of Religion and Spirituality[1]. This may be related to the fact that monotheistic religions are associated in the minds of many with dogma and ritual rather than wisdom or practical life teachings. This runs in sharp contrast to the perception of Eastern traditions such as Zen Buddhism[2]. Consider the case of Dialectical Behavior Therapy (DBT), which integrates aspects of cognitive-behavioral therapy with Zen based strategies (Robins, 2002). DBT is regarded today as the gold standard intervention for individuals with borderline personality disorder and is beginning to be examined in terms of its efficacy for treating other problems (Miller, 2015). The Zen Buddhist insights that inspired DBT, among other third wave interventions, include the following: first, the doctrine of non-self which basically implies that personal identity is delusional; second, change is the only constant and thus attachment to phenomena (internal or external) is the source of suffering; third, detachment from transient phenomena leads to the end of suffering; and fourth, life is full of paradoxes that cannot be navigated via the power of individual will, logic, or rational thinking alone. Hence, the value of radical acceptance. Interestingly, such insights are common to all spiritual traditions including Christianity, Islam, and Judaism.

In this chapter, I aim to discuss the ethic of self-transcendence in the context of Sufism, the inner mystic tradition within Islam. In the context of highlighting the ultimate motive force of Sufism being love and realizing one's innermost essence, the paradoxical yet complementary relationship between self-transcendence and compassion toward the self and others will be discussed. Relatedly, the dialectic between the heart and ego will be

---

[1] The Psychology of Religion of Spirituality is a sub-field within the field of psychology whose beginnings are typically traced back to Clark Halls' (1881) studies of "Religious Conversion in the Awakenings of Adolescence" and Williams James' (1902) "Varieties of Religious Experience".

[2] Many scholars and laypersons - alike - do not consider Buddhism a religion which may be due to the fact that the concept of religion is very much shaped by the Western understanding of religion largely associated with theism (Ashcroft, 2022).

presented paving the ground for a discussion of the inverse relationship between exerting one's will on the one hand and cultivating an attitude of surrender and acceptance on the other. Finally, the emphasis in Sufi ethics on examining one's motives and intentions will be highlighted. Ultimately, Sufism will be presented as a lens through which insights from different traditions and disciplines may be integrated and appreciated rather than a substitute for any given tradition within or outside Islam.

The Motive Force of Sufism: Love

The mystic could be defined as one who has asked himself the question: 'How can I transcend myself?' It is as an answer to this question that Sufism exists, and for no other reason, for it is by definition the way of the most direct approach to God (Ling, 1999, p. 28).

Lings' statement highlights the centrality of self-transcendence in Sufism. More importantly, it suggests that as important as self-transcendence as an ethic is, it does not represent an end in and of itself. It rather derives its importance from facilitating a pathway towards God. Working toward this motive entails overcoming psychological inner knots as a necessary, albeit insufficient, step to knowing God and realizing the deepest sense of Selfhood. To appreciate the intricate relationship between knowing God and realizing an authentic self, it is necessary to understand God not only as transcendent of all creation (i.e. that which is greater than us) but also as immanent (whose trace can be felt in our bodily life, daily experiences, and practices).

In the Qur'an, God is said to transcend all perception or imagination.

"No vision can grasp Him" (Qur'an, 6:103) and, "Nothing there is like Him" (Qur'an, 42:11). At the same time, He is "with you wherever you may be" (Qur'an, 57:4), and "withersoever you turn there is the presence of Allah" (Qur'an, 2:115).

Not only that, but His pervasive presence extends to each person's corporeal existence (Awn, 1983), for,

"He is closer to humans than their jugular vein" (Qur'an, 50:16), and "God blew into him of His own spirit" (Qur'an, 15:29;38:72).

These verses provide an exegetical basis for the complex God-human relationship as envisioned in Islam, one that is primarily based on the experience of divine lordship while recognizing the unique experience of divine intimacy and immanence (Awn, 1983).

God as the Immanent and Transcendent

Religion, in general, has been recently defined (Nelson, 2009) in terms of the relationship with the transcendent and also the immanent with different religions or streams within the same religion placing more emphasis on one rather than the other. Like all Muslims, Sufis believe that no vision can fully grasp God's love or His overwhelming presence. His essence escapes any vision or perception. Hence, an emphasis on God's transcendence of all vision and perception. At the same time, Sufis admittedly place more emphasis on God's immanence when compared to other streams within Islam with the most extreme contrast being Salafis or Wahabis, who place almost an exclusive emphasis on God's transcendence. [2] Specifically, Sufis believe that God's trace can be felt everywhere in the universe and within our own souls; in fact, both "nature" and the "human self" have been regarded as sacred books that should be carefully contemplated in conjunction with the revealed book of the Qur'an (Rustom, 2017). In line with the Qur'anic verse

"God blew into Him of His own spirit" (Qur'an, 15:29; 38:72),

Sufis believe that God's trace resides within our very own souls. However, it is only through transcending the psychological barriers and polishing our hearts, that we may allow God's reality to transpire before and within us. Ultimately, Sufis believe that is only in the context of a view of God as both transcendent and immanent that tawhid may be realized; otherwise all talk about tawhid remains an abstraction.

"Neither my Heavens nor My Earth encompasses Me - but the heart of My believing servant does encompass Me" (Hirtenstein, 2010, The Heart's Pilgrimage section, para. 4).

This hadith points to the potential the human heart has for holding God's presence. This is not a simple task however. Consider Moses' story in which he insists on having a direct encounter with God. As per the Qur'anic plot, Moses asked God to reveal Himself to him. The response Moses received was the mountain falling apart as he gazed on it. To Muslim theologians this was regarded as a testimony to God's transcendence and a warning against seeking direct encounter with Him. Interestingly, Sufis had a different, even though not necessarily contradictory, reading on the issue. To them, it was an allusion to a particular mode of seeing and

---

[3] Most intellectual movements within Islam underwent what may be described as intellectual cross-fertilization (Chittick, 1981), and traces of Sufism may be seen in various life domains across the Muslim world including Art, literature and poetry (Lings, 2005; Nasr, 1972).

comprehending reality, namely seeing with the heart, which, as will be shown later, is key to the Sufi ethical framework or vision. Considering that the fall of the mountain represented an immediate answer by God, Sufis argued that the fall of the mountain is a sign of His Ravishing presence and desire to disclose Himself to human beings (McGremor, 2021).

"I was a Hidden Treasure and I sought/loved/desired to be Known so I created the world" (Hadith Qudsi/prophetic tradition)

This hadith qudsi is often cited by Sufis to convey their understanding of the ultimate motive of creation – being the desire by the Creator to be known/revealed through his creatures. The hadith also conveys Reality's (God's) passionate yearning for self-consciousness as a dynamic process of emanation. Such yearning is described by Ibn Arabi (Awn, 1983) as a sighing, a breathing forth in love which is regarded as the source of *al-Khalq* (i.e. creation). Hence, the Sufi emphasis on meditative techniques in which the disciple pays special attention to the breath to cultivate presence with the Divine. This explains reference (Chittick, 2007, p.56) to Sufis as "the folk of the breaths" (ahl al-anfas). "Just as God created us in order for Him to be known, we too 'create' the consciousness of God within us as part of our self-discovery in order for us to be known" (Abdul Rauf, 2008, p. 593).

However, just as we are not ready to receive, let alone mirror, the sweetness of love, when we are mired in childhood unresolved traumas, disciples on a spiritual path are likely not ready to either receive or reflect back the ravishing presence or love of God when they have not cultivated psychospiritual readiness. The notion of cultivating readiness or receptivity (within the heart) is key in a psycho-ethical discourse that bases itself on Ibn 'Arabi's philosophy in which human hearts are seen as mirrors whose ultimate purpose is to empty themselves before the Beloved so that they may reflect back His presence. This is an allusion to the divine manifestation which ensues from self-effacement (Eletreby, 2023). The notion of the human self as mirror possessing no real independent reality is elucidated in the section below.

The Human Self as a Mirror Possessing No Independent Reality

In Islam all qualities belong to God and human beings have no existence separate from God's will. This is at the core of the first pillar of Islam, the *shahadah of tawheed* (i.e. testimony that there is no god but God). The *shahadah of tawheed* implies that nothing and no-one has or can have a separate existence from God (Smith, 1951/1991). In other words, all that exists actually exists as a reflection of God's presence or His will. Whereas God in His essence cannot be directly known for He is beyond all imagination or perception (transcendent), He may be known through His qualities which reflect in creation and in such knowing we may realize God's essence within (Chittick, 1989; Casewit, 2020). In Sufi discourse, the pursuit to have a direct encounter with God occurs partly through meditative practices that involve contemplating the paradoxes of being. The qualities attached to God in the Qur'an suggest that He is beautiful, merciful and compassionate, yet majestic, just and punitive. However, His compassion is said to embrace everything. Muslim scholars typically interpret this as meaning that even seemingly rigorous events that we go through are not meant to destroy us but rather to reveal aspects of our soul that we need to work through in order to reflect God's will in our lives. To be able to do this kind of work we need to acknowledge our nothingness before God and to be constantly willing to discern and exercise His will. In Sufism, independence is considered a key, if not the key form of illusion that human beings are likely to experience (Latif, 2009).

To be able to embark on the human journey in its fullness, it is thus necessary to appreciate that qualities of compassion or generosity do not belong to the individual self; rather they belong to God. Without such realization, one may commit the error of *polytheism or egoism* which often translates into attributing to oneself what ultimately belongs to God (Shah-Kazemi, 2010) or perceiving one's existence independently from the will of God. Given the autopilot mode we live in, it may be difficult to remember that the self has no real independent reality. A Qur'anic verse states,

"You threw not, [O Muhammad], when you threw, but it was Allah who threw," (Qur'an 8:17).

This verse, which descended as a commentary on Muslims' victory in the first of Muslim battles, namely, the battle of Badr, points to the Qur'anic teaching that all qualities and actions ultimately issue from Him. Relatedly, and as will be shown further in the section on motives, the potency or destiny of a given act or situation is largely determined by the underlying motive. Do we have ulterior motives such as accumulating material or social gains or pursuit of self-indignation or are we engaged in a given act in pursuit of God's face? The story (Rustom, 2017) of imam 'Ali who refrained from killing his enemy in the battle once he had gained the upper hand exemplifies this meaning. Just when 'Ali had thrust the enemy to the ground and was about to kill him, the enemy spat on 'Ali's face. When this happened, 'Ali immediately dropped his sword and walked away which left the enemy in a state of bewilderment. When asked about the motive for his action, 'Ali explained that up until the point before the man spat on his face, he was fighting for God's sake alone. However, after the man had spat on his face, the possibility of this becoming a personal affair presented itself. Hence, the ethical necessity of refraining from it.

Self-Asceticism in the Context of a Sufi Discourse of Communion

It is important to point out, at this juncture, that Sufism does not constitute one monolithic discourse. Contemporary historic treatises eloquently highlight diverse discourses within Sufism. Recently, Knysh (2016) commented that Sufism cannot be understood without an appreciation of the imaginative and constructionist processes likely to take place between the reader and the reading experience. Chittick (2007) would elaborate that Sufis' experiences cannot lend themselves completely to abstraction and logical analysis, for what Sufis seek to communicate is better expressed or hinted at in the language of symbolism and imagination as it cannot be fully captured from the outside or through rationalistic discourse. Such is the language of love. Here, it is important to differentiate between love and sentimentality for the former demands a presumption of attitudes and values rather than mere expression of emotion(s). Similar notions are being expressed today in third wave interventions such as Acceptance and Commitment Therapy (ACT) which deconstruct popular myths about romantic love, reinstating the role of values and commitment in loving relationships (Harris, 2009; Hayes et al., 1996). It is also important to differentiate between the imaginal and the imaginary (Chittick, 1989). Such a differentiation is meant to serve as a reminder that there are realms within the human experience that cannot be encapsulated within two-dimensional reality. In fact, one does not have to be a believer in a given religion to appreciate such a notion. Research on psychedelics points to the possibility of experiencing a reality that transcends the bounds of ordinary consciousness (Smith, 1964). That said, in trying to delineate common denominators between the varied discourses within Sufism, Knysh (2016) emphasized the following: first, the Qur'anic context of Sufism which does not exclude the cross-cultural exchanges that took place between practicing Sufis and other cultures that existed within the Islamic milieu including Christianity and Neoplatonism; second, the inevitably symbolic language of Sufism. In fact, early approaches to Qur'anic exegesis fostered the development of Sufism by employing imaginative, allegorical, and esoteric interpretation of the text (ta'wil). Third, the intimate relationship between the soul of the reader and the Qur'anic text leading to Rumi's saying that not only does the reader read the text but the text also reads the reader (Latif, 2009). Fourth and relatedly, the inextricable relationship between ascetic practices and mystical experiences. This point is particularly relevant for the purpose of this chapter. It has been argued that "asceticism," or *zuhd* in Arabic, is not an end in and of itself in the Islamic worldview but is one of several tools and aids for facilitating religious or spiritual development (Abdul Rauf, 2008). Knysh (2016) would elaborate that the highly ascetic and disciplined practices of Sufis cannot be understood or justified outside the goal of seeking communion with God. Such communion does not refer to some lofty paranormal or supernatural experience but to a quest of realizing one's true or innermost Self or a deep calling for wholeness within. It is in the context of cultivating readiness for receiving this state of communion that the emphasis on self-ascetic practices, including holding night vigils and extended fasting, bears its significance in Sufism.

The Psychospiritual Function of Ascetic Practices

Ascetic practices are typically utilized in a worldview in which a duality is conceived between bodily/worldly needs on the one hand and spiritual needs on the other hand (Deezia, 2017). Hence, early Muslim ascetics preached detachment from worldly possessions. By extension, celibacy was advocated by some "despite the fact that the Qur'an is clear in its unabashed commitment to sexuality and the family, and in fact to all of God's created gifts [Qur'an 57:27; 4: 1-35]" (Awn, 1983, p. 245).

A shift in appreciating the function of early Sufi asceticism is attributed to the first prominent woman mystic in Islam, Rabi'a al-Adawiya (d. 801 c.e.), who perceived the obsessive concern with denying the world as, "Ultimately as preoccupying as dedicating oneself completely to the life of the libertine" (Awn, 1983, p. 246). "For Rabi'a, the need for detachment was to provide the mystic with the freedom to focus his or her total attention on the goal of loving intimacy with God, not to fixate oneself on the ascetical practices themselves" (Awn, 1983, p. 246). In emphasizing love, Rabi'a introduced an important nuance into the Sufi understanding of the ultimate purpose of asceticism.

It should be pointed, herein, that these developments within Islamic Sufism have parallels in other spiritual traditions. According to Le Goff and Truong (2003, as cited in Deezia, 2017, p. 95), until the Middle Ages the "body was despised, condemned, and humiliated." However, in newer understandings of asceticism, specifically in Christian thought, the monastic body came to be seen as "the sublimated body of the resuscitated Christ - it does not suffer any longer but can express emotions, such as love of God. This body communicates with God through prayer, and blooms" (Deezia, 2017, p. 95). The ascetic body is appreciated as a tool to perfect contemplation (Deezia, 2017) which overlaps with the Islamic emphasis on God-consciousness as the ultimate goal of spiritual practices (Helwa, 2020).

"Fasting is prescribed for you as it was prescribed for those before you, that you might remain God-Conscious" (Quran, 2:183).

Helwa (2020) elaborates that fasting is meant to slow down the entire body, thus weakening the hold of the *nafs* (ego) over the soul. Citing Rumi she notes, "There is a hidden sweetness in the stomach's emptiness ... if the sound box is stuffed full of anything, the music of our souls could not vibrate into the world," (Helwa, 2020, p. 215).

She adds that when we fast, we are withdrawing the resources of energy from our physical senses and redirecting our focus toward spiritual awakening. To the extent that fasting supports this state then it has fulfilled its psychospiritual function.

The *Nafs* (Ego)/Heart Dialectic

The duality between the world and spirit or Satan and God is translated internally in terms of the *nafs* and the spirit or the *nafs* and the spiritual heart. The *nafs*, in the Qur'an and particularly in Sufi hermeneutics, is often equated with the ego, or the lower self, associated with instinctual impulses and more specifically, with self-centered and compulsive inclinations. These inclinations may translate to autopilot actions that are devoid of mindfulness of one's own behavior, let alone of God's signs. The *nafs* is also used in other instances of the Qur'an to refer to the totality of the human self which may be open to positive or negative influences (for a review of the variety of positions on the form and capacities of the self within Islamic discourse, see McGremor, 2021). When used in a negative manner, the *nafs* is the separative "I" translated in modern psychological literature as the ego which ascetic practices seek to transcend even if temporarily.

That said, ascetic practices also have the potential of feeding rather than transcending the ego, thus creating a veil between the human being and his or her essence. This is a nuance that was detected by the famous mystic Bayazid Bistami as conveyed through his famous statement "the thickest veils between man and God are the wise man's wisdom, the worshipper's worship, and the devotion of the devout" (Frager, 1999, pp. 55, 56). The moment one begins to focus on one's accomplishments, even if ascetical, one misses the whole point of engaging in spiritual practice, which is to humble, if not efface, oneself before God so that His light may shine through the mirror of the heart (*qalb*). For this to be possible, we need to declutter the inner space which typically involves seeing through one's ego, including *khawatir,* i.e. transient impulses, thoughts, and emotions (Ad-Darqawi, 1969) and by extension one's overall persona or false identity (Rothman, 2018). Seeing through one's ego does not entail destroying it but rather seeing it for what it is by shedding light on its workings. This is beautifully communicated in the Sufi parable about how to wisely handle a thief, who breaks into one's home. It is proposed that responding to the thief's violence with violence may lead to unnecessary destruction, when turning on the light [i.e. becoming aware] may be sufficient for getting rid of the thief [destructive egoistic inclinations]. Egoistic inclinations are Qur'anically classified into the following afflictions: (a) love of natural things such as food, drink, and sex; (b) having qualities of deception, ruse, envy, and suspicion; (c) preoccupation with lordly attributes like greatness, power over others, love of praise and fame, and self-sufficiency; and (d) most importantly still, an illusion of being independent. This latter affliction is understood to be the root of humanity's ill fortune in Sufism (Latif, 2009).

Being dominated by one's ego hardens the soul and prevents connecting with the heart. In Islamic philosophy and psychology, the heart occupies a central place. It is recognized as the seat of compassion and spiritual discernment (Saniotis, 2018), the locus of intention (Olatoye, 2013), and "the access point in which we are able to connect directly with the Divine" (Rothman, 2018, p. 36). Whereas the heart is often contrasted to the *nafs* (i.e. the ego), at other times still it is contrasted to the mind, pointing to layers of consciousness that cannot be realized through rational reasoning alone. Rothman (2018) suggests that one of the first tasks in orienting his clients towards an Islamic understanding of the self is to teach them how to center their awareness in their *qalb* - their heart - and move away from the tendency to over-identify with the mind or with one's own will (see Rothman, 2018). A practical way for discerning when we are centered in the heart as opposed to being driven by the ego lies in the following. Whenever our attention is directed toward the self and its failures or accomplishments, fortunes or misfortunes, we are feeding/engaging the ego and dispersing our spiritual energies. Whenever our gaze is turned to God, we are feeding the heart thus centering our spiritual energies. Here it is relevant to point out that Ad-Darqāwī (d. 1823), the founder of a major branch of the Shadhiliyyah Sufi Order in North Africa, warned against the dangers of becoming preoccupied with the insignificance of the self. As cited by Khalil (2020, p. 240), in one of his letters, Ad-Darqāwī (d. 1823) described how a fellow wayfarer came to him and complained, " "I am nothing," to which he retorted, "do not say 'I am nothing,' nor, 'I am something' […] But rather say 'Allāh,' and you will see wonders" (1998, 18)". In other words, Ad-Darqāwī counseled the disciple to turn his attention away from the self towards God, lest he descend into a pit of self-loathing and abasement. Another way that helps one be centered in the heart is to be clear about one's intentions and motives. This will be discussed in a separate section.

The Trap of Egoism and the Role of Self-compassion

Al-hakim al-Tirmidhi, a ninth-century mystic, drew attention to the inescapable moment of realizing that all practices aimed at transcending the self or the ego end up either ensnaring us further into the traps of the ego or realizing the limitations of the individual will (Sviri,1994). The way out of this dilemma is to train the self or the ego to watch less its achievements and failures and those of others and instead to turn its attention outside the self. Hence, the advice given by a contemporary Christian authority that practicing humility does not involve thinking less of oneself but rather thinking of oneself less, as the former may metastasize into a form of subtle narcissism blocking one's opening to the Divine (Khalil, 2020). Again, to avoid being dominated by the ego does not mean destroying it nor overlooking its tendencies. On the contrary, it has been proposed that continuous engagement of one's competing aspects is inevitable. The medieval Sufi scholar Abū ʿAbd al-Raḥmān al-Sulamī (d. 412/1021) conveyed the following inherited wisdom by his teacher Ibrāhīm Ibn Shaybān on the matter. When asked about the sign of one who admonishes (yanṣaḥa) his *nafs*, Ibn Shaybān's response was, "He pushes it toward what it hates and what is contrary to its inclination, never satisfied with it" (McGremor, 2021, p. 195). Thus, the Sufi prescription appears to be for continuous engagement between one's competing aspects rather than shunning altogether a given part. It would thus appear that self-transformation or attainment of virtue is more of "an ecosystem of balanced rivals than a drive for conquest and purity," and that it is precisely out of this effort and work "that the virtuous self may emerge" (McGremor, p. 195). In light of the above, perfectionism may be regarded as an inverted form of egoism as it carries within it a basic intellectual error in regard to the dynamics of self-transformation.

In Sufism, progress relies on exertion of human effort accompanied with a realization of the limitations of that effort, thus keeping the door open to receiving God's grace. Realization of the limitation of the human effort is meant to lead to an attitude of perpetual return to God as opposed to self-flagellation. The Sufi path uses human deficiencies as opportunities to experience God's mercy and compassion toward the self as well as others. This may be best illustrated through an interpretation of the Qur'anic myth of Adam's fall. In this myth, God's different response to Adam's and Satan's transgressions is qualified by Adam's and Satan's different reactions (Latif, 2009). In the Sufi framework, our responses to our misgivings carry as much if not even more impact on the course of our lives and overall destiny than our original misgivings which are somewhat expected. Identifying with one's misgivings as opposed to holding oneself accountable toward them creates a barrier that blocks the possibility of opening oneself to receiving the Grace of God. This is partly in line with contemporary literature on self-compassion, which emphasizes the importance of recognizing one's flawed condition as part of the human condition. It is relevant to point out here that "because self-compassionate individuals do not berate themselves when they fail, they are more able to admit mistakes, modify unproductive behaviors, and take on new challenges" (Neff, 2009).

Ultimately, what God wants is our hearts, our love, and our efforts, as deficient as they are, rather than our so-called perfect souls. Hence, the Qur'anic verse,

"But only he (will prosper) who comes to Allah with a sound heart," (Quran, 26:89).

In fact, the deficiencies seem to be part of the human being by (divine) design. When one focuses one's vision on God's presence, one becomes immersed in His love by extending compassion to oneself and others. One then also accepts one's deficiencies as well as those of others. Finally, Sufism is to be able to perceive the manifestations of Divine majesty in the Qur'an, the universe and the human being, deepen in contemplation of the workings of Divine power and advance upon the path of knowledge of God. In other words, it is to be able to know Allah Almighty with the heart (Topbas, n.d.). This entails searching for God's will and God's signs within varied aspects of our lives rather than be preoccupied with the game of self-evaluation. It also requires being mindful of one's intention and motives that lie within one's innermost self, in the heart.

Mindfulness of One's Intentions and Motives in the Context of a Multi-layered Tawhidic Beatific Vision

Human beings are not uni-dimensional and whereas they are called by the Sufi path to concentrate their efforts on the ultimate purpose of experiencing divine love, Sufi masters have been aware that conflicting motives are inevitable. Yet, in order not to betray the soul's ultimate call to connect with the divine (i.e. a force beyond the ego), it is important to refine one's vision, to be attuned to the possibility of connecting with the vastness of living beyond the individual self while also acknowledging the different needs that we have. Maslow's hierarchy of human needs has been acknowledged by Muslim scholars, albeit considered lacking in cultural and spiritual sensitivity (Bouzenita & Boulanouar 2016). Giving things their due, be it at the level of satisfying material or interpersonal needs, is considered an aspect of justice in Islam. This is exemplified in the prophet's hadith, "Your body has a right over you, and your Lord has a right over you, and your family has a right over you, so fast and break your fast, and pray and join your family and give everyone his right" (Bouzenita & Boulanouar, 2016, p. 74).

That said, satisfying all needs should be governed by the overarching quest to seek the face of God. This partly translates into having the most mundane and basic needs, such as eating or drinking accompanied with an attitude of humility and gratitude. Ultimately, all needs should be attended to while fixating one's gaze on God's presence. Awareness of God's presence should not be restricted to temples and instances of formal prayer, neither should it be reserved for those who have their basic needs saturated (Bouzenita & Boulnaoar, 2016). It should rather be practiced across different life situations and stages, and it should accompany and govern all acts, even the seemingly most mundane. According to Helwa (2020), we are not meant to eat food to pursue our materialistic needs only, "but rather we eat to honor and support our body with the energy necessary to worship God and to become vessels of His love and peace" (Helwa, 2020, p. 220). Such a mode of being is meant to facilitate the unification of the varied forces within, hence inducing a sense of wholeness that is not grandiose or self-sufficient but rather contingent on seeking God's will in our lives and recognizing our dependency on Him.

Applying this to the intrapersonal and interpersonal spheres, one should learn to consider the difference between doing things so one may increase one's reputation and status among people, and seeking to do the right thing (Sameh, 2020). Ultimately, one should learn to act for the sake of God alone even if a given deed appeared wrong in the eyes of others who may employ strict religious or social standards that foster a judgmental attitude and closed-mindedness (Helwa, 2020). One may also reconsider doing what may appear to be a good deed to the outside world if he or she recognizes that the deed is colored with ulterior motives. While recognizing the multifaceted nature of human needs and motives, it is important to point out that in the human sphere it is difficult to discern whether a behavior is spiritual by looking on its outward form. The need for recognition or the momentary urge to satisfy an impulse of anger, self-righteousness, or vengefulness may color the seemingly most spiritual or ethical acts. Someone might pray in the mosque or engage in an act of charity to gain social respect rather than for the intrinsic value attached to prayer itself. Also, someone may engage in a seemingly chivalrous act on the battlefield out of self-interest rather than in pursuit of God's satisfaction. The story of Imam 'Ali recounted previously highlights this possibility which is affirmed by the horrific accounts of shameful acts taking place today in the context of conflict and warfare. Sufi discourse recounts the different possibilities and motives that may govern a given action while highlighting that the gains and losses one is likely to incur shall depend on its underlying motive or intention. So, if one prays for social recognition, one will likely reap that benefit which in turn will detract away from the spiritual benefit. As per the prophetic hadith, "deeds are only by intentions, and every man shall have only what he intended" (An-Nawawi 1, 1999, p.1). In Islamic literature, intention is referred to as the 'action of the heart'(Olatoye, 2013).

According to Zarabozo quoting Ibn Qayyim, intention is defined as "the knowledge of a doer of what he is doing and what is the purpose behind [this action]" (Zarabozo, 1997, p. 104). Hence, the symbolic significance of prefacing acts Muslims engage in with the phrase Bismillah Al-Rahman Al-Rahim (i.e. In the Name of God, the most Compassionate and Merciful). Not only does making one's intention clear carry special significance in Sufi ethics but so does the manner in which one engages in a given behavior. There are instances in which people may have purified their intention of pursuing God's face; however, the applause of others may get to their ego resulting in distraction and a dispersal of spiritual energy. Hence, the Sufi recommendation to engage in acts of charity in a secretive manner in order to protect one's heart from whisperings of the ego. Others have suggested that whether an act is conducted secretively or in open is not the key issue as long as one does not care about others witnessing one's acts (Gulen, 2001).

Conclusion

Sufi masters teach that all events - internal or external - can lead to salvation if approached with an attitude of trust, humility, and a commitment to return to the Real (i.e. repentance; Rothman, 2018; Helwa, 2020). In the Sufi ethical framework presented herein, repentance does not equate or necessarily implicate self-flagellation or perfectionism as these could detract one's attention away from the Beloved. It rather implies perpetual return to God, the Beautiful, the Merciful, and the Compassionate. Relatedly, it implies cultivating a tawhidic beatific vision in which God's presence is appreciated in the here and now. It is such seeing or orientation, that motivates the Sufi ethic of self-transcendence.

In Sufism, the practice of ethics is not merely a willful act; it is a training program contingent on cultivating the will to see all that comes our way as a sign of God's ultimate beauty and mercy (McGremor, 2021). Individuals will likely experience moments of bitterness, anger, or mistrust of God's presence or mercy no matter how strong their faith is, for after all they are human. They may and will likely fall into the clutch of the ego even as they engage in the most seemingly spiritual or chivalrous acts. As shown throughout this chapter, the more ascetic the path of efforts actually is, the graver the risk of an inflated ego, which creates a vicious cycle: one cannot progress without making efforts and the results of the efforts are the indication of the progress (Sviri, 1994). However, when one becomes conscious of the extent of one's progress, one falls into the trap of the 'calculating' ego, thus cluttering the mirror of the heart and detracting attention away from the divine. This need not induce a sense of hopelessness or cynicism but rather an acknowledgment of the vicious cycle embedded in the game of self-attribution and/or self-evaluation and relatedly it should highlight the limitations of human will and reasoning. Such notions are not alien to the field of psychology. It has become quite salient, particularly in third wave interventions, informed by Buddhist ethics. In the Sufi framework, whereas such awareness should lead to detachment from the aforementioned processes, it should also strengthen the need to turn to God and by extension it should facilitate an attitude of love and compassion and softening toward the self as well as others. After all, we all partake in the fragility of the human condition, and we all yearn to realize a sense of wholeness within.

The beauty of Sufi ethics lies in its insistence on the importance of monitoring our personal motives and intentions as we engage in any act, even the most seemingly spiritual or honorable. It reminds us that as human beings, we are always faced with the threat of being lost in our ego and self-aggrandizing calculations. Sufi ethics provide us with practical means for ascertaining whether an act is worthy by inviting us to examine its effect on others and on our own souls. It also notes that every spiritual station, if not mystical moment, has a corresponding etiquette and behavior often referenced in Sufi literature as *adab* (Mayeur-Jaouen & Patrizi, 2017). In conclusion, the purpose of Sufi ethics may be summed up in terms of fostering a certain mode of seeing and being. Sufi ethics and related practices (e.g. invocation, meditation) not only aim at helping us do things for the sake of God but at enhancing our capacity to see things through the eyes of God. This provides an important framework for humanizing other human beings as well as the overall environment we live in (Rustom, 2017).

Ultimately, seeking love within the self is an abstract concept and a distant possibility for many people. In Islam and particularly in Sufism, the surest way into the world of love is to develop a relationship with God, and the easiest way this can be done is to foster love in one's heart for God's creatures including oneself. Through exercising compassion, one can come into the purview of the vast scope of love: "One loves every existent thing since every existent thing is His act and handiwork" (Ayn al-Quḍāt cited in Rustom, 2021, pp. 131-2). Love in Sufi literature among other spiritual traditions, including Christianity, requires inner work and attunement of the two wings of one's vision – the intellect which can decipher and analyze things, and the heart which contemplates unity and continuity between created things through relating at all times to a transcendent, loving God.

Limitations, Applications and Future Directions

Ideas offered in this chapter constitute the author's understanding of how the Sufi motive force of divine love may inform our understanding of the human potential for love, transcendence, and interconnectedness, often

THE WAY OF LOVE

challenged by unresolved wounds and a misguided tendency to be overly hard on oneself and others in pursuit of one's ideals. The Sufi ideal of connecting with a loving force in the universe need not be approached as a romantic or exotic ideal. In fact, the ethical discourse presented in this chapter on the relationship between self-transcendence, compassion, and cultivating a contemplative or beatific vision should be seen as part of a global literature that recognizes the intricate relationship between the need to detach from habitual, autopilot responses on the one hand, and contemplating possibilities for realizing the human potential to its fullness on the other hand. As psychologists and scholars, we have a responsibility to become aware of the links between the varied psychospiritual discourses before us, rather than exoticising or overlooking any given discourse. This should enable us to cultivate not only greater cultural but also spiritual sensitivity. Instead of standing outside people's traditions we should consider seeing these traditions from within in order to benefit from their insights, nuanced meanings, and acumen in transmuting apparent contradictions.

Whereas the themes tackled in this chapter are rooted in the Islamic Sufi tradition, they are not foreign to other sister traditions – be it in the Middle East (Mayeur-Jaouen & Patrizi, 2016), the Far East, or the West. There is a merit in learning how different notions and practices are contextualized across different traditions as this would help us as human beings in general and clinicians in particular achieve a number of things including: cultivating a greater openness to and respect toward each other, and facilitating a more nuanced understanding of one's own wisdom tradition and pertinent ethics and practices. Revisiting the overarching framework of this chapter, which is connected to the question of ethics, it should be noted that *adab* is "an ongoing crucible, a 'hybridization'… of encounters and patient effort to continuously create something new" (Mayeur-Jaouen & Patrizi, 2016, p. 23). In the Middle East, Muslims and Christians, who lived side by side, did not produce different cultural norms. "'Good manners' for everyone conformed to very similar criteria where each believed in the beneficial imprint of his own religion but in harmony with the world in order to be fully human" (Mayeur-Jaouen & Patrizi, 2016, p. 22). Whereas Sufism influenced oriental Christianity and Jewish pietism, it was also influenced by their presence (Knysh, 2016; Mayeur-Jaouen & Patrizi, 2016). Each tradition selectively borrowed those aspects which enhanced its understanding of its own teachings. There is no reason why we cannot be open to such exchange today. Actually, it is rather essential and necessary.

Recently, Trammel (2017) and Sun (2014) shed light on the Christian and Buddhist roots of mindfulness, with Sun (2014) noting how the original goals associated with mindfulness were lost in the secularization process. Merits of secularization, which included popularizing mindfulness, were acknowledged (Sun, 2014). At the same time, Sun (2014) and Trammel (2017) suggested that being aware of the original goals and contexts of mindfulness as practiced in Buddhism or Christianity may facilitate tapping into deeper motives. Whereas some individuals may be content to practice mindfulness as a means for relaxation or stress reduction, others may benefit more from being reminded that such a practice which has roots in their own tradition is meant to link them to a deeper mode of being or consciousness. In Buddhism, this would be through a deepened relationship of the self to the Buddha nature. In Christianity, it would be through a deepened relationship of the self to God contained in Christ, the Holy Spirit, and God the Father (Trammel, 2017). The process of learning about different spiritual traditions need not be restricted to searching for the lowest common denominator among them all (e.g. stress reduction or detachment from non-adaptive thoughts). It may also involve learning about the potential latent in a given practice or concept as articulated by forebearers of a given tradition. Consider the concept of motives and intentions which emerged in this chapter. This concept is not unique to Islam as it is extensively covered in Buddhism today, such that treatises have been written to carefully distinguish between goals and intentions. Whereas goals have been associated with envisioning a future outcome in the world, intentions have been associated with a path of practice that is focused on how you are "being" in the present moment (Moffitt, 2022). Mindfulness based interventions such as (ACT) emphasize the importance of differentiating between goals and values. This emphasis, however, is lost to many practitioners of Buddhism (Moffitt, 2022) and clinical psychology alike. A conversation across traditions may be helpful for deepening our understanding of the different layers and shades of meaning associated with these concepts. This could and should happen in the context of academic settings which fail to offer courses on wisdom traditions to graduating future clinicians.

Finally, this chapter suggested an intimate relationship between self-transcendence, self-compassion, and holding a beatific vision. Whereas self-compassion in Islam involves self-care and giving one's bodily as well as emotional needs their due attention, it also involves an acknowledgment of one's limitations as one strives to pursue certain ideals. The key element to consider Islamically is that failure to exercise self-compassion may lead to perfectionism and endless evaluations of the self that will likely block one's ability to return to God which in Islam is the ultimate ideal. Clinicians can facilitate such return by sensitizing themselves to the spiritual narratives and ideals associated with varied wisdom tradition. This requires much more than asking clients about their values; it ultimately requires fostering a dialogic space within academic settings as well as the broader community where we contemplate our own values and ethics in the context of the worldwide wisdom traditions.

References

Abdul Rauf, I. F. (2008). Asceticism in Islam. *Asceticism today, 57(4)*, 591-602.

Ad-Darqawi, M.A. (1969). *Letters of a Sufi master* (T. Burkhardt, Trans.). Fons Viate.

An-Nawawi, Y. (1999). *The 40 hadith of Al-Imam An-Nawawi.* Abul-Qasim Publishing House.

Ashcroft, R. (2022). *Is Buddhism a religion or a philosophy?* The Collector. https://www.thecollector.com/buddhism-philosophy-religion/

Awn, P. (1983). The ethical concerns of classical sufism. *The Journal of Religious Ethics, 11(2)*, 240-263.

Bouzenita, A.S. & Boulanouar, B.W. (2016). Maslow's hierarchy of needs: An Islamic critique. *Intellectual Discourse, 24(1)*, 59-81.

Casewit, Y. (2020). Al-Ghazali's virtue ethical theory of the Divine Names: The theological underpinnings of the doctrine of takhalluq in al-Maqsad as-Asna. *Journal of Islamic Ethics, 4*, 155–200. https://doi.org/10.1163/24685542-12340042

Chittick, W. (1989). *Ibn "al-"Arabi's metaphysics of imagination: The Sufi path of knowledge.* The University of New York Press.

Chittick, W. (2007). *Sufism: A Beginner's Guide.* Oneworld.

Chittick, W. (1981). Mysticism versus philosophy in earlier Islamic history: The Al-Tusi, Al-Qunawi correspondence, *Religious Studies, 17(1)*, 87-104.

Deezia, B.S. (2017). Asceticism: A march towards the Absolute. *IAFOR Journal of Ethics Religion & Philosophy, 3(2)*, 85-98. DOI: 10.22492/ijerp.3.2.06

Eletreby, B. (2023). *A universe of mirrors: the mirror metaphor in Ibn 'Arabi's thought in relation to ontology, knowledge, and perfection* [Unpublished doctoral dissertation]. The American University of Cairo.

Frager, R. (1999). *Heart, self and soul: The Sufi psychology of growth, balance, and harmony.* The Theosophical Publishing House.

Gulen, F. (2001). Ikhlas (sincerity or purity of intention). http://fgulen.com/en/fethullah-gulens-works/key-concepts-in-the-practice-of-sufism-1/ikhlas-sincerity-or-purity-of-intention

Harris, R. (2009). *ACT with love: Stop struggling, reconcile differences, and strengthen your relationship with acceptance and commitment therapy.* New Harbinger Publications.

Hayes, S.C., Wilson, K.G., Gifford, E.V., Follette, V., & Strosahl, K. (1996). Experiential avoidance and behavioral disorders: A functional dimensional approach to diagnosis and treatment. *Journal of Consulting and Clinical Psychology, 64*(6), 1152-1168.

Helwa, A. (2020). *Secrets of divine love.* Naulit Publishing House.

Hirtenstein, S. (2010). The mystic's ka'aba - the cubic wisdom of the heart according to Ibn 'Arabi. *The Journal of the Muhyiddin Ibn Arabi Society, 48. https://ibnarabisociety.org/cubic-wisdom-of-the-heart-stephen-hirtenstein/*

Khalil, A. (2020). Humility in Islamic contemplative ethics. *Journal of Islamic Ethics, 4*, 223-252.

Knysh, A. (2016). *Sufism: A new history of Islamic Mysticism.* Princeton University Press.

Latif, A. (2009). *Qur'anic narrative and Sufi heremeneutics: Rumi's interpretations of Pharaoh's character* [Unpublished Doctoral dissertation]. Stony Brook University.

Lings, M. (1999). *What is Sufism?* The Islamic Texts Society.

Mayeur-Jaouen, C., & Patrizi, L. (2016). Ethics and spirituality in Islam. In F. Chiabotti, E. Feuillebois-Pierunek, C. Mayeur-Jaouen, & L. Patrizi (Eds.), *Ethics and spirituality in Islam* (pp. 1-44). Brill. doi: https://doi.org/10.1163/9789004335134

McGremor, R. (2021). Seeing is believing: sufi vision and the formation of the ethical subject. In B. Orfali, A. Khalil., & M. Rustom (Eds.), *Mysticism and ethics in Islam* (pp. 187-202). American University of Beirut Press.

Miller, A.L. (2015). Introduction to a special issue dialectical behavior therapy: Evolution and adaptations in the 21(st) century. *American Journal of Psychotherapy, 69*(2), 91-95. doi: 10.1176/appi.psychotherapy.2015.69.2.91.

Moffitt, P. (2022). *The heart's intentions – Dharma wisdom.* Life Balance Institute.

Nelson, J.M. (2009). Introduction to psychology, religion, and spirituality. In *Psychology, religion, and spirituality (pp. 3-41).* Springer Link.

Olatoye, R. M. (2013). Towards understanding the Islamic concept of the heart and its relationships with man's intention/actions. *European Scientific Journal, ESJ, 9*(19). https://doi.org/10.19044/esj.2013.v9n19p%p

Robins, C.J. (2002). Zen principles and mindfulness practice in dialectical behavior therapy. *Cognitive and Behavioral Practice, 9*(1), 50-57. https://doi.org/10.1016/S1077-7229(02)80040-2

Rothman, A. (2018). An Islamic theoretical orientation to psychotherapy. In C. Y. Al-Karam (Ed.), *Islamically integrated psychotherapy: Uniting faith and professional practice (pp. 36–64)*. Templeton Press.

Rustom, M. (2017). Actionless action. In M. Rustom & E. Alkan (Eds.), *The door of mercy: Kenan Rifai and Sufism today, vol. 1 (pp. 122-128.)*. Nefes.

Rustom, M. (2021). Theo-fani: 'Ayn al-Qudat and the fire of love. In Orfali, B., Khalil, A., & Rustom, M. (Eds.), *Mysticism and Ethics in Islam (pp. 129-138)*. American University of Beirut.

Sameh, A. (2020). *Slaying the ego: moral education of the self in Sufism and its relations to virtue ethics.* [Unpublished Doctoral dissertation]. The American University of Cairo.

Saniotis, A. (2018). Understanding mind/body medicine from Muslim religious practices of salat and dhikr. *Journal of Religion and Health, 57,* 849–857. https://doi.org/10.1007/s10943-014-9992-2

Shah-Kazemi, R. S. (2010). *Common ground between Islam and Buddhism.* Fons Vitae.

Smith, H. (1991). *The world religions.* HarperCollins Publishers. (Original work published 1951)

Smith, H. (1964). Do drugs have religious import? *The Journal of Philosophy, 61*(18), 517-530.

Sun, J. (2014). Mindfulness in context: a historical discourse analysis. *Contemporary Buddhism, 15*(2), 394-415. *http://dx.doi.org/10.1080/14639947.2014.978088*

Sviri, S. (1994). The mysterium coniunctionis and the "Yo-Yo Syndrome": From polarity to Oneness in Sufi psychology. In J. Ryce-Menuhin (Ed.), *Jung and the Monotheisms: Judaism, Christianity and Islam.* Routledge.

Topbas O.N. (n.d.). What is Sufism. Osman. https://en.osmannuritopbas.com/what-is-sufism.html

Trammel, R.C. (2017). Tracing the roots of mindfulness: Transcendence in Buddhism and Christianity. *Journal of Religion & Spirituality in Social Work: Social Thought, 36*(3), 367-383, DOI: 10.1080/15426432.2017.1295822

Zarabozo, J. M. (1997). *A Commentary on the Forty Hadith of an- Nawawi.* Boulder. (Vol. 1). CO: Al-Basheer Company for Publications and Translations, 1999.

CHAPTER 5

Jihad-an-nafs and the Twelve Steps:
Addiction Treatment as Development of Virtue and
Purification of Character

Sarah Mohr

The work of recovery from addiction in the United States is often accomplished through the self-help program of the Twelve Steps (AA World Service, 2001; NA World Service, 2008). Recent work on recovery and Islam has suggested that the Twelve Step approach is similar to the Sufi practice of *jihad-an-nafs*, or the purification of the self (Adisa & Steiner, 2021; Mohr, 2022). Refining one's character in Twelve Step programs involves practicing spiritual principles that closely resemble the descriptions in Sufi texts of the work to purify the *nafs*, including practices like surrender, faith, intention, refinement of character, repentance, and service (al-Qadir al-Jilani, 1992; Angha, 1991; Frager, 1999). Practices of community meetings, introspection and self-examination through journaling, speaking with those who have more experience such as a shayk or sponsor, and prayer and meditation are among the means in both paths to the improvement of character, the development of virtue, and the cultivation of a happy life (al-Qadir al-Jilani, 1992; Angha, 1991; Khorasani, 2000; Raslan, 2021; Rassool, 2021). A closer look at similarities between Twelve Step practices and Sufi practices reveals deep parallels between the two paths that suggest that these practices can support and help recovering individuals progress in the development of good character and overall wellness if used in conjunction. This chapter will cover the definitions of key terms such as Sufism, *jihad-an-nafs*, and terms related to addiction treatment. It will also explore the complementary nature of Sufism and the

Twelve Steps, as well as some of the disconnects. Finally, we present a case study and conclude with recommendations for clinical practice.

Definitions

Before delving into a comparison of Sufi approaches to self-development and Twelve Step ideas of recovery, it is necessary to clarify definitions of Sufism, *jihad-an-nafs*, the Twelve Steps, the disease concept of addiction, and what is meant by recovery. These topics are covered individually in many volumes, some of which are referenced in the discussion. These definitions are offered merely as general starting places.

Sufism

Sufism is defined by many as the mystical branch of Islam, although there is not one definition according to most scholars (al-Qadir al-Jilani, 1992; Angha, 1991; Barks & Green, 2000; Ozak, 2009). Sufism is often framed as the psychological tradition within Islam, and it connects to Islam throughout the history of the religion. It has schools both in Sunni and Shia Islam, and is sometimes conceptualized as a third distinct thread, recognizing that there are historically, and even currently, a range of traditions within Islam beyond the Sunni/Shia split.

Sufism has a tradition of being the science of character development within Islam, and being the part of the Islamic tradition that develops in more detail the methods, stages, and techniques of character development. Sufism is also sometimes understood to mean simply the spiritual tradition within Islam, distinct from the legal tradition, such as Sharia, or the techniques, practices and rules of the religion, such as fiqh. Sufism historically is associated with meditation, prayer, and contemplation, including both individual and community practices; it includes a variety of practices, techniques, and methods, including poetry, for advancement on the mystical path (Bakhtiar, 1976).

The development of Sufism spans the entire Islamic tradition and is therefore quite complicated, but there are common threads of mysticism and spirituality throughout (Malik & Hinnells, 2006). Some might argue that Sufism became more a part of mainstream Islamic practice with the standardization of the tradition with Imam Al-Ghazali, who is well known to be one of the most prominent theologians, mystics, and philosophers of the Islamic tradition (Davis, 1948; Malik & Hinnells, 2006). In addition to the influence of Al-Ghazali, Sufism was introduced to the Western world through poetry, including the widely read Rumi, as well as spiritual teachers throughout the 20th century, particularly gaining speed in the spiritual renaissance of the 1960s and 70s (Malik & Hinnells, 2006; York Al-Karam, 2021).

Jihad-an-nafs

Jihad-an-nafs in translation means "the struggle against the self" and is a major focus of the Sufi path as evidenced by texts on the topic (Bakhtiar, 2002; Bakhtiar, 2019; Frager, 1999). Some have even argued that Sufism is Islam's version of psychology (York Al-Karam, 2018) and claim that *jihad-an-nafs*, including practices like *tazkiyyah*, or the purification of the self, are a distinct psychological tradition within the history of psychology (Bakhtiar, 2002; Bakhtiar, 2019; York Al-Karam, 2018; York Al-Karam, 2021). This has been a prevalent theme in the modern Islamic psychology movement, including the early Western writers in the late 20th century, such a Dr. Laleh Bakhtiar, whose work centered on *ilm-an-nafs,* or science on the *nafs*, in her groundbreaking writing dating back to the 1970s (Bakhtiar, 1976).

Historically, Al-Ghazali's main work, *Revival of the Religious Sciences*, dealt with the topic extensively, and thinkers since him have developed the topic further (Al-Ghazali, 2014; Bakhtiar, 2019). One of the major contributions of contemporary Muslim psychologists has been the advancement of a model of the self that starts from an Islamic understanding of human ontology, focusing on a four-part division of the self into *qalb* (heart), *ruh* (spirit), *aql* (mind), and *nafs* (drives; Rothman & Coyle, 2018). The *nafs* has been a focus of Sufi psychology, again going back to Al-Ghazali and farther, as an area of self-development, self-reflection, and self-purification that comprises a key foundation of Sufi practice and psychology (Angha, 1991).

The word *nafs* is used a total of 295 times in the Quran, and in fact, Islamic psychology is also called *nafsiyat* (Ul Haque, Aziz, Aqib, 2022). Islamic psychologists and scholars derive their focus on the *nafs* directly from the Quran and Sunnah, the two primary textual sources of Islamic faith and practice. For example, Bakhtiar (2019) quoting Al-Ghazzali: "Know that the key to the knowledge of God, may He be honored and glorified, is knowledge of one's own self. For this has been said: He who knows himself knows his Lord. It is for this that the Creator Most High said: *We shall show them Our signs on the horizon and within themselves, so that it will become evident to them that it is the Truth.* (Quran 41:53)…Therefore you must seek out the truth about yourself," (p. xxxiii).

There are a range of other verses on the *nafs* in the Quran including Quran 2:48 where humanity's absolute accountability to God is made clear in relationship to the *nafs*, and Quran 4:1, where our collective creation is traced back to the *nafs,* or single soul.

In the Sufi tradition there is a story of Prophet Muhammad (PBUH) coming back from a battle and saying, "We have left the lesser *jihad* to return to the greater *jihad*" (Al-Ghazali, 2014, p. 254). This idea of *jihad*, or spiritual struggle, became the foundation for *jihad-an-nafs*, or the struggle to purify and tame the self and its desires and impulses. Imam Al-Ghazali (2014) sets out the details of this struggle extensively in *Revival of the Religious Sciences*, including how it relates to the parts of the self and the division of the heart, self, soul, and mind .

The Twelve Steps

The history of addiction treatment in the United States goes back to early settlers. The use of alcohol was widespread from the early days of the invasion of the Americas, and consumption of alcohol was a social problem that was continuous and severe. The most prominent early writer on alcoholism was Benjamin Rush (1746-1813), a member of the Continental Congress and a signer of the Declaration of Independence, and a "profound influence on early American medicine" (White, 1998, p. 1). Rush believed that alcoholism was a medical condition, a belief that deviated from the ideas of the time that alcoholism was a moral failure on the part of inebriates (White, 1998, p. 2). He also included some of the first ideas on alcoholism as a hereditary condition (White, 1998, p. 2).

Fast-forward two hundred years to around the end of prohibition when there was a huge gap in US society where people suffering from alcohol abuse could not get help. Public mental hospitals were not offering treatment for individuals struggling with alcoholism. The progression of treatment for alcoholism had reached a critical juncture and by a series of events, which included Carl Jung's advice that alcoholism was connected to a disease of the spirit, two recovering alcoholics - Bill Wilson and Dr. Bob Smith (known as Dr. Bob) - banded together to form the self-help society of Alcoholics Anonymous (AA) (White, 1998). Their concept was an expansion on Rush's and others' early ideas of alcoholism as a disease, and they conceptualized drinking problems as having a cure that involved body, mind, and spirit. Wilson and Dr. Bob's early work to establish the society of AA included the authoring of the now world famous Twelve Steps which have been adapted for use in drug addiction, over-eating, codependency, gambling, sex addiction, and a proliferation of Twelve Step societies that now number over 100.

The original Twelve Steps of Alcoholics Anonymous are as follows:

1. We admitted we were powerless over alcohol—that our lives had become unmanageable.

2. Came to believe that a power greater than ourselves could restore us to sanity.

3. Made a decision to turn our will and our lives over to the care of God *as we understood Him.*

4. Made a searching and fearless moral inventory of ourselves.

5. Admitted to God, to ourselves, and to another human being the exact nature of our wrongs.

6. Were entirely ready to have God remove all these defects of character.

7. Humbly asked Him to remove our shortcomings.

8. Made a list of all persons we had harmed, and became willing to make amends to them all.

9. Made direct amends to such people wherever possible, except when to do so would injure them or others.

10. Continued to take personal inventory, and when we were wrong, promptly admitted it.

11. Sought through prayer and meditation to improve our conscious contact with God *as we understood Him,* praying only for knowledge of His will for us and the power to carry that out.

12. Having had a spiritual awakening as the result of these steps, we tried to carry this message to alcoholics and to practice these principles in all our affairs

The Disease Model of Recovery

The disease model of recovery has in fact been challenged extensively in the scientific literature and lay movements (Brown & Lewis, 1999; Thombs, 2006). Part of the challenge has been the disease model's tendency to be associated with an insistence on the impossibility of control, and the idea that the only means of attaining recovery is total abstinence. Other models of addiction recovery include behavioral models, as well as psychoanalytic, motivational frameworks, and the transtheoretical model. However, all these frameworks have increasingly been integrated into the lives and recovery of those who have utilized Twelve Step fellowships and have served to deepen understanding and recovery.

Defining Recovery

Part of the ongoing work of the addiction treatment community has been to define recovery. The Substance Abuse and Mental Health Administration (SAMSHA) defines recovery as "A process of change through which individuals improve their health and wellness, live a self-directed life, and strive to reach their full potential" (SAMSHA, 2014). The SAMSHA concept of recovery drives behavioral health care throughout the US and includes a variety of elements, including holistic healing, self-redefinition, personal change and transformation, connectedness to the community, peers, allies, empowerment, hope, and gratitude (SAMSHA, 2009). The idea of recovery in Twelve Step programs, similarly, is freedom from active addiction and being a productive, responsible member of society (NA World Service, 2008). Recovery is defined by most people as a holistic process where healing of mind, body and spirit come together to transform the lives of people suffering from alcoholism or addiction, as well as a variety of other mental health challenges.

One ongoing question of recovery is whether it requires abstinence, or whether it is defined by abstinence. There are a variety of opinions on this topic, ranging from insistence on total abstinence, to models that incorporate the goal of functional use of drugs and alcohol. However, part of the congruence of the Twelve Step model with Islamic ideas of recovery is the goal of total abstinence. Intoxicants are forbidden by the Quran, the Sunnah, and the Islamic tradition politically and socially (Badri, 1976). Twelve Step programs' intention to support a complete end to all drug and alcohol use makes Twelve Step recovery more compatible with an Islamic way of life than other models which do not rule this out.

The Comparison Between Sufism and the Twelve Steps

Sufism and the Twelve Steps have a number of similarities that will be discussed here, and some fundamental differences; or one could even go so far as to say conflicts. The way that *jihad-an-nafs* and Sufism generally connect to Twelve Step recovery include spiritual virtues and practices for spiritual development. The disconnects include a resistance, even outright rejection of any association or inclusion of religion in the Twelve Steps, and a prohibition on the open display or discussion of religion in meetings, literature, and activities associated with Twelve Step recovery.

Inventory of a Few Common Virtues

In addition to the emphasis on total abstinence, another feature of Twelve Step recovery that is highly consistent with Islamic values, and the above-mentioned *jihad-an-nafs*, is the focus on the improvement of character. The medical model of addiction does not rule out the need for changing standards of behavior or personal traits that are morally reprehensible. In fact, Twelve Step recovery programs focus on many of the same values as Sufism. The idea that Twelve Step recovery is in essence a spiritual program designed to "confront a diseased ego and promote its transcendence"

(Warfield & Goldstein, 1996) is strikingly similar to the concept of transformation of the *nafs*. It is not surprising that the spiritual concepts that form the foundation of the two paths have many similarities.

Surrender

Muslims orient their entire religion around surrender or submission to God. Islam means to surrender/submit. The wholehearted surrender of the self to the spiritual path forms the foundation and structure of the religion. The abandonment of the self and the world in submission to God is the first step of the Sufi path (Angha,1991). Frager (1999) states, "Western society places great value on personal freedom. But for many this is merely freedom to follow their own misguided inclinations. Paradoxically, submission to spiritual discipline is the beginning of real freedom, because it is the beginning of freedom from the tyranny of the *nafs,"* (p. 50).

In Twelve Steps, surrender is the main principle of the First Step. The Basic Text of Narcotics Anonymous states: "We stress the importance of surrender for it is the very process that enables us to recover" (NA World Service, 2008, p.11). The surrender of the First Step makes it possible to give up using drugs, alcohol, and other addictions because it is the admission of the inability to use drugs successfully. In that admission of powerlessness, and the resulting unmanageability that accompanies it, people in Twelve Step recovery find the strength to turn their lives around and embark on a spiritual program of self-transformation without the use of substances. This surrender is a daily struggle for many people in recovery, an ongoing battle with the impulses to get high or drunk and avoid life and pain. Surrender to the principles of recovery opens the door to a new way of life.

Faith

The driving force behind self-actualization in Sufism is faith in God. In a sense, for some teachers, faith in God is faith in oneself, in that we are manifestations of God's purpose, and the spiritual path is understanding God through going into the self through meditation, contemplation, and prayer (Khan, 1994, p. 127).

Faith is the critical foundation of Twelve Step recovery, just as it is of Sufism. The Big Book of Alcoholics Anonymous (p. 47) states, "As soon as a man can say that he does believe or is willing to believe, we emphatically assure him that he is on his way." As soon as alcoholics, or any Twelve Steppers, surrender to the program, they begin to lay a foundation of faith that grounds their journey. The Second Step states, "We came to believe in a Power greater than ourselves that could restore us to sanity." The belief in a Higher Power helps people in recovery to face their failures, challenges, and setbacks with consistency of purpose, and the emotional strength needed to persevere in the face of often overwhelming emotional pain (Kissman & Maurer, 2002).

Intention

The meaning of one of the sayings of Prophet Mohammed (pbuh) is,

> "Actions are but by intentions and every man gets but that which he intends."

Sufism emphasizes the importance of intentions as part of the Islamic tradition. Clarifying intentions is critical for the Sufi path and for *jihad-an-nafs* because without it, the path is almost meaningless. Many Sufi teachers talk about the centrality of intentions, including "confronting your intentions, your motivations" (Khan, 1994, p. 104). as understanding the meaning of both one's own life and God. For many Sufis "The study of the self is the study of God" (Khan, 1991, p. 34) and this intention to embark on the path of self-exploration is key to the entire project of spiritual awakening that Sufism represents. Imam Mehdi Khorasani (2000, p. 16) states in *The Way of Success and Happiness:* "In order to have a goal one needs a special kind of thought or intention through which to discover oneself. When this intention has taken place the real goal of God (service and good works) will evidence itself in one's life." He clarifies that the intention to know oneself is the first step toward success in life, just as it is in the process of recovery. This knowledge of self is the same as knowledge of God.

In the Twelve Steps, the intention to understand oneself and one's motives, drives, and character, as well as to transform the self towards self-realization is the heart of the steps. Step Three reads, "We made a decision to turn our will and our lives over to the care of God as we understood Him." This is essentially intention, self-exploration, self-examination, and self-purification through the path of the Twelve Steps (Mohr, 2022). The words used in the Third Step as discussed in Twelve Step literature often focus on the idea of decision, but this word means the formation of the intention, the focus of the effort to engage in recovery. The decision of the Third Step is the foundation for recovery to commit to a way of life under the guidance and care of a Higher Power, following the path of the steps (NA World Service, 1993).

Refinement of Character

Jihad-an-nafs is essentially the work to purify and transform the self. Through prayer and meditation, reflection, contemplation, and other spiritual practices, Sufi teachers instruct practitioners to develop themselves beyond the pull of base desires to a state of spiritual and moral purity and self-control. Character defects like anger, greed, and other base desires are resisted systematically as part of the spiritual path, while positive character traits like forgiveness, generosity, and other prosocial traits are actively cultivated (Al-Ghazali, 2014).

The process of the steps is at its heart an effort to improve character and transform oneself to a better way of life. Both the moral inventory of Step Four and Five and the work to remove one's defects of character in Steps Six and Seven involve an intense focus on self-reflection as a means to move from morally reprehensible actions to morally sound ones.

Both the Twelve Steps and Islam have a positive view of the self. Regarding the process of the steps, the *Narcotics Anonymous Step Working Guide* (1998, p. 31) states that it is like peeling away the layers of an onion: "the core represents the pure and healthy spirit that lies at the center of each one of us." Similar to the idea of reaching a core pure spirit that is Divine in the path of self-transformation of Sufism, the Twelve Step fellowships generally have a positive view of human nature and that the process is a restoration to an original nature that has been hidden by defects of character and unhealthy patterns. This then involves a focus on character assets as much as it is focused on overcoming defects (NA World Service, 1998).

Islam, and Sufism particularly, includes a basic belief in the fundamental goodness of human beings. Even though there is a mixed view of the *nafs,* in that it requires training and purification, other parts of the self are viewed as being pure in their origin and nature, such as the *qalb,* or heart, which is considered to be pure from birth and only polluted or confused by upbringing, training, or life experiences. Thus, the process of working with the *nafs,* and Islamic psychology generally, involves a purification and restoration of an original goodness, not a resistance to, or rejection of the core self. The Quran states,

"So direct your face [i.e., self] toward the religion, inclining to truth. [Adhere to] the fiṭrah of Allāh upon which He has created [all] people" (Quran, 30:30).

And in the hadith,

"Every child is born on the fitra" (Maliks Muwatta, 16:53).

Rothman and Coyle (2018) state of their research into the Islamic model of the self, "The consensus among participants was that fitrah posits that all human beings are born with the same sound nature, which most agreed is pure and which comes from and has a direct link to God" (p. 1735). They go on to say, "The model [of the self in Islamic psychology] posits that the soul has an inherent inclination toward growth and an upward trajectory in relation to this model, due to its primordial nature of knowing God, and that the Islamic tradition, as guided by the Qur'an and Sunnah, encourages and maps out a path for the human being to pursue this trajectory (p.1743)."

Thus, the concept of fitra which is so essential to Islamic psychology, and to Sufism, is consistent with the general view of the self in the Twelve Steps.

Repentance

Sufism emphasizes the importance of repentance, or *tawba*, as part of the spiritual path. *Tawba*, or repentance, means essentially to turn away or turn back. In the sense that it is a path of complete devotion to God, repentance is at its heart turning away from everything of the world in devotion to one's Lord (Angha, 1991). Repentance also involves setting aside sinful behavior and character traits that interfere with the pure experience of God on a moment to moment, day to day basis (Al-Ghazali, 2014).

In Twelve Steps, Steps Eight and Nine involve repenting of mistakes and misdeeds and harms to oneself, others, and society. The process of making amends, the Ninth Step, is based on a willingness to change that is the focus of the Eighth Step. Willingness in Twelve Step recovery has many similarities to the idea of *tawba*, in that it involves a similar sense of humility and self-examination that leads to personal growth and progress on the spiritual path. The *NA Step Working Guide* talks about the personal transformation that comes about as a result of the process of the Ninth Step, "We become better people. We become less willing to engage in destructive behavior because we are aware of the cost in human misery, both our own and those around us. Our self-centeredness is replaced by an awareness of other people and concern about their lives. Where we were indifferent, we begin to care. Where we were selfish, we begin to be selfless. Where we were angry, we begin to be loving ," (NA World Service, 1998, p. 89).

The idea that the process of amends makes people in recovery better people involves letting go and committing to change old harmful habits and replace them with new ones. This process of self-transformation is the core of the Twelve Steps.

Service

Service is an essential part of the Sufi path, with the refinement of character manifesting through love and service to others. Frager (1999, p. 27) states, "With positive actions the breast expands, and the Light of Practice grows. This is why service is an essential aspect of the Sufi path." Generosity, through charitable acts, as well as an overall attitude of helpfulness and giving, are central to Sufism, and all Islamic practice (Al-Ghazali, 2014).

Step Twelve, the culmination of the Twelve Step program reads, "Having had a spiritual awakening as a result of these steps we tried to carry this message to others and practice these principles in all our affairs." The idea that "service keeps you clean" is an essential component of Twelve Step fellowships, and service forms a foundation of recovery as it makes the fellowship possible, and viable. Many people report that addiction was a self-centered way of life, and the antidote is the selfless service promoted by Twelve Step fellowships (NA World Service, 1998).

Commonalities Between Tools

One interesting and important parallel between Twelve Step recovery and Sufism is the similarity of tools that people use to progress on the two paths. Meetings, writing, having a relationship with a teacher or sponsor, prayer and meditation, and reflection all feature in both traditions as important structures to implement growth and change.

Meetings

Twelve Step groups are most well-known for their meetings. Groups meet regularly throughout the world and members share their experience, strength, and hope through informal talks, literature studies, conventions, and gatherings. One of the mainstays of Twelve Step recovery is regular meeting attendance, with many members attending a meeting every day for the first few months or years and continuing to attend meetings on a lifelong basis. Engaging in mutual support groups has been shown to improve outcomes with addiction treatment and members who commit to regular meeting attendance often see better results than those who do not (Kissman & Maurer, 2002).

Likewise, gatherings and spiritual companionship are a core component of the Sufi path. Sufi groups meet regularly, often around meals, at a local center, and there are usually regular meetings led by more senior members, organized by a shaykh or order. These meetings often include a lecture, spiritual companionship (called *sohbet)*, where advice, lessons, and teaching happen, as well as chanting, singing, and occasionally dancing. Sufi gatherings provide community support for members of the order, as well as the larger community who are often welcomed free of charge or obligation other than to follow simple rules of social etiquette.

In both traditions, meetings serve as a foundation for the establishment of good character. Role modeling, mentoring, and open sharing of ideas help newer members learn the tradition, while older members benefit from sharing their experience and renewing their commitments. The importance of community is central to both Sufism and Twelve Steps, with Twelve Steppers calling their groups "fellowship" of which they are "members" and Sufis being a part of an order or *tariqah* where they are renunciates, dervishes, *saleks*, mureeds, or wayfarers.

Working on purification of character, or *jihad-an-nafs*, is integrated into the structure of both groups through active sharing, teaching, and introspection. The evolution of character through self-refinement is a central goal of both traditions, with Sufis progressing through stages of spiritual realization, and Twelve Steppers progressing through the steps. This gradual evolution leads members to achieve greater personal freedom and self-actualization.

Writing

Writing is a critical part of the Twelve Steps (AA World Service, 2001; NA World Service, 1993; NA World Service, 1998). The use of step work to address underlying issues and behavior patterns forms the foundation. For people who follow a Twelve Step program, extensive writing and assignments structure the way recovery happens. Additionally, there are emerging models of Twelve Step recovery in the Islamic tradition that emphasize writing to explore patterns of behavior and gain personal insight and facilitate self-transformation (Adisa & Steiner, 2021).

While Sufism does not center writing to the same degree as the Twelve Steps, writing forms a central part of the Sufi tradition. Mystical poetry in the Sufi tradition, for example, is one of the major ways that Sufism has been transmitted to the Western world (Acim, 2018) as well as a basic practice in the tradition (Bakhtiar, 1976). In the US, poets like Rumi and Hafiz have found their way into the homes and hearts of millions. Sufi teachers often engage in writing poetry as well. Aside from poetry, there are teachers who suggest journaling as a tool for growth (Frager, 1999). Both traditions contain the idea that the act of writing can be a tool for insight, growth and change.

Another interesting connection to make is the science of calligraphy which is a discipline in and of itself in the Islamic tradition, both as an art form, and a spiritual practice. Sharify-Funk (2018) states, "The scriptural prevalence of ideas linked to writing provided great inspiration to Sufis and Sufi calligraphers. Quranic passages conveying the idea of a heavenly pen (*al-Qalam*), for example, suggest a correspondence between human practices of writing and God's acts of teaching humanity through the creation of holy books."

She also outlines the connections between Quranic verses and writing, including the verses on the Divine Pen, which include Quran 68:1; 96:1-5, and the Eternal Book, Quran 43:4; 13:39; 85:22; 56:78.

Speaking With Individuals With More Experience for Guidance

Both Twelve Step recovery and Sufism emphasize the importance of seeking the help of a guide. In Sufism, this usually takes the form of a shaykh, who helps the student to learn about the religion, both in its exoteric and esoteric aspects. The importance of a shaykh in Sufism appears throughout the tradition (Angha, 1991; Frager, 1999; Ozak, 2001). There are clear structures for the inclusion of people aspiring to the path through gradual rites of passage into traditional orders, and less formal relationships in more modern times. While modernity has changed some structures of the shaykh/student relationship (for example places where students are encouraged to connect to a shaykh via the world wide web) traditional relationships are still central to the Sufi tradition.

In Twelve Step programs, the relationship between a member seeking recovery and a sponsor is critical (AA World Service, 2001; NA World Service, 2008). All step work, or the writing out of the steps, happens in conjunction with a sponsor. Additionally, regular contact between sponsors and sponsees provides guidance and life coaching throughout the process of recovery. Sponsors also have a lineage, like shaykhs, with sponsorship families, including the idea of grand-sponsor, sponsor sisters or brothers, and other relationships related to sponsorship lines.

Prayer and Meditation

Prayer and meditation form the backbone of *jihad-an-nafs* and Sufism generally. The Friday prayer, which is a community prayer, is supplemented by the five daily prayers, which are sometimes done communally. The practice of meditation in Sufism is central as well, with dhikr, often translated as mindfulness or mantra, through repetition of Islamic phrases, and the names of God in Arabic taking up significant parts of daily and community practice (Khan, 1991; Khan, 1994). Dhikr is seen as a way to purify the heart specifically, as well as the whole character and life of practitioners (Angha, 1991).

In Twelve Step groups, prayer and meditation are usually included in a regular program of recovery. Both the Third Step, the Seventh Step, and the Eleventh Step all center around practices of prayer. The Eleventh Step reads: "We sought through prayer and meditation to improve our conscious contact with God as we understood God, praying only for knowledge of God's will for us and the power to carry it out." Seeking to improve "conscious contact" with a Higher Power is emphasized by most members seeking outside spiritual practices, including Sufism, for further personal development. Prayer and meditation are used extensively by people in recovery and have been shown to improve outcomes and support continued abstinence (Priester et al, 2009). Additionally, these two paths are currently merging in the literature. Multiple writers commenting on Islam and recovery mention the possibilities and potential of dhikr as a tool for recovery (Adisa & Steiner, 2021; Mohr, 2022; Raslan, 2021; Rassool, 2021).

Differences and Conflicts Between Approaches

The Problem of Religion: The A.A. Preamble/What Is Narcotics Anonymous

One of the major disconnects between Twelve Steps and Sufism is the problem presented by the historical traditions represented by both the A.A. Preamble and *What is Narcotics Anonymous*, each of which is read in almost every meeting without exception in their respective fellowships. Just to explain, there are certain readings which are consistent in most Twelve Step fellowships which are read at the beginning of each meeting, prior to speakers, open sharing, or literature studies. These readings generally discourage religious affiliations being expressed in meetings or Twelve Step related events.

The A.A. Preamble states, "A.A. is not allied with any sect, denomination, politics, organization or institution; does not wish to engage in any controversy, neither endorses nor opposes any causes." *What is Narcotics Anonymous* includes this language: "We are not connected with any political, religious, or law enforcement groups, and are under no surveillance at any time." These documents have been historically connected to a resistance of allowing discussion of religious affiliations within Twelve Step meetings. It has also led to some members being quite resistant to other members wearing open symbols of a religious tradition, which has historically mostly focused on the crosses and Christian symbols, but also definitely includes resistance, and at times outright hostility to, the hijab. The idea that Twelve Step groups are not connected to religion, and that they do not endorse religions, however, is not universally held to mean that religion, the wearing of religious symbols, and other associations by individual members are strictly prohibited in meetings and events, in spite of sporadic and sometimes vehement views of individual members or groups.

The Problem of "Outside Issues"

Another issue that can hinder the free association of Sufism with the Twelve Steps is the tradition that Twelve Step fellowships have no opinion on "outside issues." As background, Twelve Step groups and fellowships are run entirely by members, thus the idea of self-help groups. The service structure of the groups is organized around the Twelve Traditions. Of these, the original Tradition 10 reads: "Alcoholics Anonymous has no opinion on outside issues; hence the AA name ought never be drawn into public controversy." This tradition is shared by most Twelve Step fellowships who unanimously agree that any fellowship should not express any views on any outside issue beyond the explicit goals of sobriety or abstinence endorsed by that particular fellowship (alcohol in Alcoholics Anonymous, drugs in Narcotics Anonymous, cocaine in Cocaine Anonymous, codependency in Codependents Anonymous, and so forth.) For many members, seeing a member at a meeting wearing religious symbols such as a hijab violates this principle. It also means for some that any mention of the name of a god associated with a specific religion (Allah, Jesus, Krishna) is a violation of this principle. There is however another group of people who are vocal in their belief that anything that relates to recovery is valid for meetings, and have no problem with these types of references. It varies from member to member, and from group to group.

Case Study

Clearly, there are both similarities and differences between the two paths, conflicts, and points of harmony. How can they come together in practice? There are many examples of people who participate in both groups, representing diverse experiences. The author provides here a case study of a person in recovery who utilized the two paths and how it benefited them to provide insight into one example of how the paths of Twelve Steps and Sufism can come together to complement each other. There is little quantitative data about the prevalence of the use of both paths worldwide. However, the presence of Twelve Step orders in countries where there are strong Sufi orders such as Iran and Turkey, as well as all over the world, would suggest this case study has many counterparts globally.

A young woman had come to recovery in her early twenties and struggled with staying clean, although she followed the Twelve Step model with some success. She had developed habits of step work and prayer and meditation and had re-enrolled in school after dropping out. When a comparative religions teacher introduced her to Islam, she had an instant interest and found a contact in the phone book who happened to be a Sufi teacher. Over the next fifteen years she studied with him, and his coaching and unconditional love led her to embrace the path of Islam which greatly enhanced her recovery, including finally enabling her to settle down and have a family which had been eluding her with the Twelve Steps. In times of trial, the paths played different and supporting roles for her, alternatively helping her stay off drugs and on track with life and increasing her level of spiritual connectedness which she believed greatly enhanced her quality of life.

Part of this was a result of the jihad-an-nafs which is intrinsic to the practice of Islam. Self-control is a consequence of the rigorous practices of the Islamic faith including daily prayer and regular fasting. It is also clear that the strong prohibitions against alcohol and drugs in Islam have the potential to be supportive of a clean and sober lifestyle where people's urges to indulge, party, and let loose are restricted, although this is not uniform across all believers.

One challenge that this woman had in integrating the two paths was the conflict between the sometimes anti-religious nature of Twelve Step groups and her eventual decision to wear hijab. However, members were often supportive, and the pressure to conform was in large part merely an echo of societal norms in the larger world.

In her case at least, there were many benefits of bringing both paths together. She experienced a deeper sense of spirituality. She developed a greater sense of self-control and higher levels of self-actualization as a result of the stringent requirements of the Islamic faith, and the ongoing self-examination of the Twelve Steps. Happily, she met other people who had taken the same path of combining the Twelve Steps with Islam and Sufism, and shared many of the joys and challenges that she has faced.

Possibilities of a Dual Approach With Sufism and the Twelve Steps

For Recovering Individuals

As the case study reflects, individuals can reap greater rewards from both paths, particularly with the problems of facing substance use alone, or spiritual growth alone. The benefits of community, structures of guidance and support, and proven successes of others lead to increased opportunities for self-actualization for individuals who choose to use both Twelve Steps and Sufism. One of the major problems with embracing a path like Sufism without the foundation of the Twelve Steps is the dangers of not being able to integrate into a society with high demands for personal practice, and vice versa. The familiar expectations of a spiritual community, particularly one that demands total abstinence from drugs and alcohol, makes integrating the potential gains smoother. Deepened self-understanding, self-refinement, and self-realization both in character development generally, and in prayer and meditation and conscious contact with a Higher Power, are potential benefits of following both paths simultaneously.

For Psychologists Supporting Recovery

The compatibility of Twelve Step recovery with Sufism offers many opportunities for mental health professionals. Some of these involve the potential to leverage the two frameworks in motivation enhancement, the possibility of increased effectiveness of the transtheoretical model through cultural congruence, stronger interventions for harm reduction strategies, and an overall increase in available tools for recovery through integration of spirituality in substance abuse treatment.

Motivational interviewing (MI) and motivation enhancement is an evidenced-based and widely utilized therapeutic intervention for clients who present with substance use disorders (Miller & Rollnick, 2013). The basic ideas of MI, to follow the lead of the client and address ambivalence through empathy, awareness, open ended questions, and reflective listening, are generally secular in focus. One major tool of MI is the idea of developing discrepancy between client's personal goals and the impact of their substance use. In this respect, many people present with spiritual goals, which is often an underutilized focus in MI given how central a feature of internal life it is for many clients. Before giving feedback in MI, the therapist asks for permission. Then there is often an introduction of ideas or information, or a highlighting of focus that the clinician uses to explore options with the client. The emphasis on the importance of mutual support groups, the transformative power of prayer and meditation, and recovery as a spiritual path also supports the idea that the therapist accompanies the client on the journey of change, rather than leading through expertise as much of the transformative work of recovery is expected to occur outside of the context of therapy (Priester, 2000). Sufism, and the influence of religious ideas of the development and refinement of character present an underutilized opportunity for exploration of motivation for change.

The transtheoretical model generally, often used in conjunction with MI, also known as the Stages of Change model, could also potentially benefit from the inclusion of ideas of Sufism and *jihad-an-nafs*, as well as introducing the idea of the Twelve Steps for clients who already are culturally or religiously Muslim (Prochaska & DiClemente, 1983). The idea that change happens gradually through stages includes the idea that the therapist takes an active role in clients' change process. In pre-contemplation, spiritual ideas can provide insight into other ways of living that might be healthier or less destructive. In contemplation, the motivation to live spiritually could be explored as a catalyst for change. Exploring religious paths and Twelve Step fellowships could provide community support, a proven factor in successful change, in preparation, and action. Healthy community support, and the above congruence of spiritual practices

THE WAY OF LOVE

could make maintenance more fluid, and relapse less likely as added incentives become central to the life of the client.

Harm reduction is an evidenced-based intervention that continues to gain prominence in the recovery community (Des Jarlais, 2017). The ideas of Sufism and the purification of the self could support more clear moves towards healthier choices for people seeking freedom from suffering due to drug and alcohol use. Many people in the harm reduction community have familiarity with the Twelve Steps and embrace some parts of the model but have a hard time applying the entire program. Integration of the two approaches has the potential to increase healthy options for help seeking behaviors.

Another interesting application of the congruence of Sufism and Twelve Step recovery is spiritually integrated approaches to therapy, including spiritually integrated psychotherapy such as spiritually modified CBT and Traditional Islamically Integrated Psychotherapy (TIIP) (Keshavarzi, Khan, Ali, & Awaad, 2021; York Al-Karam, 2018; 2020). Research on CBT indicates that incorporating spirituality can improve the efficacy of interventions with clients (Hodge, 2011). Religion and spirituality provide an abundant source of thought modification possibilities for clients, and in the case of clients engaged in both Sufism and Twelve Steps, spiritually modified CBT has tremendous potential as shown already by its efficacy in the literature on alcohol treatment (Hodge, 2011).

For Non-Muslims

In addition to solutions for the alcohol and drug related problems of Muslims, Sufism could also potentially help non-Muslims in their recovery. Just as meditation and mindfulness drawn from the Buddhist tradition have contributed greatly to the lives of people in recovery, Sufism has much to offer. Specifically, as a path of psychology, Sufism offers insight into the process of self-refinement for people in recovery. Also, tools like the creative use of poetry have value. Many people in recovery draw a great deal of inspiration from Sufi poetry, for example, loving Rumi or Hafiz. The beauty of the Islamic tradition has a great deal to offer to expand the spiritual horizons of everyone in recovery, not just Muslims, enriching their path, and their experience of recovery.

Ideas for Future Research and Exploration

The use of Sufism and Twelve Step recovery together for addiction treatment is significantly under-explored in the literature. Few books and articles exist, little quantitative or empirical research, and there are minimal avenues for exploration of these ideas in the broader society. Substantial work is needed to clarify how these two paths can supplement each other and support recovery for individuals seeking help, self-transformation, and freedom from active addiction. Given the prevalence of Sufi orders in places like Turkey, Iran, and India, much of this work could be done internationally, although there remains fertile ground for research in the United States. Studies that document the influence of dhikr on overall wellness of recovering individuals, the benefits of reading and listening to Sufi lectures and talks, the benefits of Twelve Steps for Muslims seeking to establish a lifestyle of abstinence from drugs and alcohol, and many other possible interventions would benefit mental health professionals and the broader public. Additionally, with the increasing use of group interventions in the Muslim community, the possibility for recovery groups is vast, with some already existing such as Millati Islami, and many more group forums popping up all the time.

Clearly this is the work of many decades. If anything, the crisis of addiction calls for attention by Muslims as a public health emergency, which affects our society generally, as well as the Muslim community specifically. Leveraging both modern and traditional tools to help those suffering is a critical and pressing task that calls for aggressive action on the part of the Muslim mental health community. The traditional prohibition of drugs and alcohol and the low rates of addiction in the Muslim community should encourage us to engage in sharing the religion with those in need. As the hadith states,

"Your religion is not complete until you love for others what you love for yourself."

References

Acim. (2018). The reception of Sufism in the west: The mystical experiences of American and European converts. *Journal of Muslim Minority Affairs, 38*(1), 57–72. https://doi.org/10.1080/13602004.2018.1432145

al-Qadir al-Jilani, A. (1992). *The Secret of secrets: Hadrat Abd al-Qadir al-Jilani* (Bayrak, T., Trans.). Cambridge, England: The Islamic Texts Society, 1992. (Original work published XXXX)

Adisa, A., & Steiner, J.A. (2021). *Overcoming addiction: An Islamic approach to recovery: 12 Steps for the Muslim & the Muslim Addiction Recovery Program.* Tayba Foundation.

Alcoholics Anonymous (AA) World Service. (2001). *Alcoholics Anonymous: The story of how many thousands of men and women have recovered from alcoholism (4ᵗʰ ed.).* Alcoholics Anonymous World Service.

Al-Ghazali. (2014). *Mukthasar: ihya ulum ad-din.* (Khalaf, M.,Trans.) Spohr Publishers Limited.

Angha, N. (1991). *Principles of Sufism.* Asian Humanities

Badri, M. B. (1976). *Islam and alcoholism.* American Trust Publications.

Bakhtiar, L. (1976). *Sufi: Expression of the mystic quest.* Avon Books.

Bakhtiar, L. (2002). *Al-Ghazzali: His psychology of the greater struggle.* Kazi Publications.

Bakhtiar, L. (2019). *Quranic psychology of the self: A textbook on Islamic moral psychology.* Kazi Publications

Barks, C., & Green, M. (2000). *The illuminated prayer: The five-times prayer of the Sufis as revealed by Jellaludin Rumi and Bawa Muhaiyadeen.* Ballantine.

Brown, S., & Lewis, V. (1999). *The alcoholic family in recovery: A developmental model.* The Guilford Press.

Brown, S., Lewis, V.M., & Liotta, A. (2000). *The family recovery guide: A map for healthy growth.* New Harbinger Publications.

Davis, G. W.(1948). Sufism from its Origins to Al-Ghazzali. *The Muslim World (Hartford), 38*(4), 241–256. https://doi.org/10.1111/j.1478-1913.1948.tb00983.x

Des Jarlais, D.C. (2017). Harm reduction in the USA: the research perspective and an archive to David Purchase. *Harm Reduction Journal, 14*(51), 1-7. https://doi.org/10.1186/s12954-017-0178-6

Frager, R. (1999). *Heart, self, and soul: The Sufi psychology of growth, balance, and harmony.* Quest.

Hodge, D. (2011). Alcohol treatment and cognitive-behavioral therapy - enhancing effectiveness by incorporating spirituality and religion. *Social Work (New York), 56*(1), 21–31. https://doi.org/10.1093/sw/56.1.21

Khan, H.I. (1991). *The mysticism of sound and music.* Shambhala.

Khan, P.V.I. (1994). *That which transpires behind that which appears: The experience of Sufism.* Omega Publications.

Kheshavarzi, H., Khan, F., Ali, B., & Awaad, R. (Eds.). (2021). *Applying Islamic principles to clinical mental health care: Introducing traditional Islamically integrated psychotherapy.* Routledge.

Khorasani, M. (2000). *The way of success and happiness.* Islamic Society of California.

Kissman, K., & Maurer, L. (2002). East meets West: Therapeutic aspects of spirituality in health, mental health and addiction recovery. *International Social Work, 45*(1), 35–43. https://doi.org/10.1177/0020872802045001315

Malik, J., & Hinnells, J. (Eds.). (2006). *Sufism in the west.* Routledge.

Mohr, S. (2022). *Loving the present: Sufism, mindfulness, and recovery from addiction and mental illness.* Resource Publications.

Narcotics Anonymous (NA) World Service. (1993). *It works: How and why.* Narcotics Anonymous World Service.

Narcotics Anonymous (NA) World Service. (1998). *Narcotics Anonymous step working guides.* Narcotics Anonymous World Service.

Narcotics Anonymous (NA) World Service. (2008). *Narcotics Anonymous: Sixth Edition.* Narcotics Anonymous World Service.

Miller, W. R., & Rollnick, S. (2013). *Motivational interviewing: Helping people change* (3rd ed.). The Guilford Press.

Ozak, M. (2009). *Love is the Wine: Talks of a Sufi master in America.* (Frager, R., Ed.). Hohm, .

Ozak, M. (2001). *The unveiling of love: Sufism and the remembrance of God.* Pir Press.

Priester, P. E. (2000). Varieties of spiritual experience in support of recovery from cocaine dependence. *Counseling & Values, 44*(2), 107. https://doi.org/10.1007/s11089-009-0196-8

Priester, P.E., et al. (2009). The frequency of prayer, meditation and holistic interventions in addictions treatment: A national survey. *Pastoral Psychology, 58*(3), 315–322. https://doi.org/10.1007/s11089-009-0196-8

Prochaska, J. O., & DiClemente, C. C. (1983). Stages and processes of self-change of smoking: Toward an integrative model of change. *Journal of Consulting and Clinical Psychology, 51*(3), 390–395. https://doi.org/10.1037/0022-006X.51.3.390

Raslan, M.S. (2021). *The danger of personal drug abuse: Addiction and the breakdown of society* (Imran, A., Trans.). Muktabaturlirshad Publications.

Rassool, G.H. (2021). *Mother of all evils: Addictive behaviors from an Islamic perspective.* Islamic Psychology Publishing.

Rothman, A., & Coyle, A. (2018). Toward a framework for Islamic Psychology and psychotherapy: An Islamic model of the soul. *Journal of Religion and Health, 57*(5), 1731–1744. https://doi.org/10.1007/s10943-018-0651-x

Substance Abuse and Mental Health Administration. (2009). Recovery: A philosophy of hope and resilience. *SAMSHA News, 5*(17), 1-7. https://taadas.s3.amazonaws.com/files/682584680804252211-aphilosophyofhopeandresilience.pdf

Substance Abuse and Mental Health Administration. (2014). *Recovery.* SAMSHA National and Regional Resources. https://www.samhsa.gov/sites/default/files/samhsa-recovery-5-6-14.pdf

Sharify-Funk, M. (2018). Geometry of the Spirit: Sufism, Calligraphy, and Letter Mysticism. Society for the Arts in Religious and Theological Studies, https://www.societyarts.org/geometry-of-the-spirit-sufism-calligraphy-and-letter-mysticism.html

Thombs, D. L. (2006). *Introduction to addictive behaviors(3rd ed.).* The Guilford Press.

Ul Haque, M.A., Aziz, S., Aqib, M. (2022). Language as motive: A rhetorical analysis of Surah Ash-Shams (The Sun). *Pakistan Journal of Educational Research, 5* (2), 655-672.

Warfield, & Goldstein, M. B. (1996). Spirituality: The key to recovery from alcoholism. *Counseling and Values, 40*(3), 196–205. https://doi.org/10.1002/j.2161-007X.1996.tb00852.x

White, W. L. (1998). *Slaying the dragon: The history of addiction treatment and recovery in America.* Chestnut Health Systems.

York Al-Karam, C. (2018). *Islamically integrated psychotherapy: Uniting faith and professional practice.* Templeton Press.

York Al-Karam, C. (2021). *Islamic psychology in the United States: Past, present, and future trajectory. International Association of Islamic Psychology.*

CHAPTER 6

————— ❖•❖ —————

Spiritual Virtues: Linguistic Definitions and Counselling Applications

Misbah Rafiq, Ph.D. and Shawkat Ahmad Shah, Ph.D.

Abstract

The primary objective of this chapter is to provide linguistic definitions of spiritual virtues in the Quran in order to facilitate their incorporation into counselling and psychotherapeutic spaces. Section 1 gives the rationale for this work. It answers the following questions: What is spirituality? How does spirituality feature in Islamic psychology? What is the nature of the relationship between psychological and spiritual well-being? What are spiritual virtues? Why is it important in the context of Islamic counselling to furnish linguistic definitions of spiritual virtues that are essentially Arabic words mentioned in the Quran? Section 2 details the methods used to achieve the objectives of this work. The outline of the methods used is as follows: a) searching the Quran for verses which feature a spiritual virtue, b) choosing a Quranic lexicon, c) using the lexicon to furnish definitions of spiritual virtues, d) integrating the underlying commonalities of these definitions in order arrive at a framework for operationalising spiritual virtues in more concrete terms, and e) suggesting some practical ways through which these spiritual virtues can be integrated in counselling spaces. Section 3 is comprised of the findings of the work which feature linguistic definitions of spiritual virtues. Section 4 unravels the framework for operationalising the spiritual virtues and also puts forth practical ways of incorporating these spiritual virtues in counselling practices. Lastly, section 5 concludes the discussion by offering a brief summary and recommendations for applying the techniques in order to evaluate their effectiveness.

The primary objective of this chapter is to provide linguistic definitions of spiritual virtues in the Quran in order to facilitate their incorporation into counselling and psychotherapeutic spaces. These objectives warrant certain clarifications. Firstly, what is spirituality? Secondly, how does spirituality feature in Islamic psychology? Thirdly, what is the nature of the relationship between psychological and spiritual well-being? Fourthly, what are spiritual virtues? Fifthly, why is it important within the context of Islamic counselling to furnish linguistic definitions of spiritual virtues that are essentially Arabic words mentioned in the Quran?

To begin with, defining spirituality is a daunting task owing to the subjectivity of its experience and the interdisciplinary scope of this concept. The interdisciplinary variation in the concept of spirituality is very aptly demonstrated by Jaberi et al., (2019). They provide theological, psychological, sociological and philosophical definitions of spirituality which is summarised below.

In theological literature, spirituality is the existence and nature of God, both the relationship to the divine to the world and the human response to God (Meraviglia, 1999). In psychological literature, spirituality is an expression of one's internal motives and desires concentrating on the self instead of God (Pargament, 1997). Sociological literature holds that spirituality entails the spiritual practices and rituals of groups of people as well as the social morality within personal relationships (MacQuarrie, 1992). Lastly, the philosophical view about spirituality is that it is a sense of unity with the cosmos...the source of cosmic order, the harmony of the universe (Bloomfield & Kory, 1978).

Hence, some of the common denominators of spirituality include: transcendence, purposefulness and meaningfulness, faithfulness, harmonious interconnectedness, integrative power, multidimensionality, and holistic being.

It is interesting to note that despite differences in conceptualising spirituality, this concept has been used across disciplines to foster spiritual health which contributes to holistic well-being. One of the disciplines that places spirituality at its centre to foster well-being is the relatively recent discipline of Islamic psychology. In Islamic tradition, spirituality is associated with the relationship with a transcendent God "Allah" and it is subsumed within religion. Therefore, ontology and epistemology of the Islamic tradition extend to encompass the unseen realm of metaphysics and the nature of Being and Divine revelation as a source of knowledge. With this understanding of spirituality subsumed in the religion of Islam, it is integrated in Islamic psychology with the aim of boosting holistic well-being.

However, the fundamental question underlying integration is the nature of the relationship between psychology and spirituality. Besides the statistical correlation between spirituality and psychological well-being, there are some philosophical underpinnings which support the argument that the two concepts are overlapping. For instance, it is assumed that "psychological development without the dimension of surrender, mystery, and imagination is incomplete and spiritual development without psychological grounding is immature" (Hoenkamp-Bisschops, 2000, p. 255). Furthermore, it is held that "the self-enclosed life ultimately stagnates. It is through openness to another in silence, listening, and obedience that......meaning flows" (Wolff-Salin, 1988, p. 134). Therefore, these arguments suggest that spiritual and psychological development can facilitate each other.

Given this overlap, it is assumed that instilling spiritual virtues in counselling can foster well-being. But how do we define spiritual virtues? Spiritual virtues are what the spirit craves. For instance, spirit is considered to be "a throng of intuitive feelings arising within us, spontaneously or called forth by outer circumstance, the emotion and attitudes concerned with what we earnestly desire and especially with what we regard as our best selves as our highest aspirations" (Sinnott, 1956, p.178). The words which define the spiritual pursuit in this definition, like 'emotion', 'attitude', 'highest aspiration', tend to make the abstract concept of spiritual virtues somewhat tangible. In a similar vein, Utz (2011) defines Islamic psychology as "the study of the soul; the ensuing behavioral, emotional, and mental processes; and both the seen and unseen aspects that influence these elements" (p. 34). This definition also refers to the tangible manifestations of a spiritual core through behaviours, emotions, and mental processes. Likewise, this work aims at operationalising spiritual virtues in the holy scripture – the Quran – by providing linguistic definitions of these Arabic terms which do not seem to have English equivalents. Although there is a lot of Islamic literature about the spiritual virtues (especially Sufi manuals), yet their operational linguistic definitions seem to be missing in the field of Islamic psychology. While this work underscores the importance of providing linguistic definitions of Arabic terms of spiritual virtues in the Quran, Badri (2018) also points out the need for providing comprehensive linguistic translations of the important Arabic terms in English in order to prevent losing the essence of the Arabic terms. Through providing linguistic definitions, this work is, therefore, expected to facilitate the application of these spiritual virtues in Islamic counselling spaces.

Method and Procedure

While underscoring the importance of providing linguistic definitions of Arabic terms of spiritual virtues in the Quran, the methods used in this work are outlined in what follows: a) searching Quran for the verses which feature a spiritual virtue, b) choosing a Quranic lexicon, c) using the lexicon to furnish definitions of spiritual virtues, d) integrating the underlying commonalities of these definitions in order arrive at a framework for operationalising an abstract spiritual virtue in more concrete terms, and e) featuring some of the practical ways through which these spiritual virtues can be integrated into counselling spaces.

Searching the Quran for Verses Which Feature a Spiritual Virtue

Given the definition of the spiritual virtue, which is essentially a virtue that the soul craves through connecting to the Divine, nine Quranic verses were selected, each featuring a spiritual virtue. These verses are:

1. Shukr (Gratitude): "Work O family of David in thankfulness, though few of My servants are *thankful*" (34:13).

2. Sabr (Patience): "And those who are *patient* in misfortune, hardship, and moments of peril. It is they who are the sincere, and it is they who are the reverent" (2:177).

3. Raja (Hope): "What ails you that you do not *hope* for Allah with dignity" (71:13).

4. Hub (Love): "And something else you *love*: help from God and a victory nigh. So give glad tidings to the believers" (61:13).

5. Ikhlas (Sincerity): "Unto us our deeds and unto you your deeds, and we are *sincere* toward Him" (2:139).

6. Taqwa (Reverence): "O Children of Adam! Should there come unto you messengers from among yourselves, recounting My signs unto you, then whosoever is *reverent* and makes amends, no fear shall come upon them, nor shall they grieve" (7:35).

7. Tawakkul (Reliance): "So turn away from them and *trust* in God. God suffices as a Guardian" (4:81).

8. Ihsan (Benevolence/Virtuousness): "Whenever you did good (ihsan), it is to your own advantage and whenever you commit evil, it is to your own disadvantage" (17:7).

9. Ijtinaab (Abstinence): "If you shun the grave sins that you are forbidden, We shall absolve you of your evil deeds and cause you to enter at a noble gate" (4:31).

It should be noted that although this work assumes that there are not exact English equivalents of the Arabic terms for the selected spiritual virtues, we acknowledge the need for doing away with linguistic barriers. As such, Nasr's (et al., 2015) commentary of the Quran - The Study Quran - was used to furnish the one-word English translations of the selected words.

Choosing a Quranic Lexicon

After identifying the spiritual virtues in the Quran, "Lexicon of Words of the Quran" (*Mufradaat alfaz al Quran,* 1994) was consulted in order to furnish their linguistic definitions. This lexicon is written by Al Husain bin Muhammad bin al-Mufazal, popularly known as Raaghib al-Isfahani who was born in the Iranian city of Isfahaan. He was a scholar of the Arabic language and the Quran in the 12th century which was a knowledge-driven time in the history of Islamic traditions. His famous works are "Book of Lexicon of Uncommon Words in the Quran" (*Kitaab ul Mufradaat fi Ghareeb bil Quran*) and a Quranic exegesis titled *Jaamiul Tafsir*. However, his lexicon is a must read for every student of the Quran. It falls in the genre of lexicographical exegeses as it lists the Quranic words in alphabetical order. Therefore, choosing this lexicon for furnishing the linguistic definitions made sense.

Integrating Commonalities to Arrive at a Framework for Operationalising Spiritual Virtues

These definitions were analysed to uncover their underlying commonalities in order to operationalise spiritual virtues. It was found that an abstract spiritual core, which is a relationship with God, is manifested in concrete realms in terms of human thoughts, emotions, or behaviours and manifests vertically towards a transcendental God and horizontally towards other people.

Practical Ways to Integrate Spiritual Virtues in Counselling Spaces.

After arriving at operational definitions of each spiritual virtue, it becomes easier to incorporate them into counselling spaces. When a succinct manifestation of a spiritual virtue is described, it can then be used to formulate clear goals for spiritual counselling. Since it is the spiritual core which craves a relationship with the Divine in the form of various spiritual virtues, we suggest techniques of contemplation and meditating on the Divine names can be used to instil these spiritual virtues in counselling practices.

Findings

Linguistic Definitions of Spiritual Virtues

The following spiritual virtues are defined: gratitude (shukur), patience (sabr), reliance (tawakkul), hope (raja), reverence (taqwa), sincerity (ikhlas), love (hub), benevolence (ihsan), and abstinence (ijtinaab). It should be noted that while providing the linguistic definitions of these spiritual virtues, which are originally extracted from the Arabic language, it should be kept in mind that the Arabic words have a primary and a secondary meaning. Therefore, it is often the interplay of these meanings which carries the essence of the term. Consequently, comprehensive linguistic definitions of these Arabic terms can help to capture the nuance of spiritual virtues and aid their operationalisation to some degree.

Shukur (Gratitude)

Shukur is an Arabic word that translates as gratitude. Shukur is reflecting over blessings or favours and expressing it. Its antonym is *kufr* which means forgetting the blessing or favour and hiding it. Shukur is filling with the remembrance of the One who bestows the blessing. There are three stages of gratitude (shukur): gratitude of the heart, gratitude of the tongue, and gratitude of bodily limbs. Gratitude of the heart involves contemplating the blessing. Gratitude of the tongue involves praising the One who bestows the blessings or favours. Gratitude of bodily limbs involves appropriate use of the favours as is demanded by them (Al-Ishfahani, 1994).

There is a verse in the Quran which reflects the third stage of gratitude which is being grateful through doing good deeds. It states:

"Do good, O family of Dawud, in thankfulness. And few from My slaves are thankful," (39:13).

It commands Prophet Dawood to do good deeds as a token of thanks for the blessings bestowed on him and not just to merely chant the prayers of thankfulness. It indicates that gratitude operates at various levels: at a cognitive level through contemplating the blessing, at an emotional level through filling the heart with remembrance of the bestower, and lastly, at a behavioural level through using the blessing for a good purpose. Consequently, gratitude is a cognitive, emotional, as well as a behavioural characteristic of human personality. That is to say, in order to be grateful, one needs to develop the following habits: thinking about one's blessings, remembering the One who blesses, and using blessings for a good purpose. It is the amazing richness of the Arabic language which communicates the comprehensiveness of the word 'shukr' through its linguistic analysis only.

Sabr (Patience)

Sabr is an Arabic word that translates as patience. Sabr means to stop oneself or to exercise restraint. It means to restrain oneself from doing something which is reprehensible either to reason or to the law or to both. Sabr has a common usage in language. However, it has different names in different situations. The most common usage of the word sabr is to prevent an emotional response of fretfulness in the face of tribulations, quarrel, and misfortune. It also includes keeping secrets (Al-Ishfahani, 1994). For instance, it is stated in the Quran:

> "Of course, the patient in hardships and sufferings and when in battle! Those are the ones who are true and those are the God-fearing," (2:177).

This verse exalts the status of those who are patient in face of hardships and sufferings. In addition, there are a few verses in the Quran which use sabr to mean steadfastness. For instance, it is stated:

> "O those who believe, be patient, be more patient than others, and guard your frontiers, and fear Allah, so that you may be successful," (3:200).

Allah encourages people to compete with each other in exercising patience. Another verse of the Quran mentions the rewards of exercising patience. It is stated:

> "Such people will be rewarded with a high place because they observed patience and will be received therein with prayers of their eternal life and peace," (25:75).

At yet another place, showing patience in difficult times is exhorted. It is stated:

> "So, patience is best," (12:18).

There are also a few Arabic variants of the word sabr which reflect the linguistic nuances of the word, like 'saboor' and 'sabaar'. The former means someone who has potential to show patience and the latter means someone who shows patience in the face of difficult times. This indicates that there needs to be an actualisation of the potential of patience. It is stated in a Quranic verse:

> "Surely in this, there are signs for everyone who is ever-patient, fully grateful," (34:19).

Another connotation of the word sabr is 'waiting'. As patience is an essential component of waiting, the Quran has used the word sabr to indicate the meaning of waiting as well, as it states

"So, remain patient with your Lord's judgment," (68:48).

That is, it exhorts its reader to exercise patience and wait for God's decree.

Consequently, the spiritual virtue of sabr manifests itself at various levels. At an emotional level, it involves preventing an emotional response of fretfulness in the face of tribulations. At a behavioural level, it involves exercising restraint in various situations.

Tawakul (Reliance)

Tawakul is an Arabic word that translates as trust or reliance. As it is used within the context with Allah, it means to entrust one's affairs to a Divine Power, to appoint Him as one's deputy, and to rely on Him completely (Nasr, et al., 2015). There are many verses in the Quran which encourage placing trust in Allah. These verses build strong arguments for establishing that Allah is strong and powerful enough to be relied on. For instance, it says:

"And Allah is enough to trust in," (4:81).

Moreover, there is a famous prayer invoked often by Muslims especially in times of danger, which is translated as,

"God suffices us, an excellent Guardian He is," (3:173),

and,

"And Allah is enough to trust in," (4-81).

These verses indicate that it is Allah who is the best disposer of affairs, therefore, it encourages its readers to entrust all affairs to Allah and to consider Him to be an excellent disposer of affairs.

There are numerous verses in the Quran which carry a deep spiritual connotation of placing trust in Allah:

"And in Allah the believers must place their trust," (14:11);

"And whoever places his trust in Allah, He is sufficient for him," (65:3).

It is also stated:

"O our Lord, in You alone we trust, and to You alone we turn for help, and to You is the final return," (60:4).

Furthermore, it is also stated:

"And in Allah you must place your trust, if you are believers," (5:23).

Tawakkul operates at a cognitive level as it involves thinking in one's head that there is a deity powerful enough to take care of one's affairs and encourages reliance on Him completely.

Rajaa (Hope)

Rajaa is an Arabic word that translates as hope. Rajaa means a thought which makes one happy. Essentially hope is expecting a pleasant outcome. However, although hope leads to happiness, it is somehow also surrounded with the fear of not achieving the desired thing (Al-Ishfahani, 1994). The Quran uses the word raja in the sense of a combination of hope and fear. It is stated in various parts of the Quran:

> "While you hope from Allah what they do not hope. And Allah is All-Knowing, All-Wise," (4:104),

and,

> "And there are others whose matter is deferred till the command of Allah (comes): either He punishes them or relents towards them. And Allah is All-Knowing, Wise," (9:106).

Etymologically, rajaa means 'a happiness-evoking thought' therefore, it pertains to human cognition.

Taqwa (Reverence)

Taqwa is an Arabic word that translates in English as reverence. It comes from the word, "wikayah" which means to protect something from that which is harmful. In this regard, it is stated in the Quran:

> "So Allah will save them from the evil of that day, and will grant them bloom and delight," (76:11).

> "And He will save them from the torment of the Hell," (44:56).

> "And for them there is none to save them from Allah," (13:34).

> "O those who believe, save yourselves and your families from a fire," (66:6).

In essence, the word taqwa means to save oneself from everything that one apprehends to be harmful. Therefore, sometimes taqwa and fear are used interchangeably. In the domain of Islamic law, taqwa means to save oneself from everything which becomes liable for sins or things which even lead to sins. There are many verses in the Quran which exhort its readers to practice taqwa and list its enormous spiritual benefits. It is stated:

"O children of Adam, if messengers from among you come to you narrating My verses before you, then, whoever fears Allah and corrects (himself), for them there shall be no fear, nor shall they grieve," (7:35).

"Surely, Allah is with those who fear Him and those who are good in deeds," (16:128).

"And those who used to fear their Lord will be led towards the Jannah in groups, until when they reach it, while its gates will be (already) opened (for them), and its keepers will say to them, salamun-'alaikum (peace be on you). How good are you. So, enter it to live here forever" (39:73).

"And be fearful of a day when you shall be returned to Allah, then everybody shall be paid, in full, what he has earned. And they shall not be wronged" (2:281) (Al-Ishfahani, 1994).

As taqwa concerns the attitude of human beings towards God, it conveys a sense of fear, mindfulness, and a constant awareness of God's Presence and Power (Nasr et al., 2015). It indicates that taqwa is an attribute which operates at a cognitive level as it pertains to one's thoughts about God. It is being mindful of God and saving oneself from His wrath. It also operates at a behavioral levels as it involves protecting oneself from causing spiritual harm to oneself.

Ikhlas (Sincerity)

Ikhlas is an Arabic word that translates as 'purification' or 'sincerity'. Ikhlas and *saafi* are synonyms. Saaf refers to something which is essentially pure and ikhlas refers to something that might have been impure in the beginning and then it has become cleansed. Another meaning of ikhlas is 'to get separated from others' or simply 'to withdraw'. In this sense, it is stated in the Quran:

"So when they lost hope in him, they went aside for consultation," (12:80).

This verse pertains to the discussion among the brothers of Prophet Yusuf (AS) about their younger brother, Bin Yamin. It uses the Arabic word 'khalasu' to indicate that they went aside from the king to have a consultation among themselves. Another verse uses the word 'mukhlis' to indicate faithfulness toward Allah. It is stated:

"Would you argue with us about Allah, when He is our Lord as well as your Lord? For us our deeds, and for you your deeds! And to Him we are faithful," (2:139).

Yet another verse uses the word 'mukhlis' for Prophet Yusuf (AS) and Prophet Musa (AS) to indicate 'chosen-ness'. It is stated:

"Surely, he (Yusuf) is among Our chosen slaves," (12:24)

and

"And mention in the Book (the story of) Musa. Indeed, he was a chosen one and was a messenger, a prophet," (19:51).

Therefore, the word ikhlas is used in the Quran to describe the attributes of the prophets.

In essence, ikhlas is withdrawal or purification from every other purpose and to solely intend to please Allah in every thought and action (Al-Ishfahani, 1994). It is a cognitive characteristic of personality as it entails purification of intentions from every other purpose and maintaining the exclusivity of the purpose of pleasing Allah.

Hub (Love)

Hub is an Arabic word that translates as love. Linguistically, "habun" means a seed of a fragrant plant. Another meaning of the word hub is 'intense love'. Love toward something can be merely for pleasure or for its benefit or for its excellence. Moreover, love or hub toward something involves a will to attain it (Al-Ishfahani, 1994). A Quranic verse indicates the desire or intention involved in love where it is stated:

"Allah shall bring a people whom He loves and who love Him," (5:54).

In this verse, Allah's love towards people means His immense blessings for them and people's love toward Allah means their desire for His nearness.

There are many places in the Quran which set the standards for Allah's love. For instance, it is stated:

"Surely Allah loves those who are most repenting, and loves those who keep themselves pure," (2:222),

and,

"Surely, Allah does not like anyone arrogant, proud," (31:18).

In addition, the Arabic language captures the subtleties of the emotion of love that humans have for Allah by indicating that although love is an emotion, it is cognitively initiated through being purpose-oriented (and the purposes may vary from the mundane to profane) and it is behaviorally manifested through the willful pursuit of seeking the beloved.

Ihsan (Benevolence/Virtuousness)

Ihsan is an Arabic word that translates into English as benevolence, beneficence, virtuousness, favour, or kindness. The word ihsan comes from the word "hasan" which means anything delightful, intellectually or sensuously (Al-Ishfahani, 1994). A thing can be pleasing to one's different senses. That is, some things appeal to our reason, some appeal to our lowly desires, and yet some are appealing to our eyes. Therefore, the word 'hasana' indicates every blessing whose attainment becomes a source of happiness. The word 'hasana' is used in the Quran in terms of good fortune. It is stated in the Quran:

> "So when something good came to them they said, 'This is our right'," (7:131).

In common parlance, the word 'hasan' is used for beauty that is appealing to the senses, but the Quranic usage of this word is usually used to refer to the beauty which is appealing to reason. For instance, it is stated:

> "And to parents you shall be good (Ihsaanaa), and to near of kin and to orphans and the needy. And say to the people what is good (Husna)," (2:83).

In this verse, the word ihsan is used to refer to the good behavior that the Quran exhorts its readers to show toward their parents and it uses the word 'husna' to refer to the pleasant ways of interpersonal communication.

Besides the linguistic definitions, the practical connotations of the word 'ihsan' are with respect to oneself, others, and God. With respect to oneself, ihsan means to act in excellent ways. For instance, it means more than 'doing usual favours'. It is stated in one verse:

> "If you do good (ahsantum), you will do it for yourselves, and if you do evil, it will be for you, too," (17:7).

Ihsan is an even greater good than justice. The Quran separately exhorts its readers to be just and benevolent. It states:

> "Allah commands to do justice and be good," (16:90).

Justice demands giving oneself and others what is due, and ihsan demands doing more than what is due (Al-Isfahani, 1994). With respect to others, it means, "loving for one's brother what one loves for oneself" (Nasr et al., 2015, p. 681). With respect to God, it means, "worshipping God as if you saw Him"(Nasr et al., 2015, p. 681). Ihsan is, therefore, a behavioral attribute which is reflected in the excellence in one's deeds.

Ijtinaab (Abstinence)

The root letters of the word *ijtinaab* is 'ja-na-ba' which has two meanings: to be on one's side or to get away from something. As a spiritual virtue to be practiced, the word ijtinaab means "to protect", "to abstain" or "to refrain from" (Al-Ishfahani, 1994). In this respect, it is stated in the Quran:

> "Those who abstain from the major sins and from shameful acts, except minor involvements," (53:32)

and,

> "So refrain from the filth of the idols and refrain from a word of falsehood," (22:30).

The Arabic root word "ja-na-ba" may also mean either "to get away from harm" or "to get deprived from good" (Al-Isfahani, 1994). For instance, it is stated in the Quran:

> "And when Ibrahim said, 'My Lord, make this city peaceful, and keep me and my children away from worshiping idols'," (14:35).

Abstinence is essentially shunning certain thoughts or deeds and it therefore pertains to the realm of human behaviour.

Framework for Operationalising Spiritual Virtues

In the above-given section, nine spiritual virtues were defined. Given the linguistic definitions of these spiritual virtues, there are some underlying commonalities that run across definitions. For instance, each spiritual virtue is manifested across thinking, feeling, or behaviour. In other words, an inner spiritual core of human essence which craves for spiritual virtues is manifested through concrete or material aspects of human existence which are thoughts, feelings, and actions. In this respect, Utz's (2011) definition of Islamic psychology also captures this idea of studying spirituality through physical manifestations and thereby substantiates the framework of this work. She defines Islamic psychology as "the study of the soul; the ensuing behavioral, emotional, and mental processes; and both the seen and unseen aspects that influence these elements" (Utz, 2011, p. 34). Therefore, the framework for operationalising a spiritual virtue involves seeing its manifestations in cognitive, emotional, and behavioural terms. Furthermore, it also includes a vertical (toward God) and horizontal (toward others) manifestation of a given a spiritual virtue.

Practical Ways to Integrate Spiritual Virtues in Counselling Spaces.

Spiritual virtues can be integrated into the counselling space by setting them as goals of the process of counselling. This can be achieved using various techniques. In the following section we propose examples of techniques clinicians can use with clients. We remind that these spiritual goals have various dimensions including cognitive, emotional, and behavioral and can be vertical or horizontal. Although there exists a significant overlap among the spiritual virtues in the categories of the dimensions, there are some characteristics which predominantly fall into a particular category. However, this categorisation is given merely to demonstrate the fact that spiritual virtues in the Quran operate at these diverse levels and dimensions.

Techniques for Instilling Spiritual Virtues

The analysis of the definitions of these spiritual virtues reveals that they seek a loving, sincere, and comforting relationship with the Divine, which is manifested through one's thoughts, feelings, and behaviours as well as through vertical (toward God) and horizontal (towards others) dynamics of one's relationships. Therefore, we suggest a few techniques to instil these virtues, such as contemplation, meditating on the divine names of Allah, and a few other practices. The rationale for developing these techniques was that they contribute across all levels and dimensions of one's thoughts, feelings, and behaviours. For instance, contemplation allows bringing God into consciousness and meditating on a Divine name of Allah involves strengthening one's relationship with Him. These practices will help a person to make some positive changes in one's behaviour. The following section presents examples of these techniques in order to instil these spiritual virtues.

Instilling Shukur (Gratitude)

Gratitude has three components: contemplating the blessing, praising the bestower, and appropriate use of the blessing. One of the techniques to instil gratitude can be contemplation. The following section outlines the technique of contemplation for instilling gratitude.

Technique: Contemplation

1. List 10 blessings which are essential for life. In other words, things that a person cannot do without.

2. Now think about how independent humans are in securing these blessings for themselves.

3. Conclusion:

4. List five of your signature blessings from Allah, that is, those blessings which are unique to you, which make you who you are:

5. Do you feel special because of the blessings you possess?

6. List 5 favours that you received from others for which you are grateful.

121

Instilling Sabr (Patience)

Patience is essentially emotional constraint. One way of instilling patience can be contemplating the transience of the material world and the permanence of transcendental realms. A brief outline of contemplative practice over a Quranic verse which may lead to an increased acceptance of one's problems is given below.

Technique: Contemplation

Contemplate the statement:

> "We certainly belong to Allah, and to Him we are bound to return." (Quran, 2:156).

In context of the above statement, list your problems and rate your acceptance of each problem on a rating scale of 0-5 where 0 means no acceptance at all and 5 means complete acceptance.

Tawakkul (Reliance)

Reliance is entrusting one's affairs to Allah. One way of instilling this spiritual virtue is meditating on a Divine name of Allah which reflects His attribute of being a Trustee (Al-Wakeel) for His creation. The technique which involves description of the Divine name (Al-Wakeel) and the instructions for meditating on this Divine name is outlined below.

Technique: Meditation on a Divine Name

Al-Wakeel (The Trustee) is someone to whom you entrust your affairs. The God we believe in is our trustee. He is the One on whom His creation places their trust and He, out of His might, sets their affairs right. Moreover, it is through acknowledging that Allah is one's Trustee, one places trust in Him. Placing trust in Allah (tawakkul) itself is a therapeutic and liberating experience as life gets exhausting dealing with problems and our own limited abilities to fix them. It is at that time when the belief in a deity who is able to dispose our affairs and take care of our problems no matter how difficult they are comes to our rescue. Placing trust in Allah (tawakkul) is associated with some of His other attributes as well such as His Oneness and His Forgiveness.

Technique: Meditation

1. Try to fix a time (10-15 minutes) two times a day to meditate on the divine name Al-Wakeel.

2. Find a quiet and comfortable place and time, where you have no distractions.

3. Sit in a comfortable position after any of the five daily prayers, preferably after Fajr and Isha.

4. Focus on the divine name Al-Wakeel.

5. Breathe normally, relax and repeat "Ya-Wakeelu" as you are inhaling and exhaling.

6. While repeating this name, focus on its meaning and remind yourself of the times when you felt that Allah took care of all your affairs.

7. Lastly, establish your relationship with Allah, who has the attribute of being Al-Wakeel, The Trustee.

Rajaa (Hope)

Hope is expecting positive outcomes from Allah. One way of instilling hope is through contemplating the effectiveness of supplications. The technique which involves bringing one's attention to the power of supplications is outlined in what follows.

Technique: Contemplation

1. Do you have any story which shows how supplication (duaa) worked amazingly at any point in your life?

2. Supplicate to Allah whatever you want to achieve, or to get rid of. However, observe the etiquette of the supplications.

3. While supplicating, consider humbly that you are asking the Being who has the power of providing you with your needs.

Taqwa (Reverence)

Reverence is mindfulness or constant awareness of Allah and protection of oneself from spiritual harm. One of the ways to instil reverence can be through meditating on the Divine name of Al-Baseer (All-Seeing), as it attunes one to the presence of the Divine Being who is ever present. The description of the Divine name Al-Baseer and the instructions for meditating using this Divine name is given below.

Technique: Meditation

Al-Baseer (All-Seeing) is derived from the word 'basr' which means "seeing or sight." Therefore, the god that Muslims believe in is All-Seeing. It is stated in the Quran:

> "Say: 'Shall I tell you what is far better than that? For those who fear (Allah), there are with their Lord gardens beneath which rivers flow where they shall live forever, and wives purified,

and approval from Allah. And Allah is watchful over His servants," (3:15),

"And fight them until there is no Fitnah (disorder or disbelief) and total obedience becomes for Allah. So, if they desist, then, Allah is indeed watchful over what they do," (8:39),

and,

"Surely, with regard to His slaves, He is All-Aware, Ever-Watchful," (42:27).

It is Allah who sees the depths of oceans, the darkness of night, the states of hearts and the conditions of temperaments. In order to internalise this divine name, one should be mindful of a Being who is watchful. Therefore, considering that Allah is seeing everything one does, one should not commit any act in isolation that one would not commit in the presence of others.

Technique: Meditation

1. Try to fix a time (10-15 minutes) two times a day to meditate on the divine name Al-Baseer.

2. Find a quiet and comfortable place and time where you have no distractions.

3. Sit in a comfortable position after any of the five daily prayers, preferably after fajr and isha.

4. Focus on the divine name Al-Baseer.

5. Breathe normally, relax and repeat "Ya-Baseeru" as you are inhaling and exhaling.

6. While repeating this name, focus on its meaning and try to relate to Allah as someone who sees your internal and external conditions.

7. Lastly, establish your relationship with Allah, who has the attribute of being Al-Baseer, The All Seeing.

Ikhlas (Sincerity)

Sincerity is exclusivity of intentions for the pleasure of Allah. This spiritual virtue involves attaching to Allah's approval and detaching from people's approval. One way of instilling this spiritual virtue can be through contemplating the unnecessary concern for people's approval and replacing it with the concern for Allah's approval. The technique outlining the contemplation of this sort is given below.

Technique: Contemplation

1. If you think that you are too much affected by others' praise or by their criticism, think that it is only Allah whose approval should matter.

2. Therefore, whenever you have to evaluate your thoughts or deeds, keep Allah's approval as your standard not the peoples' standards.

Hub (Love)

Love is yearning for Allah. It is a spiritual virtue which can be inculcated through the techniques of meditating on specific Divine Names. The description of the love-invoking Divine Names and the method for meditating on them is given below.

Technique: Meditation on a Divine Name

Al-Wadood (The Most Loving): This divine name *wadood* is derived from "wudd" which means "extreme love or sincere affection." Therefore, the god that Muslims believe in is The Most Loving, whose love reflects the most sincere and genuine form of love. Allah says in the Quran about this love,

"Allah shall bring a people whom He loves and who love Him," (5:54).

Our love for our Lord is mutual, we love Him and He loves us;

"And seek forgiveness from your Lord, then turn towards Him in repentance. Surely, my Lord is very merciful, most loving" (11:90).

Moreover, reflect on the following verse in which Allah says that He is the one who creates love:

"Surely, those who believe and do the righteous deeds, for them the Rahman (All-Merciful) will create love". (19:96).

Love means to give up one's desires for The Beloved, to stay engrossed with The Beloved, to leave comfort for The Beloved, and to be sincere in one's pursuit.

Technique: Meditation

1. Try to fix a time (10-15 minutes) two times a day to meditate on the divine name Al- Wadood.

2. Find a quiet and comfortable place and time where you have no distractions.

3. Sit in a comfortable position after any of the five daily prayers, preferably after fajr and isha.

4. Focus on the divine name Al-Wadood.

5. Breathe normally, relax and repeat "Ya-Wadoodu" as you are inhaling and exhaling.

6. While repeating this name, focus on its meaning and try to relate to Allah, who is The Most Loving, and remind yourself of the ways in which Allah loves you and of the ways in which you love Him.

7. Lastly, establish your relationship with Allah, who has the attribute of being Al-Wadood, The Most Loving one.

Instilling Ihsan (Benevolence)

Benevolence is behavioural excellence with respect to oneself, others, and Allah. This spiritual virtue needs a lot of contemplation in order to understand what one's unique needs are, in order to achieve excellence across different facets of one's life. One of the ways to instil benevolence is through contemplating the following set of questions.

Technique: Contemplation

1. How do you think you can show excellence (ihsan) towards Allah?

2. How do you think you can show excellence (ihsan) towards others?

3. How do you think you can show excellence (ihsan) towards yourself?

4. Try these ways and emulate prophetic excellence in your life.

Practicing Ijtinaab (Abstinence)

Abstinence involves observing behavioural restraint through shunning certain practices. One of the ways to instil the spiritual virtue of abstinence can be through contemplating what needs to be shunned and then cultivating the habit of abstinence from it. This technique is summarised in the following lines.

Technique: Contemplation

1. Think about acts which you think earn Allah's displeasure. What are they?

2. Consider leaving these acts for three days. Then for a week. Then for a month. Notice how leaving these acts made your life better.

3. Try giving up these habits for a lifetime through prayer and protection from Satan.

Conclusion

Spirituality is defined in various ways in various disciplines, yet there are some common denominators such as transcendence, purposefulness, meaningfulness, faithfulness, harmonious interconnectedness, integrative power, multidimensionality, and holistic being. Given these positive aspects of spirituality, it can be integrated into psychology and psychotherapeutic practice to foster well-being. This work attempted to integrate psychology and spirituality through defining and instilling spiritual virtues and thereby, informing counselling practices.

Linguistic definitions of the selected spiritual virtues indicated their underlying commonalities which allowed an abstract spiritual virtue to be manifested in concrete terms, specifically in terms of one's thoughts, feelings, and behaviours. This allowed for operationalising these spiritual virtues in more concrete terms in order to facilitate their incorporation in counselling spaces.

Incorporation of these spiritual virtues can be achieved through making them goals of the Islamic counselling process and through techniques of contemplation, meditating on a Divine name, and a few other practices. These techniques are arrived at through a research-oriented, bottom-up approach which was based on the premise of strengthening spirituality at cognitive, emotional, and behavioural levels. Consequently, these techniques might strengthen these spiritual virtues as contemplation helps to facilitate positive thinking, meditating on a Divine name helps to better nurture a relationship with Allah, and the practices of abstinence may be of help for behavioural regulation.

The application of these techniques in counselling spaces is recommended in order to elaborate the techniques further and to see their effectiveness in terms of reducing symptoms or enhancing the client's well-being and the inculcation of these spiritual virtues can work both for primary and secondary prevention.

References

Al-Isfahani, A. R. (1994). *Mufradaatul Alfaazul Quran*. (Lexicon of the words of Quran). Darul Ma`arif.

Badri, M. (2018). *Contemplation: An Islamic psychospiritual study (New Edition)*. International Institute of Islamic Thought (IIIT).

Bloomfield, H. H., & Kory, R. B. (1978). The holistic way to health & happiness: A new approach to complete lifetime wellness.

Hoenkamp-Bisschops, A. (2000). Spiritual direction, pastoral counseling and the relationship between psychology and spirituality. *Archive for the Psychology of Religion, 23*(1), 253-263.

Jaberi, A., Momennasab, M., Yektatalab, S., Ebadi, A., & Cheraghi, M. A. (2019). Spiritual health: A concept analysis. *Journal of Religion and Health, 58*, 1537-1560.

Macquarrie, J. (1992). Paths in Spirituality. Harrisburg.

Meraviglia, M. G. (1999). Critical analysis of spirituality and its empirical indicators: Prayer and meaning in life. *Journal of Holistic Nursing, 17*(1), 18-33.

Nasr, S. H., Dagli, C. K., Dakake, M. M., Lumbard, J. E., & Rustom, M. (2015). *The study of Quran. A new translation and commentary*. HarperCollins.

Pargament, K. I. (2001). *The psychology of religion and coping: Theory, research, practice*. Guilford press.

Sinnott, E. W. (1956). Biology and Spiritual Virtues. *The Journal of Religion, 35*(3), 177-189.

Utz, A. (2011). *Psychology from the Islamic perspective*. International Islamic Publishing House, p. 34

Wolff-Salin, M. (1986). *No other light: Points of convergence in psychology and spirituality*. Crossroad.

CHAPTER 7

Ethics, Morals, Virtues, and Character Strengths: A Comparison Between Islamic Psychology and Positive Psychology

Sálua Omais, Eman Tarif & Manoel Antônio dos Santos, PhD

The study of human virtues has been, for many years, a wide theme of discussion in several fields, such as philosophy, psychology, and theology. Positive psychology, a movement which began in the late 1980s and led by Martin Seligman, identifies factors that influence happiness and well-being, including the importance of virtues and character strengths (Seligman, 2004; 2011). In positive psychology, character strengths are considered personality traits that connect with human virtues and enable personal development through practice, leading to a positive emotional state and resulting in a higher level of engagement (Peterson & Seligman, 2004). For centuries many of these elements were present in Islam, through its religious teachings, to guide Muslims in their lives. However, despite the similarity between virtues in both western and Islamic perspectives, within an Islamic context these behaviors are not only limited to the individual or social scope but are also a way of worshiping God. This means that, besides the personal and social dimensions, these practices are also guided and supported by religious and spiritual motivations. The Quran, as well as the *sunnah (prophetic traditions)*, places a lot of emphasis on ethical behavior and rules of conduct with religious values at an individual and social level. Two terms that are widely used in the Islamic view when addressing this issue are *akhlaq*, which is linked to the noble qualities of character, ethics and morals, and *adab*, which identifies and explains good manners and behaviors. Both these terms refer to adequate behaviors that one needs when living in society. Islamic traditions and sources such as the Quran and the *sunnah*, show a clear incentive for the adoption of positive behaviors both individually and socially. Such behaviors are also considered an important part of faith, as they reinforce religious values and the connection with God and humanity.

The 1990s introduced a new field in psychology, as the then-president of the American Psychological Association (APA), psychologist and researcher Martin Seligman, raised a series of questions about the exclusive focus of psychology on pathologies, pain and human suffering, and the scarcity of research dedicated to factors that can contribute to the enhancement of human qualities, satisfaction, and well-being (Seligman & Csikszentmihalyi, 2000). The idea driving positive psychology would be to invest in studies on what "does good" and not only on the elements that limit human beings. This movement created a broad field of research that encompasses not only studies focused on Psychology itself, but on other areas of knowledge that encourage the promotion of behaviors and emotions that can contribute to mental health and well-being, which are found present in diverse areas such as genetics, biology, anthropology, sociology, neurosciences, and also in the fields of religion and spirituality. After years in search of theoretical models that could explain human happiness, Seligman (2011) released the PERMA model, formed by five main elements related to well-being: positive emotions, engagement, relationships, meaning, and accomplishment. Among these elements, a large part of the research within positive psychology has focused on the study of virtues and strengths of character, which are part of the "engagement" element of the PERMA model. However, this theme is not new in the scientific field. The field of human virtues has a long history in Greek philosophy, as well as in religious teachings due to their connection with the aspect of morality and ethics.

Nevertheless, despite its great relevance in the lives of individuals, religion has not always been included in psychological theories. For this reason, in recent decades, another great movement has emerged seeking more decolonial perspectives in science. With the dissemination of indigenous psychologies, the need of new epistemologies raises the importance of aligning theoretical perspectives with the beliefs and way of life of different people, cultures, and religions. One of these epistemologies is in the field of Islamic psychology, which emerged as a movement that seeks a more holistic psychology aligned with the worldview of Muslims. Islamic psychology can be defined as a holistic and interdisciplinary approach that combines Islamic sciences and practices with the study of the soul, affections, cognitions, and behaviors through an evidence-based paradigm, using the teachings of the Qur'an and *sunnah* as the basis of their studies (York Al-Karam, 2018a, 2018b; Rassool, 2021). It is a framework that seeks to fill the gap in the classical theoretical conceptions of psychology, which, according to Badri (2016), were built under a Eurocentric, atheistic, and universalizing bias. The need to create this new psychological paradigm arises with the aim of including the particularities of the Islamic faith and offering subsidies for a service that is more connected to the practices, habits, and lifestyle of this group, whose behaviors are permeated and shaped by religious traditions (Badri, 2016, 2018; Elzamzamy, Ahmed, Hassan, El Mahdi, 2021).

The purpose of this chapter is to draw a parallel between the concepts and elements linked to human virtues and character strengths, from the perspective of Islamic psychology and positive psychology, pointing out the differences and similarities between them. Besides being a subject already explored in Islamic literature by philosophers and theologians, due to the importance of rescuing pro-social behaviors and attitudes, the content present in this chapter includes ideas and reflections related to the refinement of character and the practice of virtues such as justice, love, wisdom, and other behaviors that could influence the individual and his or her surroundings. We also develop a discussion to understand how religion establishes and encourages the practice of virtues, through teachings, guidelines, and ethical-moral precepts arising from Islamic sources, as a way to contribute to the expansion of the theoretical framework of Islamic Psychology.

The Quran and Sunnah as Resources for the Development of Character and Virtues

Revealed over 1,400 years ago, the Quran is considered a divine revelation that guides and inspires the behavior of many Muslims around the world, along with the Sunnah, a set of traditions from Prophet Muhammad, whose role was fundamental to the teaching of religion and good manners. In Islam, it is not possible to talk about human virtues or character strengths without morals and ethics. Such elements have an intrinsic relationship with the religious behavior of Muslims and the principles of the Islamic faith.

The Quran is a book that is used in the daily lives of Muslims, as it provides guidelines for conduct and behavior, as well as descriptions and reflections regarding the spiritual dimension. Virtues and character strengths are widely present in the Quran, in different forms and contexts, and this is one of the reasons why it is considered a code of life for Muslims around the world. For this reason, a source that implies such a powerful influence on people's lifestyle, not only spiritually, but in worldly affairs, can work as an ally of techniques used by counselors and psychologists, both preventively and therapeutically.

Qur'anic verses can sometimes be interpreted with positive or negative lenses by individuals, and this varies according to several factors, such as subjective interpretations, lack of adequate comprehension of the verse's contents, and the influence of cultural background. This is why it is important to understand Islamic values and prescriptions in Muslim behaviors and lifestyles, both from a societal and research perspective.

Considering the increase in research on Muslim mental health, it is important to consider the sources that influence the lives of this population. The Eurocentric approach present in most psychological theories, including the specific characteristics and lifestyle of the Muslim population, ended up creating the need for an epistemology that could incorporate contents and values aligned with the beliefs and way of life of the clientele (York Al-Karam, 2018; Badri, 2016, Haque & Rothman, 2021; Pasha-Zaidi, 2021). Given this scenario, Islamic psychology has emerged to study and investigate common themes in psychology, such as cognition, emotions, and behaviors, using the knowledge of Islamic sources, such as the Quran and Sunnah, and rescuing the contributions of Muslim scholars in the past centuries related to this field. Furthermore, this epistemology also includes research on behaviors based on ethical and human values, which are an essential theme within the field of psychology (Rasool, 2021).

Character, Virtue, and Correlations with Ethics and Morals

The study of character strengths emerged from the work of Christopher Peterson and Martin Seligman (2004), through extensive research carried out over three years, in 52 countries around the world, with the objective of identifying the most valued human qualities and virtues among the different cultures, countries, and religions of the world. In addition to the various research sources used such as books, magazines, newspapers, documentaries, etc., the study included different doctrines and religions such as Buddhism, Islam, Christianity, Judaism, and Confucianism, as well as other philosophical texts. After collecting data and refining the results obtained through pre-established criteria, the Character Strengths Values (CSV) was created and, up to the present day is considered the backbone of positive psychology. The Character Strengths Values (CSV) brings together the 24 most common strengths in human beings, organized under six major groups of human virtues: wisdom, courage, humanity, justice, temperance, and transcendence. From this, a new instrument is also created, the Values in Action Inventory of Strengths (VIA-S), a psychological assessment of personality that aims to identify the character strengths most present in a given individual (Seligman, 2004). The result of the assessment serves as a tool for therapists and coaches to help the client to enhance their strengths in different areas of their lives, as well as to use them to face challenging situations (Omais, 2018; Seligman, 2004).

Table 1

Virtues and Character Strengths

Virtues						
	Wisdom and Knowledge	**Courage**	**Humanity**	**Justice**	**Temperance**	**Transcendence**
Character Strengths	Curiosity	Bravery	Love	Citizenship	Forgiveness	Appreciation of beauty and excellence
	Creativity	Persistence	Kindness	Fairness	Humility	Gratitude
	Perspective	Integrity	Social intelligence	Leadership	Prudence	Hope
	Judgement	Vitality			Self-regulation	Humor
	Love of Learning					Spirituality

Note: Adapted from Peterson, C.; & Seligman, M. E. P. (2004). *Character strengths and virtues: a handbook and classification.* Oxford University Press.

Strengths are highly desired and encouraged moral characteristics, both individually and socially, and can be applied in youth, families, work environments, and relationships, in order to enhance the individual's personal development (Peterson & Park, 2009). For this reason, several studies have shown benefits of using human strengths and virtues in relationships and institutional environments, such as higher levels of satisfaction with life, engagement, positive affect, self-efficacy, optimism, resilience, and also a reduction in levels of depression, stress, and anxiety (Niemiec, 2019, 2020; Niemiec & McGrath, 2019a; Rashid & Seligman, 2019; Peterson & Seligman, 2004; Snyder & Lopez, 2009).

One of the criteria established in the classification of character strengths by Peterson and Seligman (2004) is that they are morally valued characteristics. Hence the importance of better understanding the relationship between these two elements. The moral aspect of character develops internally through observation and learning, which makes it important to understand the influence of values and principles on personal and social behavior. This is why the authors emphasize that character strengths would be the foundation of the human condition. Therefore, the investigation and development of this theme in the field of psychology would help to identify positive traits and behaviors that contribute to well-being and excellence. However, they make it clear that character strengths are not something to be practiced with the intention of obtaining some recognition or for other external reasons, since this would mischaracterize its genuine nature and connection to good character. These strengths would function as an external manifestation of the individual's traits linked to moral aspects. Some of them can be externalized regardless of the context, as the so-called tonic forces, and others can be manifested in the face of specific situations that demand them at that moment. It is important to remember that the 24 elements of the VIA Classification were not based solely on a single culture, country, or religion, but were the result of those qualities most valued jointly by the countries in which they were screened. In addition, it is important to note that the VIA Character Strengths is not the only existing classification about this subject, as there are other studies in the literature that identified these and other human qualities. This is why the authors point out that the 24 forces are not an exclusive or exhaustive list, and are expected to be expanded over time (Peterson & Seligman, 2004).

However, even the forces listed in the CSV that are not directly linked to the moral aspect, will somehow be involved in some context that ends up having this connection. Niemiec (2019) affirms that, although not all character strengths have a direct connection with morality, the therapeutic process often involves reflections brought by the individual on moral values and virtues, such as kindness, or in the search for a personal evolution whose objective is to be a better person in their environment (Niemiec, 2019; Niemiec, Russo-Netzer & Pargament, 2020a).

For Abdullah (2014), although some terms of positive psychology, such as character strengths, were created with the intention of being explored in the field of psychology with a different perspective from philosophy, this theme is basically the same one treated in the field of ethics and religion. Alternatively, Kristjánsson (2013) emphasizes from a philosophical perspective that the conception of characters and virtues from the view of positive psychology still does not have a total consonance with ethics in its deepest sense, given the complexity that the theme requires. For him, despite having a relationship with positive emotions and well-being, the use of forces aimed only at achieving happiness, without a real education for character, creates gaps that can weaken the effective use of these resources in practice. The author also criticizes the conception brought by positive psychology regarding "signature strengths," warning that a strength or virtue cannot be compensated at the expense of others, since all

134

are necessary, and a possible "specialization" in only certain forces could culminate in gaps or deformities in the individual's character. According to him, strengths and virtues should not be treated logically and independently, but in an integrated way so that there is a balance, since, depending on the circumstances, there may be a conflict between them, which would require the choice to detriment the other, as when faced with the choice between justice and compassion, or between prudence and courage. That is why he emphasizes the need for a dominant and unifying master virtue that plays the role of "arbitration" in situations that demand a decision between one force and another.

Virtues and Character Strengths From the Perspective of Positive and Islamic Psychologies: Differences and Similarities

A deeper understanding of the concepts of virtues and strengths in the view of Islamic psychology and positive psychology shows some similarities and differences between them. Peterson and Seligman (2004, p. 13) define the virtues as "core characteristics valued by moral philosophers and religious thinkers" explaining that virtues such as wisdom, humanity, justice, temperance, courage, and transcendence would be essential values for building good character. As for character strengths, they describe them as "the psychological ingredients – processes or mechanisms – that define the virtues."

In addition to the objective of building content through a more psychological than philosophical perspective, character strengths differ from virtues because they are characteristics that can be measured, especially because of their concreteness. According to the authors, while virtues are abstract, strengths would be a concrete way for someone to put them into practice. This is why different character strengths were included in each group of virtues. Furthermore, the authors explain character strengths are different paths that an individual can use to achieve the same virtue. This diversity of options to attain a certain virtue would be necessary, since it would be difficult for a person to have or exercise all these strengths at same time. That's why they claim that "a given individual will rarely, if ever, display all of them" (Peterson & Seligman, 2004, p. 13). And they complement by saying that just a few of these forces would be enough to characterize a good character affirming that "we are comfortable saying that someone is of good character if he or she displays but 1 or 2 strengths within a virtue group" (Peterson & Seligman, 2004, p. 13).

From an Islamic perspective, there doesn't seem to be a specific distinction between virtues and character strengths in terms of nomenclature because "character strengths" is a term coined in positive psychology with the aim of distinguishing the psychological paradigm of this subject from traditional philosophical concepts. Character in the Arabic language is a word that derives from the term *akhlaq*. Muslim philosophers like Ibn Miskawayh (2003), a Muslim philosopher of the 20th century, explain the word *akhlaq* or *khuluk* as a state of the soul where the individual performs actions without the need to deliberate it. Abdullah (2014) explains that virtue ethics (*akhlaq*) focuses on the study of character, and the moral qualities of an individual. Thus, character is understood as an internal state of the soul that manifests itself through actions. That's why Miskawayh emphasizes the importance of cultivating virtues, since it is not just something to be taught, but above all a process that needs to be constantly practiced in order to become integrated into the individual's nature. For a better understanding of this process, Miskawayh divided the study of Islamic ethics into three parts: how to cultivate virtue, how to preserve it, and how to keep the soul away from vices (Abdullah, 2014; Rahim, 2013).

From a religious perspective, it is important to highlight that building and strengthening character was one of the main missions given to Prophet Muhammad (SAW), which he confirms when he says,

"I was sent to perfect good character," (Sahih Al-Bani).

The Qur'an also confirms this mission and the role of Prophet Muhammad (SAW) as an ethical model to be followed when Allah mentions,

"And verily, you (Muḥammad) are on an exalted standard of character," (68:4).

The level of importance given to character in Islam is so high that in some hadith, it is even placed in an equal or even superior position to acts of religiosity/spirituality. This is shown when Prophet Muhamad (SAW) stated,

"The believers most complete in faith are those who have the best character,"

or when he said,

"By his good character a believer will attain the degree of one who prays during the night and fasts during the day," (Sunan Abu-Dawood).

Thus, the importance of character is emphasized in various Islamic teachings, representing one of the highest forms of faith and religiosity that a Muslim can have.

Virtues and character strengths have a broad and direct relationship with spirituality, especially because they are non-materialistic behaviors and are often linked to a greater purpose in life. Littman-Ovadia and David

(2020) emphasize this relationship by stating that every strength of character is a reflection of spirituality, given that both are linked to morality, which is why it is important to better explore this reciprocal relationship between them. Based on this premise, it is extremely important to investigate this interrelationship from the different forms of spirituality, and investigate how they can favor and encourage the use and practice of virtues and pro-social behaviors.

This is why one of the biggest differences observed between Islamic psychology and positive psychology is the position that spirituality occupies in all this system of virtues and strengths. Thus, unlike the way it appears in Peterson and Seligman's (2004) classification, spirituality in the Islamic perspective is not simply an isolated virtue or force, but the basis of all of them. Spirituality occupies a central position and directs the other virtues. The Qur'anic prescriptions, along with the various prophetic guidelines that encourage Muslims to cultivate virtuous character and behavior, would work as guiding elements for the practice of virtues, as well as a way to complete an important requirement of the Islamic faith. Character formation in Islam follows the prescriptions and guidelines of the Sunnah and the Qur'an, which represent the primary sources of Islamic ethics (*Ilm al-akhlaq*) whose aim is to make the individual raise virtuous conduct to an optimal level (Rahim, 2013). When asked about the character of Prophet Muhammad (SAW), Aisha (R.A.), the prophet's wife, succinctly replied that "His character was the Quran" (Sahih Al-Bukhārī). With this, we can understand that the cultivation of character goes hand in hand with the absorption of religious teachings, simultaneously with that virtue linked to religion as an important element of faith. In Islam, the practice of virtues is confused with the practice of spirituality, as both are an integrated whole, while in the Western model represented by positive psychology, spirituality is an isolated strength, which may or may not accompany the others. Thus, the motivation for an individual to practice a virtue or not depends exclusively on his or her free will and conscience. In Islam, in addition to the free will and conscience of each individual, the pursuit of spiritual evolution at a worldly and transcendental level is encouraged by Islamic contents and prescriptions, which work as an additional motivator for the development of character and practice of virtues. Thus, virtuous behavior is not merely an individual's discretion, but is also linked to a purpose of pleasing God, as well as being rewarded for one's actions. This is noted in the Quran when it says

"[…] And do good, for Allah certainly loves the good-doers," (2:195),

or even when the practice of good deeds is associated with the worship saying,

"[...] worship your Lord, and do what is good so that you may be successful," (22:77).

Peterson and Seligman (2004) explain that the formation of good character and the practice of virtues should not be something conditioned to rules or laws, because in this way, good character would be linked to external conditions and not something arising spontaneously from the individual him or herself. In an Islamic view, however, ethical principles are not separated from religious laws, the *shariah*, which is based on divine revelations to regulate the rules of conduct. The notion of what is good or bad is not always within human reach. Many addictions occur due to the difficulty of human beings in taming their desires, supported solely and exclusively by their sense of responsibility and free will. Divine law through *shariah* aims to establish limits based on a broader divine wisdom, in order to protect individuals from excesses and conduct that compromise social well-being. Therefore, Islamic ethics and *shariah* are not separated dimensions, given that one has a direct relationship with the other (Rahim, 2013).

In the Quran, virtuous behavior is also linked to the idea of reward. It states:

"Allah has promised those who believe and do good His forgiveness and a great reward" (5:9).

This is a point that diverges a little from positive psychology, since, according to Peterson & Seligman (2004), the practice of virtues is not something linked to external elements, but an inherently rewarding action for the individual. However, would it be possible to say that all human beings, from the most diverse cultural, educational, social, and economic contexts, would be able to practice the different virtues without linking such practices to a greater purpose? Knowing that the practice of certain virtues requires the abdication of certain desires, a struggle of the soul against its own desires, would it be possible that all individuals manage to renounce their will in a totally unmotivated way? Thinking widely, it is somewhat difficult to imagine that all of humanity can reach this level of evolution unpretentiously, without any limits and without any future expectations, considering the various human weaknesses and social inequalities that we have in the world.

It is possible to find in the Qur'anic text all the human virtues and character strengths cited by Peterson and Seligman (2004) as well as others that are not present. Some of the ethical-moral values that stand out in the Quran, aimed more specifically at the individual, are sincerity (8:27), gratitude (31:12), humility (17:37), critical thinking (30:9), forgiveness (24:22), prudence (31:19); integrity (2:283), trust (3:159), patience (46:35), firmness (5:8), loyalty (5:2), and the pursuit of knowledge in different forms (20:114). On the other hand, the qualities directly linked to social relationships most prominent in an Islamic perspective are humanity, confidentiality, cordiality, fairness, civic spirit, generosity, simplicity, cooperation, responsibility, compassion, empathy, wisdom, kindness, love, justice, dignity, and pro-social attitudes, among others (Bensaid and Machouche, 2019).

Another frequent element in the Quran that is not specifically listed among the character strengths of the Via Character Strengths is patience. In Islam, patience and faith are understood as a "summary" of faith (Pasha-Zaidi, Al-Seheel, Bridges-Lyman, Dasti, 2021a; Yasien, 2006). However, according to Yasien (2006) Al-Isfahani reveals that gratitude would be superior because it promotes contentment with God and a kind of transcendence for being a practice carried out even in the face of difficult situations, while patience is necessary for moments of sadness to contain oneself in the face of adversity (Yasien, 2006).

Perhaps it is possible to make an analogy of patience with the strength of self-control or the prudence of the VIA test since patience is a characteristic linked to temperance and impulse management. However, in the Quran, patience is presented with different meanings, depending on the context in which it is brought, especially in the sense of persistence (3:200), of resignation (reference), of faith (3:200), of waiting (10:109), of hope (11:115), of acceptance (16:127), of tolerance (20:130), or even in the temporal sense. These are just some of the many meanings of the word patience, an attitude that is greatly emphasized in Islam.

Miskawayh (2003) states that the best way to achieve happiness would be through wisdom, both intellectually and spiritually. According to him, upon reaching this stage, an individual would present more energy, self-confidence, optimism, tranquility, strength, and satisfaction. Furthermore, he highlights the importance of friendships for human happiness, revealing that an individual is not able to fill this gap effectively alone. He emphasizes that, in addition to love, these bonds will only be maintained when they are based on kindness and virtuous behavior.

Many Muslim thinkers claimed that virtues would be the way to happiness, both in the earthly life and the afterlife. The practice of good deeds is clearly encouraged in the Qur'an, which states,

> "Each one has a goal set by Him. Engage in the practice of good deeds, for wherever you are, God will make you all appear before Him, for God is Almighty" (2:148).

Yasien (2006) highlights that for Al-Isfahani, one of the great scholars of the 8th century, virtue does not only depend on intellect, but also must be connected to the emotional and spiritual life of the individual. For this, it would be necessary for human beings to cultivate the virtues of the soul, the virtues of the body, and the external virtues. Along with the virtues of the soul, elements connected to one another include wisdom, courage, temperance, generosity, and justice. Therefore, in order to exercise generosity, a person would need the courage to part with their possessions, and need wisdom and a sense of justice to perform this action. He also cites humanity and noble-mindedness as virtues that encompass all others, as they are qualities directly linked to human beings and their actions. He argues that although the highest mundane virtue is wisdom, in an extramundane world, the highest virtues would be the spiritual or theological ones such as faith, sincerity, and piety (Yasien, 2006).

In positive psychology, despite the 24 strengths, an individual is advised to focus on the practice of signature strengths, which are represented by those that occupy the first five positions of the VIA test. Such forces would have the characteristic of being stable and naturally performed by the individual (Niemiec & McGrath, 2019a). On the other hand, Niemiec (2019) states that despite the stable characteristic, forces can be developed over time through interventions, situational issues, changes in the social role, or the simple practice of new habits. In addition to acting together, the author explains that the number of forces expressed simultaneously increases in the face of more complex or challenging situations. Thus, he states that both strengths and virtues do not operate in isolation, but in a combined way, and depending on the context in which they are used, in an interdependent way. Such an interrelationship between the forces can generate several positive results in the cognitive, emotional, and social aspects of the state of happiness (Niemiec, 2019).

This plural characteristic of forces and virtues converges with an Islamic perspective, which emphasizes that virtues cannot be understood in isolation, but rather in an integrated way in a relationship where one depends directly on the other. This is how many Islamic scholars approached the subject. Al-Ghazali (1997) in his work Ihya Ulum al-Din, written in the 11th century, lists four virtues from which, according to him, all other character traits come: wisdom, justice, courage, and temperance. Wisdom, according to him, aims to guide the soul to the distinction between right and wrong, and therefore involves qualities such as discernment, discretion, and critical thinking. Courage is linked to qualities such as nobility, firmness, affection, endurance, and bravery. Temperance, in turn, would be directly linked to patience, generosity, modesty, tolerance, contentment, and control of desires. Wisdom and justice would be the most present virtues in the Quran (Fakhry, 1991). Yet from an Islamic perspective, the concept of justice is expressed in different ways, at times where justice is to the individual himself, to other people, and to God (Yasien, 2006).

Another philosopher who also talked about this integration of virtues was Ibn Miskawayh (2003) defended the idea that the practice of virtues carried out by the individual methodically and systematically will lead to a habit, and when repeated, such practices are then exercised without effort or difficulty, thus contributing to the formation of their character and the achievement of happiness. He emphasizes that the virtue of justice responsible for equity and balance would only be possible from the harmony between the virtues of wisdom, courage, and temperance, and their respective subdivisions. Among the virtues of wisdom are intelligence, prudence, common sense, and ease of understanding. Among the virtues of courage, he cites firmness, strength, bravery, self-confidence, and endurance. About the virtue of temperance, he cites some behaviors such as modesty, self-control, honesty, serenity, contentment, mildness, self-discipline, piety, generosity, and sweetness. And within the virtue of justice, he cites friendship, reciprocity, honesty, kindness, and conciliation. An interesting point is that Miskawayh (2003) makes an analogy between morality and medicine, stating that cultivating character is a way of preserving the health of the soul, and this would be possible through "moral therapy" or "restoration of moral health," which mainly involves the eradication of anger, fear, and arrogance.

In the aspect of temperance, the Qur'an encourages moderation and discourages all kinds of excesses in food, financial spending, sexual behavior, ostentation, vanity, and other behaviors linked to hedonic pleasures. Koenig and Al-Shoaib (2014) state that Islam's strongest basis for healthy behaviors is belief in and submission to God, which influences the most diverse decisions and behaviors of adherents. According to the authors, the Islamic religion influences the health of the individual not only directly, but also indirectly through the psychological, social, and behavioral aspects of religious prescriptions. Self-regulation and self-control, for example, are stimulated in different ways by religions, both by religious restrictions that seek to contain human impulses, the management of emotions in the face of adversity, and also through the future perspective of reward and punishment that aims to encourage self-responsibility (Falb & , 2014).

Making an analogy with the virtue of humanity in positive psychology, an emphasis on love, along with the other elements associated with it, is observed in the Islamic perspective. Miskawayh (2003) talks extensively about love, dividing it into three categories: the natural love that unites people in their social relationships, the love between spouses, and the love of human beings towards God, which resembles the love of children towards their parents. The latter would only be possible through obedience and worship to God. In an even more integrated view, Yasien (2006) reveals that love appears in the Qur'an as a divine attribute and is usually associated with other qualities such as forgiveness, mercy, gratitude, generosity, and kindness. Both love and friendship are social virtues, considered virtues of the soul. The author reveals that, according to Al-Isfahani, love for God is the greatest source and the highest form of this feeling, from which human beings learn to love others. Human love is the basis of all relationships, whether marital, parental, or social. He points out that in addition to being the greatest source of cooperation between people, love is an even nobler quality than justice, since where there is love, there is no injustice. Love would be, in this perspective, the great engine of justice, because it would be from it that the impetus to act justly would arise. It is noted that in Islamic literature, justice is a virtue that receives a lot of attention and, in addition to being one of the greatest virtues along with love, it is also considered the ultimate goal of all other virtues (Bakhtiar, 2019; Fakhry, 1991; Miskawayh, 2003). This strong relevance given to justice in Islam can be clearly noticed in some Qur'anic verses such as,

> "Surely Allah loves those who are just" (5:42) and also "Be just! That is closer to righteousness," (5:8).

Virtue and Ethics in the Quran

Islam has an intense focus on morals which, according to Al-Kaysi (2003), is the basis of someone's self-confidence and strength. This converges with the ideas of positive psychology, developed by Petterson and Seligman (2004) and Niemiec (2019), which highlights that the practice of virtues and character strengths energizes individuals and improves the quality of their relationships. Similarly, from an Islamic perspective, the practice of virtues does not have an objective of improving behaviors only individually but also aims to positively impact the social environment since many of these behaviors are pro-social and can benefit human relationships in general. These virtues are elements strongly inserted in the scope of Islamic spirituality, but the difference relies on the basis from where they are built and developed, which starts with the individual's faith and religious values, being consolidated and materialized through his actions (Othman, 2016).

The word ethics has its etymological origin in the Greek *ethos*, meaning abode, lifestyle, and a pattern of character. The translation of *ethos* into Latin generated the term *mos, moralitas,* which, in turn, created the word, "moral" (Gontijo, 2006). Despite being similar words, there are subtle differences between them. Ethics is a concept linked to the external world in a broader context, thus becoming an object of study and reflection of good practices and customs among people. Morality is related to the more internal and subjective scope of character and choices, between right and wrong, good and bad, vice and virtue, and good behavior (Ali, 2015). Ethics, from an Islamic perspective, is also connected with the pure nature of humans (*fitrah*) and is directly involved in character development. According to Khazaei (2009), the moral aspect of the agent who practices an action is more important than the moral aspect of the action itself, despite both having reciprocal effects on the constitution of character. She emphasizes that it is necessary to develop different aspects of character so that there is a natural balance in the subject.

Depending on how it is understood, morality can be interpreted as something rigid that restricts the freedom of individuals. However, this restriction is often necessary for the balance of a society. Social life becomes extremely difficult without a code of conduct linked to the moral aspect. This theme was studied for a long-time in philosophical, religious, legal, and social fields, but not sufficiently explored in psychology. Classical Muslim thinkers described the science of morals and ethics as the foundation of all sciences, stating that the main purpose of Qur'anic moral psychology is to contribute to the formation of a just and sensible individual (Bakhtiar, 2019).

According to Al-Kaysi (2003), the purpose of good manners (*adab*) is to encourage the individual's daily remembrance of God through virtuous actions, since virtue is a behavior that has a fundamentally divine nature. This is why the combination of faith and good deeds is essential in Islamic routine. *Adab* and *akhlaq* are ways of encouraging awareness and consistency in the right behaviors. For example, Al-Kaysi (2003) emphasizes the importance of humility and modesty in the Muslim's life, as well as moderation, stating that pride, arrogance, exaggeration, and ostentation are all condemned in Islam. Besides this, from a social point of view, Islam seeks not only to discourage bad behaviors, but to encourage responsibility and mutual help. However, it is important to remember that some character traits are acquired while others need constant practice to be developed and solidified as a habit (Fakhry, 1991).

The Relationship Between Well-Being, Ethics (*adab*) and Character (*akhlaq*)

From an Islamic perspective, individual well-being is, at least in part, a reflection of social well-being, hence the strong presence of guidelines on human relationships in the Quran and sunnah, prescribing rules regarding ethical behavior and good manners (*adab*), and instructions on how someone can build *ahlaq*, which means the noble qualities of character (Omar, 2013). From an Islamic perspective, both of these concepts are an important part of happiness, alongside submission to the divine will. Yasien (2006) affirms that for Miskawayh, the improvement of the individual occurs through cognition and actions, and this is why, according to him, cognition is perfected through knowledge, while the individual's actions are perfected through character and morals (Yasien, 2006).

Islamic ethics and morals connect directly to faith, giving special priority to social well-being over individual well-being. Due to the inherent weaknesses in human nature, behaviors and the concept of right and wrong are imperfect, taking into account each person's interests, subjectivity, and what satisfies their own needs and aspirations. However, when meeting the needs of a single person, the results of their choices will not always advocate the broader concept of morals and ethics that attempt to serve the interests of an entire community, utilitarian theories, or themselves. Because the ultimate goal is the well-being of the entire society, Muslims use the Qur'an, divine wisdom, and prophetic teachings to guide their decisions, actions, and conduct, even if it displeases or falls short of their desires, wishes, impulses, or interests. In other words, from an Islamic perspective, a Muslim sacrifices their personal interests for the benefit of social interest, not the other way around. Hence one of Islam's most striking characteristics: the surrender and submission to God and his orders (Al-Aidaros & Shamsudin, 2013; Bensaid & Machouche, 2019).

One of the things that distinguishes Islamic psychology from positive psychology is the emphasis on the well-being of society as a whole rather than simply the individual. In positive psychology, the practice of virtues and character strengths aims at increasing the engagement and well-being of the individual, while in an Islamic view, the main objective of these behaviors is social well-being, even if some conducts require certain abdications from the individual. That is why Bensaid and Machmouche (2019, p.62) reinforce that the use of human virtues and qualities must go beyond the individual sphere, stating that:

Effective moral instruction should focus on the reflective experience of social fields work as a genuine channel of moral development and maturity, or else it may turn to a mere exercise of intellectualism, meditation or individual spiritual luxury, lacking the profound experience necessary to accommodate and adapt to the changing context.

The Quran is considered a kind of holistic interpretation of human nature, and also a Code of Conduct, hence the great diversity of themes given the reciprocal influence between them. According to Ali (2015), the foundations of Qur'anic morality focus primarily on a God-centered

144

approach (*tawheed*), the expectation of an afterlife (*akhirah*), and the purity and sincerity of intentions (*tasawwuf*). Thus, the main motivator of moral action in Islam, in addition to laws, rationality, and human conscience, is God-consciousness (*taqwa*) since, without these solid beliefs, the laws in society would be insufficient to contain human actions.

Ali (2015) relates that just as moral behavior affects the social sphere, it also affects economic issues, which in turn affect education, and this affects politics, and thus various fields of education. This shows how these areas of study complement each other, requiring an integral understanding. It is for this reason that this theme is studied, from an Islamic perspective, as a multidisciplinary subject that links the study of psychology, theology, and jurisprudence (Shariah), thus making an integrated connection of aspects of character a necessity both in the individual and social spheres (Fakhry, 1991).

The Formation, Refinement, and Solidification of Character

In positive psychology, it is possible to identify some special emphasis on the "signature strengths." This is a nomenclature given to those strengths that are naturally present in the individual as a personal trait. They are usually identified by the top five results in the VIA Survey of Character Strengths (Peterson & Seligman, 2004). Thus, it is observed that in an Islamic view, the focus is not directed only on those virtues or strengths that are innate, familiar, or "effortless" to the individual as explained by the literature of positive psychology, but on all of them, including those that are not so striking in someone's nature (Al-Ghazali, 1997).

Besides that, in Islam it is not the individual's set of traits that define the strengths that are more natural or familiar, but the context and the level of spirituality that will make it more or less easy to put virtues into practice, no matter if they are or are not part of his or her constellation of traits. From an Islamic perspective, the development of character strengths is not dependent on the individual's will or personality in isolation, but directly to his or her spiritual development. The more one is connected to God, the more he or she will be connected to his or her pure nature (*fitrah*), and this facilitates the practice and adoption of virtuous behaviors, not only the easy but also the challenging ones.

Differently from the perspective of virtues mentioned in positive psychology and traditional philosophy, in Islam, the practice of virtues and refinement of character are strongly connected to both religiosity and spirituality, and this might be considered the most significant difference between the eastern and western views regarding this subject. The adoption of virtues and positive behaviors from an Islamic perspective is part of the process of purification of the soul (*tazkiyat*) since it is from good conduct that the individual improves his behavioral inclinations (*nafs*). This purification of the soul (*tazkiyat el nafs*) takes place through the union of faith, rituals, and virtuous behaviors, which contribute to the spiritual evolution of the individual. It is possible to infer that sincere devotion to God and good manners, *akhlaq,* are intrinsically linked, as the former is related to the sincere intention of the heart, while the latter is the realization of this intention in the form of acts and behaviors. They need each other reciprocally to build strong qualities and behaviors (Al-Ghazali, 1997; Bensaid & Machouche, 2019). In other words, the development of character and the purification of the soul requires the union of internal and external dimensions to be consolidated. The internal dimension, represented by spirituality and faith, is the intrinsic motivation that will drive the individual to the external dimensions, which are symbolized by the rituals and the practice of virtues.

Keshavarzi and Nsour (2021) call this process behavioral training, reinforcing that the practice of virtues should be started in childhood so that it can then be consolidated in adult life as an automatic behavior. Such actions, to become consistent over time, need to be initiated through small acts that do not require so much effort, until they are solidified. The authors compare behavioral inclinations (*nafs*) to a muscle that, if it is overloaded with a weight greater than it is capable of supporting, can end up being damaged. Therefore, in the first moment, the focus is to invest more in the constancy of the exercise (*riyadat*) than in its complexity, since the practice of virtues is a habit that needs to be repeated. Once automated, these practices begin to require less effort on the part of the individual both in the execution of actions and in the decision-making process, which often involves a conflict between the desires of the ego and moral conduct.

According to Al Ghazzali (1997), there are four elements that purify the soul: the action itself, the power to perform it, the knowledge of both, and the quality of the soul. He explains that refinement of character can only be achieved through knowledge and training of the soul (*tarbiya*). This process can be bitter and unpleasant at first, as the person will need to refrain from cravings, old habits, or previous behaviors. Therefore, it takes effort, commitment, persistence, self-determination, and a firm resolve from the individual until the habit is internalized. He also mentions that our psychological states and dispositions, called *kayfiyyat nafsanyya*, can sometimes be firm (*malakat*) or fragile (*ahwal*). The fragile ones can be lost or removed easily, while the firm ones are more solid in the individual's character, being innate (*tabiiyya/fitriyya*) or acquired *(adiyya)*. These innate qualities are natural in the individual, but those that are acquired require determination and repetition until one clings to the individual's nature and daily life. This is important in psychology, as we can understand why some people adopt some changes more easily than others, and what we should do when qualities we want to achieve are not present or easily achieved. That is why Al-Ghazali (1997), as well as other authors, emphasize that the basis for building character is controlling ego and emotions (Abdullah, 2014).

The individual's tendency towards virtue is an innate characteristic, which is born through a pure nature (*fitrah*), and remains within a person as if it were a drive. Virtues are considered in an Islamic view as divine characteristics given to humans, hence are linked to goodness. However, several factors throughout life lead the subject to distance oneself from one's good nature, moving him or her away from these actions (Rothman, 2022; Rothman, 2018; Keshavarzi & Ali, 2021). The distance from virtuous behavior leads one to disconnect from one's self and from the divine dimension, while the practice of virtues makes one closer to God and the pure nature from which one was created, leading to a state of tranquility, satisfaction, and contentment, as is attested in the Qur'an:

"Whoever does good, whether male or female, and is a believer, We will grant a pleasant life and reward with a reward, according to the best of deeds," (16:97),

or yet another passage that says,

"And by the soul and by Him who formed it, then with the knowledge of right and wrong inspired it! Successful indeed is he who purifies his soul, and damned is he who corrupts it!" (Quran, 91:7-10).

This is the purpose of training the soul, the *riyadat al-nafs*, where someone is supposed to train oneself until becoming accustomed to certain behaviors. The *riyadat al-nafs* is divided into 3 stages: refining morals through knowledge, purifying actions through sincerity, and fulfilling the rights of praxis. The abandonment of desires or bad habits, or *tahliya*, would be the first step in improving someone's behaviors and purifying the soul. This is because, according to Islamic scholars, abandoning something bad would be easier at the beginning than trying to adopt a new behavior that someone is still not used to. However, none of this will be possible if there is no sincere intention for God, for yourself, and for others (Al Ghazzali, 1997).

Al Ghazzali (1997) emphasizes that good character traits can only be acquired through self-discipline to then become part of the individual's nature as a reciprocal relationship between the heart and the limbs, as the soul and the body. According to him, this self-discipline is strengthened through the connection of the heart with the limbs of the body that consequently initiate the movement towards action. Reciprocally, the effects caused by the body are also supposed to have repercussions on the heart. This cycle of integrated repetitions between the heart and the limbs of the body creates a kind of habit that functions as a circular movement. The constancy and repetitions of such habits and conduct are extremely important to evolve the individual, and when it comes to good character, this is one of the ways to achieve the purification of the soul (*tazkiyat*). He claims that "a balance of character traits makes the soul healthy, while any deviation from that balance constitutes a disease and disorder within it" (Al Ghazzali, 1997, p.39)

Conclusion

The increase in research on Muslim mental health has raised the need to build an approach that includes the main sources that influence the lives of this population. There is also a need to develop frameworks of psychology rooted in Islam as a valuable endeavor in and of itself. As exposed in this chapter, there are some differences regarding the subject of virtues through the viewpoints of positive psychology and of religions and spiritual philosophies, as well as classical philosophical theories, whose focus is on the field of ethics and morals. Studying happiness and well-being not only includes individual aspects, but also those arising from social relationships, which directly influence feelings and emotions. However, the excessive emphasis of psychological theories on the self as the main object of human satisfaction ended up confronting some values, virtues, and moral precepts whose content not only reaches the individual but as a whole collectivity.

Developing good character means changing and improving our behaviors. This is an extremely important point that is quite neglected in the field of psychology. The approach to human virtues integrates different areas of knowledge and also of psychological science itself, making an integration between health psychology, social psychology, and the psychology of religion. This reciprocal relationship where beliefs, religious teachings, and positive behaviors are intrinsically connected can be an important tool to be used in Islamically integrated therapies and interventions linked to the promotion of well-being. If we consider that most people suffer as a result of their behavior or the bad behavior of others, we can get a sense of how important this issue of *adab, akhlaq*, and *tazkiyat nafs* is for the emotional health of an individual and the people around them.

References

Abdullah, F. (2014). Virtues and character development in Islamic ethics and positive psychology. *International Journal of Education and Social Science, 1*(2), 69-77.

Al-Aidaros, A. H., & Shamsudin, M. F. (2013). Ethics and ethical theories from an Islamic perspective. *International Journal of Islamic Thought*, 4, 1-13. https://repo.uum.edu.my/id/eprint/21941

Al-Ghazzali, Winter, T., & Islamic Texts Society. (1997). *Al-Ghazali on disciplining the soul: Kitab Riyadat Al-Nafs; & on breaking the two desires: Kitab Kasr Al-Shahwatayn: Books XXII and XXIII of the revival of the religious sciences: Ihya Ulum Al-Din.* Islamic Texts Society.

Ali, S. S. (2015). The Quranic Morality: An Introduction to the Moral-System of Quran. *Islam and Muslim societies: A Social Science Journal, 8*(1), 94-108. https://muslimsocieties.org/Vol8_1/The_Quranic_Morality.pdf

Al-Kaysi, M. I. (2003). *Morals and Manners in Islam: A Guide to Islamic Adab.* The Islamic Foundation

Asamarai, L. (2018). Utilization of Islamic principles in marital counseling. In C. York Al-Karam (Ed..), *Islamically integrated psychotherapy: uniting faith and professional practice.* Templeton Press.

Badri, M. (2016). *The dilemma of muslim psychologists.* Islamic Book Trust.

Badri, M. (2018). Contemplation:: An Islamic Psychospiritual Study. International Institute of Islamic Thought (IIIT).

Bakhtiar, L. (2019). *Quranic psychology of the self: a text book on Islamic moral psychology.* Kazi Publications.

Bensaid, B., & Machouche, S. (2019). Muslim morality as foundation for social harmony. *Journal of Al-Tamaddun, 14*(2), 51–63. https://doi.org/10.22452/JAT.vol14no2.5

Elzamzamy, K.; Ahmed, R. M.; Hassan, W.; EL Mahdi, M. (2021). The Journey of Islamic Psychology in Egypt: The Case of Muhammad 'Uthman Nagati. In: Haque, A.; Rothman, A. (Eds.), *Islamic psychology around the globe.* Seattle, Washington: International Association of Islamic Psychology (1914-2000).

Fakhry, M. (1991). *Ethical theories in Islam.* E. J. Brill.

Falb, M.D., Pargament, K.I. (2014). Religion, Spirituality, and Positive Psychology: Strengthening Well-Being. In: Teramoto Pedrotti, J., Edwards, L. (Eds.), *Perspectives on the Intersection of Multiculturalism and Positive Psychology. Cross-Cultural Advancements in Positive Psychology*, vol 7. Springer. https://doi.org/10.1007/978-94-017-8654-6_10

Gontijo, E. D. (2006). Os termos 'Ética' e 'Moral'. *Mental,* 4(7), 127-135. http://pepsic.bvsalud.org/scielo.php?script=sci_arttext&pid=S167 9-44272006000200008&lng=pt&tlng=pt.

Haque, A., & Rothman, A. (2021). *Islamic psychology around the globe.* International Association of Islamic Psychology.

Keshavarzi, H., & Ali, B. (2021). Foundations of traditional Islamically integrated psychotherapy (TIIP). In H. Keshavarzi et al. (Eds.), *Introducing traditional Islamically integrated psychotherapy.* Routledge.

Keshavarzi, H., & Nsour, R. Behavioral (Nafsānī) psychotherapy character development and reformation. In H. Keshavarzi et al. (Eds.), *Introducing traditional Islamically integrated psychotherapy,* 236-265. Routledge.

Khazaei, Z. (2009). The role of religion in shaping moral character: an Islamic perspective. *JPTR,* 79, 1-10.

Koenig, H. G., & Al-Shohaib, S. (2014). *Health and well-being in Islamic societies.* Springer.

Kristjánsson, K. (2013). *Virtues and vices in positive psychology.* Cambridge University Press.

Littman-Ovadia, H., & David, A. (2020). Character strengths as manifestations of spiritual life: Realizing the non-dual from the dual. *Front. Psychol.* 11:960. doi: 10.3389/fpsyg.2020.00960

Miskawayh, A. (2003). *The refinement of character (Tadhib al-Akhlaq).* Seyyed H. N. Trad. Kazi Publications.

Niemiec, R. (2019). *Character Strengths Interventions: A Field Guide for Practitioners.* Hogrefe Publishing.

Niemiec, R.M. (2020). Six Functions of Character Strengths for Thriving at Times of Adversity and Opportunity: a Theoretical Perspective. *Applied Research Quality Life,* 15, 551–572. https://doi.org/10.1007/s11482-018-9692-2.

Niemiec, R. M. & McGrath, R. E. (2019a). *The power of character strengths.* VIA Institute Character Press.

Niemiec, R. M., Russo-Netzer, P. & Pargament, K. I. (2020a). The decoding of the human spirit: A synergy of spirituality and character strengths toward wholeness. *Front. Psychol.,11*(2040). https://doi.org/10.3389/fpsyg.2020.02040 .

Omais, S. (2018). *Manual de Psicologia positiva.* Qualitymark.

Omar, M. N. (2013). Ethics in Islam: a brief survey. *Social Sciences, 8*(5), 387-392. https://medwelljournals.com/abstract/?doi=sscience.2013.387.392

Othman, N. (2016). A preface to the Islamic personality psychology. *International Journal of Psychological Studies, 8*(1), 20-27. http://dx.doi.org/10.5539/ijps.v8n1p20

Pasha-Zaidi, N. (2021). Indigenizing an Islamic psychology. *Psychology of Religion and Spirituality, 13*(2), 194-203. https://doi.org/10.1037/rel0000265

Pasha-Zaidi, N., Al-Seheel, A., Bridges-Lyman, K., Dasti, R. (2021a). Gratitude and wellbeing: Cultivating Islamically-integrated pathways to health and wellness. In Pasha-Zaidi (Ed.), *Toward a positive psychology of Islam and Muslims: Spirituality, struggle, and social justice,* 207-234. Springer.

Peterson, C., & Park, N. (2009). Classifying and measuring strengths of character. In S. J. Lopez & C. R. Snyder (Eds.), *Oxford handbook of positive psychology.* Oxford University Press.

Peterson, C., & Seligman, M. E. P. (2004). *Character strengths and virtues: a handbook and classification.* Oxford University Press.

Rahim, A. B. A. (2013). Understanding Islamic ethics and its significance on the character building. *International Journal of Social Science and Humanity, 3*(6), 508. https://doi.org/10.7763/IJSSH.2013.V3.293

Rashid, T., & Seligman, M. (2019). *Psicoterapia positiva: manual do terapeuta* (S. M. M. Rosa, Trans.). Artmed.

Rasool, G. H. (2021). *Islamic psychology: human behaviour and experience from an Islamic perspective.* Routledge.

Rothman, A. (2022). *Developing a model of Islamic psychology and psychotherapy: Islamic theology and contemporary understandings of psychology*. Routledge.

Rothman, A., & Coyle, A. (2018). Toward a framework for Islamic psychology and psychotherapy: an Islamic model of the soul. *Journal of Religion and Health, 57*(5), 1731-1744. https://doi.org/10.1007/s10943-018-0651-x

Seligman, M. E. P., & Csikszentmihalyi, M. (2000). Positive psychology: An introduction. *American Psychologist,* 55(1), 5–14. https://doi.org/10.1037/0003-066X.55.1.5

Seligman, M. E. (2004). *Felicidade Autêntica* (N. Capelo, Trans.). Objetiva.

Seligman, M. E. (2011). *Florescer: uma nova compreensão sobre a natureza da felicidade e do bem-estar* (C. P. Lopes, Trans.). Rio de Janeiro: Objetiva.

Snyder, C. R., & Lopez, S. J. (2009). *Psicologia positiva: uma abordagem e prática das qualidades humanas.* Artmed.

The Clear Quran. (n.d.). (M. Khattab, Trans.). https://www.clearquran.org/

The hadith of the Prophet Muhammad (سلم و عليه الله صلى) at your fingertips. www.sunnah.com. https://sunnah.com/.

Yasien, M. (2006). *The path to virtue: The ethical philosophy of Al-Rāghib Al-Iṣfahānī.* International Islamic University Malaysia (IIUM).

York Al-Karam, C. (2018a). *Islamically integrated psychotherapy: uniting faith and professional practice.* Templeton Press.

York Al-Karam, C. (2018b). Islamic psychology: Towards a 21st century definition and conceptual framework. *Journal of Islamic Ethics, 2* (2018), 97–109.

CHAPTER 8

———— •◦•• ————

Maladies of the Nafs

Shahid Ijaz, Muhammad Tahir Khalily, PhD,

& Carrie M. York, PhD

Abstract

This chapter examines the concept of maladies of the self within the Islamic tradition, focusing on their ontological composition and relevance to the process of tazkiya (self-purification). The chapter begins with an introduction to the subject, providing an overview of the significance of comprehending and treating these maladies. It then examines the Islamic view of the self, including the roles of the ruh (soul), qalb (heart), nafs (self), and aql (intellect) in spiritual development. It then provides a detailed definition and analysis of nine specific maladies: lying, backbiting, anger, avarice, arrogance, slander, envy, ostentation, and sarcasm. Each malady is analyzed in terms of its manifestation and effect on a person's personality and spiritual health. The chapter then investigates the global ramifications of these maladies. It emphasizes the necessity of addressing them for the betterment of society by discussing their effects at different levels. The need for additional research and investigation, especially development of evidence-based treatment protocols and training programs in this area is also highlighted.

"Maladies of the self" is an extremely important topic in the Islamic tradition because it addresses the spiritual illnesses that people suffer from, and that obstruct their spiritual growth and relationship with Allah. These maladies include a range of unfavorable characteristics and behaviors that pollute the heart and divert one from the path of righteousness. The tazkiya process, which entails the purification and refinement of the self, depends critically on recognizing, understanding, and treating these maladies. It is essential to recognize these maladies of the self in order to surmount one's weaknesses and become a better Muslim. This aids in acquiring a deeper comprehension of oneself and one's relationship with Allah. The tazkiya path encourages people to develop virtues like humility, patience, and sincerity, which are necessary for a fruitful spiritual path.

Additionally, self-improvement and the pursuit of Allah's closeness are stressed in the teachings on maladies of the self. People can identify and change the unfavorable traits and behaviors that obstruct their spiritual growth through introspection, self-reflection, and self-discipline, and can work toward spiritual wellness and a closer relationship with Allah by purging their hearts of these maladies. One can strive for a more virtuous and fulfilling spiritual life by developing a deeper understanding of the significance of treating oneself of maladies during the tazkiya process.

We next examine Islamic human ontology and how these maladies manifest in different ways and how they harm people's spiritual health.

The Self From an Islamic Perspective

The notion of fitrah—the inherent character and disposition that each human is born with—serves as the foundation for the ontological justification of the human self (Bhat, 2016). Islamic ontology views the self as a complex entity that includes both material and spiritual aspects. From an Islamic perspective, humans have a physical body (jism) and a spiritual essence that make up their dual nature (ruh). The spiritual essence is eternal and derives from the divine realm, whereas the physical body is composed of earthly substances and is transient (Hadi & Uyuni, 2021).

Islam holds that the self is endowed with a natural desire to acknowledge and submit to Allah's existence and oneness as a creation of Allah (Tawhid). Every individual is believed to be born with fitrah, an innate ability to discern the divine that predisposes them to pursue a relationship with the divine (Bhat, 2016). However, because Allah has granted us free will, we have the ability to transgress against our natural inclinations. This departure from the fitrah causes spiritual illnesses like haughtiness, greed, and carelessness that separate people from their true selves and their relationship with Allah (Parrott, 2017).

According to Islamic ontology, the goal of the human self is to become closer to Allah, to cultivate a healthy heart which is free from maladies of the self, and to align one's actions and intentions with the will of the Almighty. The Quran's and Sunnah's teachings, worship, sincere repentance, introspection, and the pursuit of knowledge are all ways to aid in this process of self-purification and spiritual development (Abdullah, 2014).

Composition of the Human Being in Islamic Thought

Understanding the ontological constitution of the human being is a subject of utmost importance in Islamic philosophy and spirituality. It entails the interaction of various elements, including the Ruh (soul), nafs (self), qalb (heart), aql (intellect), and physical body (Abu-Raiya, 2012). The function of these components within the framework of Islamic thinking is examined in the following section.

Islam acknowledges the value of both the material body and the spiritual side of the human person. The body serves as a vehicle through which human experiences are realized in the physical world. It equips people with the resources they require for their endeavors, interactions, and spiritual practices. A comprehensive vision of life is viewed in Islam as necessitating the maintenance of one's physical health.

In the framework of the human experience, the nafs has two distinct meanings. It first refers to the expression of anger and sexual desire. Second, it alludes to the core of the self or person. According to Imam al-Ghazali, al-nafs al-ammara (the commanding self), al-nafs al-lawwama (the reproachful self), and al-nafs al-mutma'inna (the contented self) are the three states that the self goes through (Ghazali, 2001; Ghazali, 1993).

The al-nafs al-ammara is a representation of the self that gives in to impure cravings and passions without protest or rebuke. The Quran says about it:

"Truly, the nafs is a relentless enjoiner of evil, save for those for whom My Lord has mercy" (12:53).

It is related to the ego and manifests as egotism, arrogance, and indulgence in materialistic pursuits. Constant conflict between satisfying immediate desires and adhering to moral principles defines the lower self (Uthmani, 2008).

On the other hand, the "al-nafs al-lawwama" refers to the self that commits an error but afterwards holds it accountable. It is stated in the Quran:

"But nay! I swear by the reproachful nafs" (75:2).

This nafs refers to an inner conscience that holds individuals accountable for their actions. It examines moral violations and encourages self-improvement. The self-accusing self encourages individuals to recognize their shortcomings, feel regret, and seek forgiveness. It serves as a catalyst for personal and spiritual growth (Uthmani, 2008).

The self that complies with divine precepts and is unaffected by earthly passions is referred to as al-nafs al-mutma'inna. It is stated in the Quran:

> "To the righteous it will be said, 'Oh reassured soul, return to your Lord well-pleased and pleasing to Him" (89:27–28).

This nafs is characterized by a profound sense of calm, contentment, and submission to Allah's will. The tranquil self is liberated from the control of base desires and has a profound spiritual connection with the divine. It embodies inner peace and reaches a state of tranquility (Uthmani, 2008).

The idea of nafs is linked to other ideas like qalb, 'aql, and ruh, which are intricately related to one another. The Arabic word qalb for heart denotes both the physical and spiritual components of the organ. In terms of anatomy, the heart is an organ in charge of moving blood around the body. The heart symbolizes a dynamic, formless, unseen power that is connected spiritually to the soul.

Ruh refers to a physical component of the heart that, like an electric current coursing through the veins, causes vibrations to spread throughout the body. It can also refer to the soul, a spiritual essence that is distinct from life itself. The concept of ruh is addressed by God in the Qur'an:

> "They ask you about the ruh" (17:85).

Aql, on the other hand, has several meanings, but there are only two that are widely accepted. First of all, it denotes intelligence, allowing understanding of the true essence of tangible objects found within the soul. Second, it alludes to having the knowledge—an attribute—to comprehend the inner workings and depths of numerous fields. Despite the fact that both the quality and the container are referred to as aql, or intellect, it is important to distinguish between the two. The first creation of God, according to a statement attributed to Muhammad (SAW), was intellect. Despite being immaterial, knowledge needs the physical intellect to exist and function (Akhtar, 2017).

These ontological elements interact in a complex and dynamic way. The physical body is animated by the ruh, which enables it to do tasks and have sensory experiences. The nafs communicates with the outside world through the body under the influence of its inclinations and desires. The qalb connects a person to Allah and directs their moral and ethical decisions. It also acts as a portal into the spiritual world. The successful operation of these parts is essential for achieving spiritual development and understanding the higher purpose of life. People can transcend the confines of the physical world and achieve spiritual enlightenment by purifying their nafs, correcting their qalb, and cultivating a strong bond with Allah.

Maladies of the Nafs and Tazkiya

The nafs is often understood to refer to the self, psyche, or ego, and the maladies refer to negative states or aspects of the self that can lead to wrong actions and deviation from the righteous path. Maladies of the self, also known as spiritual illness or diseases of the heart, are undesirable states, attitudes, or conduct that obstruct a person's spiritual development, well-being, and adherence to Islamic teachings. These ailments can appear as internal conflicts, unfavorable feelings, and moral failings that lead one away from the righteous path and a close relationship with Allah. They result from the nafs' propensity for worldly desires, egotistical tendencies, and the desire for personal gratification. They are reflections of the lower, baser desires that jeopardize moral rectitude and spiritual advancement. They obstruct the soul's path to spiritual enlightenment and closer ties with Allah by distorting the spiritual faculties.

Self-purification, or tazkiya in Islamic terminology, is highly valued since it is seen as a prerequisite to the ultimate aim of life - the worship and service of God. Both the Quran and the hadith, the two fundamental Islamic sources, address the importance of tazkiya and provide instruction on how to cleanse oneself of the negative actions, beliefs, and attitudes that constitute the maladies of the self (Hamjah, 2022). According to various passages of the Quran, including Surah Al-Baqarah, verse 151, one of the fundamental goals of prophethood is to direct people toward tazkiya or self-purification. This places a strong emphasis on the prophet's function as a mentor for personal development and purification. Tazkiyya, or self-purification, is therefore a fundamental practice in Islam.

Overcoming Maladies of the Self: Islamic Scholars' Perspective

The journey of spiritual development involves recognizing and overcoming the maladies of the self. Islamic scholars have offered deep understandings of these maladies, directing believers toward the path of purification and illumination (Haque, 2004).

The well-known human psyche expert Imam Ibn al-Qayyim (d. 1350) identified a number of maladies of the self that pollute the heart and keep people from Allah. These include haughtiness, rage, envy, a love of things, and a disregard for worship (Rasool & Luqman, 2022). The remedy for these maladies, according to him, was "Qalb e Saleem." The Arabic term Qalb-e-Saleem means "sound heart" or "clean heart." It denotes an interior state of purity, sincerity, and devotion to Allah. It is a heart devoid of spiritual diseases and replete with faith, love, and obedience to Allah (Amin et al., 2022).

Famous for his writings on Islamic spirituality, Imam Al-Ghazali (d. 1111) covered a wide range of maladies of the self and their treatments. He listed some of the frequent illnesses that obstruct spiritual development such as arrogance, wrath, fury, and devotion to material pursuits. Al-Ghazali placed a strong emphasis on the need for self-awareness and the necessity to seek atonement via a number of spiritual practices, including reflection, penitence, and remembering Allah. By resolving these issues, people can strengthen their spiritual health and relationship with Allah.

Al-Ghazali and Ibn Qayyim both believed that turning away from God was the root of the maladies of the nafs. This departure is not only the source but also the cause and effect of these maladies, thus creating a vicious cycle. The same concept is outlined in the diagnostic criteria by many other Islamic scholars. These classical Islamic thinkers present a comprehensive understanding of the mind within the framework of tawhid, emphasizing the concept of divine unity (Arroisi & Rahmadi, 2022).

The theory of Imam Junayd al-Baghdadi (d. 910) includes mitsaq (covenant with God), fana (dissolution or annihilation for God), and tawhid (oneness of God). Maladies of the nafs occur when people deviate from their state of origin, their connection with God. Mitsaq aspires to regain his status as a servant of God, while Fana directs the means to this end. Junayd emphasizes God's role in its attainment (Setiawan et al., 2020).

Al-Iskandari (d. 1309), a well-known Sufi master, also explored the idea of maladies of the self. He emphasized the value of submitting to fate and accepting it for what it is, knowing that fate ultimately belongs to God. By letting go of self-control and valuing God's wisdom, people can grow transformatively and achieve a harmonious balance between their true, ideal, and real selves. Al-Iskandari examined the complexities of human psychology and the significance of God's servitude in his renowned work, al-Hikam al-'Ata'iyya. He understood that the human body can be afflicted by many diseases that impede one's spiritual growth and relationship with the divine. Pride, avarice, and attachment to materialistic desires are just a few examples of the impurities of the heart that characterize these maladies of nafs. Al-Iskandari encouraged self-examination as a way to spot and get rid of these impurities, allowing people to develop a stronger bond with God and reach enlightenment (Kardas, 2018).

Islamic scholar Maulana Ashraf Ali Thanvi (d. 1943) concentrated on diagnosing and curing maladies of the self. Detachment from fitrah, nature, and humanity increases the likelihood of developing maladies of the self, whereas attachment to God is the basis for treatment. Thanvi identifies various stages of attachment to God and categorizes maladies as either organic or functional. Detachment from God and humanity is viewed as the primary cause of a malady, leading to cognitive disturbances and abnormal symptoms. Importantly, treatment focuses on resolving the conflict between constructive and destructive forces (Khattak & Mustafa, 2022).

Ali Hajveri (d. 1072) emphasized the importance of self-purification and self-control in overcoming maladies of the self. He emphasized the significance of consulting a knowledgeable spiritual guide (Murshid) in order to successfully navigate the difficulties of the spiritual path. The importance of self-control, self-discipline, and adhering to the Quran and sunnah as a way to purify the heart and achieve spiritual enlightenment was stressed by Ali Hajveri (Fiza & Nazeer, 2020).

Collectively, these Islamic scholars stress the significance of introspection, spiritual practice, and guidance in curing the maladies of the self. Individuals can purify their hearts, strengthen their relationship with Allah, and achieve spiritual growth and enlightenment by recognizing, acknowledging, and actively addressing their maladies.

Other significant Islamic works that explored maladies of the self includes "Signs, Symptoms, and Cures of the Spiritual Diseases of the Heart" by Imam Mawlud (Yusuf, 2023)), translated and commented on by Hamza Yusuf. This work elucidates the signs, symptoms, and treatments for these spiritual diseases, thereby enhancing the discourse on these ailments. The book "Roh ke Bemariyan" by Molana Shah Hakeem Akhtar (Akhtar, 2017)) addresses diseases of the soul and provides practical advice for recognizing and overcoming them. The "Ihya Ulum al-Din" by Imam Ghazali provides profound insights and guidance for spiritual purification regarding the ailments of the self. "Tazkiya Nafs" by Molana Ameen Ahmed Islahi examines the purification of the self, highlighting self-awareness, discipline, and repentance as remedies. These works contribute significantly to the academic discourse on these conditions by providing valuable insights, treatments, and advice. They strengthen the scholarly basis for understanding and treating these spiritual diseases within the Islamic tradition, emphasizing the significance of self-reflection, seeking remedies, and approaching Allah.

Important Maladies

The nine most prevalent maladies that have been selected for discussion in this chapter include lying, backbiting, anger, avarice, arrogance, slander, envy, ostentation, and sarcasm. They were selected using a meticulous and stringent methodology. A comprehensive literature review comprising the works of prominent Islamic scholars who extensively discussed maladies of the self was conducted. Examining the works of scholars such as the scholars previously mentioned provided valuable insight and perspectives on these ailments. In addition, Islamic theology and spirituality experts were consulted for their opinions and insights to ensure a thorough understanding of the subject. The compatibility of the selected maladies with Quranic teachings and hadith literature was crucial to their justification. A thorough examination of pertinent Quranic verses and authentic hadith revealed explicit references to these diseases and their negative effects on individuals and society.

1. Lying: Lying is defined as providing misleading information with the goal to mislead another person. The Quran instructs believers to "avoid false speech and anything that is prohibited" (2:42). One's credibility and one's relationships are two of the numerous things that might suffer when one lies (DePaulo & Kashy, 1998; Vrij, 2008). It hinders a person's spiritual growth because they are less likely to cultivate honesty and integrity, qualities that are seen as essential for serving Allah and reaching the objective of human life. In order to heal from this inner illness, one must first recognize its presence and then make a concerted effort to cultivate honesty and integrity in one's actions and ideas.

2. Backbiting: Backbiting is described as speaking negatively about others behind their backs, which is a kind of betrayal and disrespect (Coyne, et al., 2012). Furthermore, it implies superiority and judgment of others. It is unethical and dishonest since it may involve the dissemination of incorrect or misleading information.

3. Anger: Anger is a powerful sensation of discontent or frustration. It is an unpleasant emotion that can lead to bad thoughts and actions. Anger can affect one's judgment, leading to poor decision-making. Negative actions, such as vengeance and violence, that are harmful to oneself and others might also result (Fernandez, & Johnson, 2016). In addition, anger can develop a negative outlook that results in feelings of resentment and bitterness, which can be destructive to one's relationships and overall health. Without good control, rage may be damaging and incapacitating.

4. Avarice: Avarice (miserliness) is characterized by an overwhelming desire for worldly gain and a refusal to share it. This may cause individuals to emphasize material achievement over more important concepts such as empathy and compassion (Seuntjens, 2016). Avarice can result in destructive behaviors such as greed and egotism that impair relationships and general well-being. A life that is unsatisfying and out of balance may be the outcome of avarice since it can lead to a lack of

160

gratitude and contentment, a relentless pursuit of more material things, and other associated issues. As people who are avaricious have a tendency to hoard opportunities and resources while others experience shortages, this can further exacerbate poverty and inequality cycles (Erzi, 2020).

5. Arrogance: A person who is arrogant has a disproportionately high opinion of himself or herself. The lack of humility, overconfidence in one's own talents, high opinion of oneself, conviction of one's own superiority, inability to empathize with others, and indifference to the thoughts and feelings of others are all hallmarks of arrogance (Gregg, & Mahadevan, 2014). A lack of motivation to learn and grow can stem from a feeling of superiority in one's knowledge. This makes it harder to connect with others and can lead to feelings of loneliness and isolation, thus affecting relationships. So, it may be harmful to one's psychological well-being.

6. Slander: Slander is defined as the act of making false statements with the intent to damage someone's reputation. Spreading false or inaccurate information about people with the purpose of damaging their reputation is a destructive act. Since this action entails misleading people and disseminating false information, it violates the values of honesty and integrity. Slander can have negative effects on relationships and reputations that can be severe and long-lasting (Alicke, 2000). Spreading incorrect information can be considered defamation and result in legal action, which can have negative professional and legal ramifications. It may also result in the loss of prospects and one's reputation in one's personal and professional life.

7. Envy: Feeling envious of another person's success or good fortune while also holding animosity towards that person is referred to as "resentful envy." Jealousy can take the shape of resentful envy if one feels wrath or animosity against another person's good circumstances. Lack of gratitude for one's blessings can be a root cause of this unpleasant mood. As a result, people may become less hospitable and close, which is bad for their relationships and their health as a whole (Hill & Buss, 2008; Salovey, 1991).

A lack of thankfulness and contentment, both of which are necessary for living a meaningful life, can result from jealousy fueled by resentment. Someone can start dwelling on their shortcomings rather than counting their many positives. They may stop being content with their current situation and start looking for ways to improve it. A person's emotional and psychological well-being can take a serious hit if their jealousy is fueled by resentment, which can then manifest as feelings of depression, anxiety, and low self-esteem. A person's self-esteem can prevent them from realizing their greatest potential.

8. Ostentation: In Islam, doing good things for the sake of others' appreciation is called ostentation, or riya. Seeking approval from others instead of Allah can be harmful to one's psyche, and Islam places a premium on good intentions. Inadequacy, low self-esteem, worry, and a loss of touch with one's authentic self are all possible outcomes. A lack of contentment and moral rectitude may emerge from an unhealthy preoccupation with external validation. Islam promotes honesty and doing things with no other motivation than to please God (Riquelme, et al., 2011).

9. Sarcasm: The use of irony or wit to ridicule or show disdain is called sarcasm (Filik, et al., 2016). In Islam, this is a very serious offense. It's unhealthy for health and relationships if a person can't empathize with other people. A lack of regard for others may result from insults and jokes about them. As people stop trusting one another, anger and isolation may set in. The victim's emotional well-being may suffer as a result, and they may experience emotions of sadness, nervousness, or poor self-esteem. A person's entire potential may be thwarted because they feel inadequate and inferior. Potential negative outcomes include haughtiness and overestimating one's own value. This may be harmful to a person's relationships and health as a whole because of the difficulty in interacting with people and the accompanying emotions of loneliness and isolation.

Maladies of the Self in Global Context

When an individual is plagued by the maladies of the nafs, it can negatively affect their personality in a number of ways. Maladies of the self which are discussed above cause a lack of empathy and understanding for others; a tendency to lash out in anger or frustration (Fernandez, & Johnson, 2016); focus on material gain at the expense of spiritual well-being (Kasser, & Sheldon, 2000; Piff, et al., 2012); feelings of dissatisfaction, emptiness, lack of satisfaction in life, isolation, loneliness, depression (Cleary et al., 2015); feelings of insecurity and inadequacy, anxiety (Dijkstra, & Buunk, 2002; Feder et al., 2010); addiction problems, (Kim et al., 2021; Sussman, et al., 2011); high scores on personality disorders, low self-esteem, and neuroticism (Weiss & Miller, 2018; Young, 2014). These studies provide evidence of a relationship between personality issues and disorders characterized by character problems like arrogance, envy, backbiting, jealousy, etc. However, pathways are intricate and multifaceted and affected by genetics, the environment, and life events. Thus, a holistic and multidisciplinary approach to comprehending the intricate interactions between mental health and maladies of the self is necessary. The negative effects of the maladies of the self are not limited to the individual alone; they can also have a significant impact on the individual's familial and social relationships.

Maladies (anger, jealousy, backbiting, and arrogance) make it difficult for the individual to connect with their family members (Lammers, et al., 2011; Fitness & Fletcher, 1993; Tandler & Petersen, 2020). They cause frequent conflicts with their spouse or children, which can lead to distance in the family and thus make it hard for them to build and maintain healthy relationships.

At the social level, maladies (greed and arrogance) can strain relationships among communities as they increase hoarding and decrease helping and volunteer behaviors; a sense of superiority makes it hard for them to connect with others on an equal level and decreases compassion and empathy for the needs of others (Piff, et al., 2012; Kasser, & Sheldon, 2000; Williams & DeSteno, 2008).

At the global level, maladies (greed, anger, and arrogance) can contribute to social and economic inequality, which causes a concentration of wealth among a few, escalates the chances of confrontations and war, and leads to a lack of collaboration among nations (Kasser, 2002; Banerjee & Duflo, 2011; Gudykunst, 2004; Bond & Smith, 1996). Overall, maladies of the self can have a significant impact on global and political levels, exacerbate social and economic inequality, and make it more difficult for people from different countries and cultures to collaborate and understand one another.

Future research directions

Future research should focus on the development of evidence-based treatment therapies specifically to treat the maladies of the self, especially tailored according to the culture and beliefs of people, as the expression of maladies is affected by cultural factors. Traditional therapies may not be designed to address these maladies. Therapies tailored for them can be used by clinicians to treat psychological conditions that are related to maladies of the self, such as personality disorders, character issues, and addiction. Proactive programs that can prevent maladies of the self through educational training and skill building can be developed. They will be beneficial for changing behaviors and attitudes in educational and organizational settings. Overall, research and studies in the area of maladies of the self can ameliorate issues at individual, familial, social, and global levels.

References

Abdullah, F. (2014). Virtues and character development in Islamic ethics and positive psychology. *International Journal of Education and Social Science, 1*(2), 69-77.

Abu-Raiya, H. (2012). Towards a systematic Qura'nic theory of personality. *Mental Health, Religion & Culture, 15*(3), 217-233.

Akhtar, H. M. (2017). *Rooh ki bimariyan aur un ka ilaj [Spiritual Diseases and Remedies, Urdu].* Khanqah Imdadiyah. Accessed at: https://d3irrwpfbszm5l.cloudfront.net/media/documents/AT020-Rooh%20ki%20bimariyan.pdf

Al-Ghazali. (1993). *Ihya 'Uloom-id-Deen* (F. ul-Karim, Trans., Vol. 3). Darul Ishaát.

Alicke, M. D. (2000). Culpable control and the psychology of blame. *Psychological bulletin, 126*(4), 556.

Amin, M. I., Trisnani, A., Nasif, H., & Puspita, E. D. A. (2022, November 8). *Qalbun Saliim: The Concept of A Clean Heart as A Foundation for Mental Health According to Ibn Qayyim al Jauziyah.* [Paper presentation]. International Conference on Psychology, Mental Health, Religion, and Spirituality. UIN Sunan Ampel Surabaya.

Arroisi, J., & Rahmadi, M. A. (2022). Theory of Mind on Ghazali and Ibn Qayyim Al Jauzi Perspective (Analysis Model on Islamic Psychology). *International Journal of Islamic Psychology, 5*(1), 8-22.

Banerjee, A. V., & Duflo, E. (2011). *Poor economics: A radical rethinking of the way to fight global poverty.* PublicAffairs.

Bhat, A. M. (2016). Human psychology (fitrah) from Islamic perspective. *International Journal of Nusantara Islam, 4*(2), 61-74.

Bond, M. H., & Smith, P. B. (1996). Cross-cultural social and organizational psychology. *Annual review of psychology, 47*(1), 205-235.

Cleary, M., Walter, G., Sayers, J., Lopez, V., & Hungerford, C. (2015). Arrogance in the workplace: Implications for mental health nurses. *Issues in mental health nursing, 36*(4), 266-271.

Coyne, S. M., Ridge, R., Stevens, M., Callister, M., & Stockdale, L. (2012). Backbiting and bloodshed in books: Short-term effects of reading physical and relational aggression in literature. *British Journal of Social Psychology, 51*(1), 188-196.

DePaulo, B. M., & Kashy, D. A. (1998). Everyday lies in close and casual relationships. *Journal of Personality and Social Psychology, 74*(1), 63-79.

Dijkstra, P., & Buunk, B. P. (2002). Jealousy as a function of rival characteristics: An evolutionary perspective. *Personality and Social Psychology Review, 6*(2), 131-148.

Erzi, S. (2020). Dark Triad and schadenfreude: Mediating role of moral disengagement and relational aggression. *Personality and Individual Differences, 157*, 109827.

Feder, J., Levant, R. F., & Dean, J. (2010). Boys and violence: A gender-informed analysis. Psychology of Violence, 1(S), 3–12. https://doi.org/10.1037/2152-0828.1.S.3 .

Fernandez, E., & Johnson, S. L. (2016). Anger in psychological disorders: Prevalence, presentation, etiology and prognostic implications. *Clinical Psychology Review, 46*, 124-135.

Filik, R., Țurcan, A., Thompson, D., Harvey, N., Davies, H., & Turner, A. (2016). Sarcasm and emoticons: Comprehension and emotional impact. *Quarterly Journal of Experimental Psychology, 69*(11), 2130-2146.

Fitness, J., & Fletcher, G. J. (1993). Love, hate, anger, and jealousy in close relationships: a prototype and cognitive appraisal analysis. *Journal of personality and Social Psychology, 65*(5), 942.

Fiza, M., & Nazeer, S. (2020). From our soul to the horizon of self: the sacred psychology of self-affirmation through self-annihilation in hazrat ali hajveri's unveiling the veiled. *Iqbal Review, 61*(4), 5.

Ghazali, A. H. (2001). *Kimya I Saadat (Alchemy of Eternal Bliss).* (M. A. Bilal, Trans., J. Dr. M. A. Mughal, Rev.). Kazi Publication.

Gregg, A. P., & Mahadevan, N. (2014). Intellectual arrogance and intellectual humility: An evolutionary-epistemological account. *Journal of Psychology and Theology, 42*(1), 7-18.

Gudykunst, W. B. (2004). *Bridging differences: Effective intergroup communication.* Sage publications.

Hadi, A., & Uyuni, B. (2021). The Critical Concept of Normal Personality in Islam. *Al-Risalah: Jurnal Studi Agama dan Pemikiran Islam, 12*(1), 1-19.

Hamjah, S. H. (2022). Tazkiyah al-Nafs in the Islamic Counseling Process from al-Ghazali's Perspective. *Ibn Khaldun International Journal of Economic, Community Empowerment and Sustainability*, *1*(1), 19-28.

Haque, A. (2004). Psychology from Islamic perspective: Contributions of early Muslim scholars and challenges to contemporary Muslim psychologists. *Journal of religion and health*, *43*, 357-377.

Hill, S. E., & Buss, D. M. (2008). The evolutionary psychology of envy.

Kardaş, S. (2018). Ibn Ata Allah al-Iskandari and al-Hikam al-'Ata'iyya in the Context of Spiritually-Oriented Psychology and Counseling. *Spiritual Psychology and Counseling*, *3*(2), 115-137.

Kasser, T. (2002). *The high price of materialism.* MIT Press.

Kasser, T., & Sheldon, K. M. (2000). Of wealth and death: Materialism, mortality salience, and consumption behavior. *Psychological Science, 11*(4), 348-351.

Khattak, A. Z., & Mustafa, R. (2022). Islamic psychology in the view of maulana ashraf ali thanvi: a literature review. *Al Misbah Research Journal*, *2*(04), 11-20.

Kim, H., Schlicht, R., Schardt, M., & Florack, A. (2021). The contributions of social comparison to social network site addiction. *PloS One*, *16*(10), e0257795.

Lammers, J., Stoker, J. I., Jordan, J., Pollmann, M., & Jordan, J. (2011). Power Increases Infidelity Among Men and Women. *Psychological Science, 22*(9), 1191-1197.

Parrott, J. (2017). Reconciling the divine decree and free will in Islam. NYU. https://archive.nyu.edu/bitstream/2451/40069/2/Reconciling%20t he%20Divine%20Decree%20and%20Free%20Will%20in%20Isla m.pdf

Piff, P. K., Stancato, D. M., Côté, S., Mendoza-Denton, R., & Keltner, D. (2012). Higher social class predicts increased unethical behavior. *Proceedings of the National Academy of Sciences, 109*(11), 4086-4091.

Rassool, G. H., & Luqman, M. (2023). Ibn qayyim al-jawzīyah's islāmic psychology: psychological and spiritual diseases. *Journal of Spirituality in Mental Health*, *25*(2), 144-159.

Riquelme, H. E., Rios, R. E., & Al-Sharhan, N. (2011). Antecedents of ostentatious consumption in Kuwait. *Journal of Islamic Marketing*,

Vol. 2 No. 3, pp. 295-308.
https://doi.org/10.1108/17590831111164813 .

Salovey, P. (Ed.). (1991). *The psychology of jealousy and envy.* Guilford Press.

Setiawan, C., Maulani, M., & Busro, B. (2020). Sufism as The Core of Islam: A Review of Imam Junayd Al-Baghdadi's Concept of Tasawwuf. *Teosofia: Indonesian Journal of Islamic Mysticism, 9*(2), 171-192.

Seuntjens, T. G. (2016). *The psychology of greed.* Tilburg University.

Sussman, S., Lisha, N., & Griffiths, M. (2011). Prevalence of the addictions: A problem of the majority or the minority? *Evaluation & the Health Professions, 34*(1), 3-56.

Tandler, N., & Petersen, L. E. (2020). Are self-compassionate partners less jealous? Exploring the mediation effects of anger rumination and willingness to forgive on the association between self-compassion and romantic jealousy. *Current Psychology, 39,* 750-760.

Uthmani, M. M. S. (2008). Ma'arif-ul-Qur'ān (Vol. 5). Maktaba Ma'arif-ul-Qur'ān.

Vrij, A. (2008). *Detecting lies and deceit: Pitfalls and opportunities.* John Wiley & Sons.

Weiss, B., & Miller, J. D. (2018). Distinguishing between grandiose narcissism, vulnerable narcissism, and narcissistic personality disorder. *Handbook of trait narcissism: Key advances, research methods, and controversies,* 3-13.

Williams, L. A., & DeSteno, D. (2008). Pride and perseverance: the motivational role of pride. *Journal of personality and social psychology, 94*(6), 1007.

Young, J. E. (2014). Schema-focused therapy for personality disorders. In *Cognitive behaviour therapy* (pp. 215-236). Routledge.

Yusuf, H. Signs, symptoms and cures of the spiritual diseases of the heart. Translation and Commentary of Imām Mawlūd's Maṭharat al-Qulūb. Cited in https://www. fussilatbd. com/Islamic/English/Hamza-Yusuf/Hamza-Yusuf_Purification-of-the-Heart. pdf (accessed May 27, 2023).

About the Editor

Carrie M. York, PhD is founder and president of the Alkaram Institute, a 501c3 non-profit research and educational institution dedicated to advancing Islamic psychology to benefit society and improve lives and whose vision is to become the first Muslim graduate school of psychology in the United States. She is also publisher of Alkaram Press. She has a PhD in transpersonal psychology from Sofia University, a Master's degree in Middle East Studies from the American University of Beirut, and is currently pursuing a graduate certificate in non-profit management at Harvard University. Dr. York's areas of interest include Islamic psychology, spiritually integrated psychotherapy, Islamic spirituality, and virtue and character development. She has taught, researched, and published extensively on these and related topics at the intersection of psychology and religion. She was an associate editor of the American Psychological Association's journal *Spirituality in Clinical Practice* ® for four years where she also guest edited a special issue on Islamic spirituality in clinical contexts. Her books include *Mental Health and Psychological Practice in the United Arab Emirates* (2015), *Islamically Integrated Psychotherapy: Uniting Faith and Professional Practice* (2018), a children's character development book *Maya and the Seven Limbs* (2020), and *The Way of Love: Towards an Islamic Psychology of Virtues and Character Development* (2023). Her forthcoming book *Heartfulness: Islamic Mindfulness, Meditation, and other Psycho-Spiritual Practices* is due 2024. Having lived outside her native United States in various countries for nearly 17 years, she now lives in Great Falls, Virginia. In her free time, she enjoys jogging, traveling, and spending time with loved ones.

About the Contributors

Shaykh Hasan Awan, MD has been a physician of internal medicine in private practice in Baltimore, MD, since 2007 and has served the Islamic Society of Baltimore Free Health Clinic since 2015. He is a spiritual teacher rooted in the Islamic traditions of Qādirī and Shādhilī Sufi spirituality. He teaches to all seekers and emphasizes direct experience in his teaching methodology. He is the founder of Hudur Institute, which seeks to revive the contemplative disciplines of Islam in contemporary living. He regularly delivers sermons in local mosques in the greater Baltimore-Maryland region. He began studying basic Islamic sacred sciences with local scholars at the age of 17. During medical school, he began to study Islamic theology, philosophy, spirituality, and comparative religion with teachers who were specialists in both theory and practice. His interests include wellness medicine, meditation, external and internal martial arts, chi gong, yoga, and mindfulness practice. He has studied and practiced meditation and self-inquiry with various teachers inside and outside the Islamic tradition. He is a member of the teaching faculty of the Alkaram Institute and Albalagh Academy, where he teaches various courses on Islamic meditation, including methods found in Islam's spiritual traditions and how to apply them to contemplatively living and Prophetically embodying the Five Pillars of Religion. He calls his approach to meditation, contemplative inquiry, and spiritual guidance the practice of presence (ḥuḍūr). His forthcoming books include *The Practice of Presence in Islamic Spirituality: A Guide to Meditation, Retreat, and Contemplative Living* and *Islam of the Heart: Living Religion with Presence*.

Anisah Bagasra, Ph.D. is an Associate Professor in the Department of Psychological Science at Kennesaw State University who specializes in behavioral health research in the Muslim American and African American faith communities. Her experience building traditional and online undergraduate curriculum led to the creation of a Psychology major at Claflin University, where she also spearheaded the launch of online degree programs prior to joining KSU. She teaches a wide range of psychology courses and mentors students engaged in undergraduate research with a focus on culturally competent research in minority communities. Specific research interests include Islamic Psychology, acculturation, measuring religiosity, and perceptions of mental illness. Her recent publications include three edited volumes, "Working with Muslim Clients in the Helping Professions"; "The Changing Faces of Higher Education: From Boomers to Millennials" and "The Impact of HBCUs in the 21st Century". She also conducts CE workshops in the area of religious and spiritual competencies for psychologists, conflict resolution, and community-based research.

Maneeza Dawood, PhD is a postdoctoral associate at the Yale Center for Emotional Intelligence, an Assessment and Efficacy Scientist at BrainPOP, and an Islamic Psychology Research Fellow at the Alkaram Institute. She completed her doctoral degree in social psychology at Columbia University. Her research broadly studies insider and outsider dynamics and the ways in which people feel included or excluded in society, with a particular focus on Muslim adolescents. She focuses on the social environments through which adolescents build some of the most powerful resources in their lives - their social connections - and how social connections can trigger a cascade of positive psychological outcomes, such as strengthened identity, character development, increased civic engagement, and improved academic performance. Her work as a fellow at the Alkaram Institute is aimed at developing a framework of Islamic social psychology.

Shahid Ijaz is a doctoral candidate at the International Islamic University Islamabad (IIUI). He is working toward a Ph.D. in the area of Islamic psychology. His research focuses on the intersection of psychology and Islam. Shahid completed his Bachelor of Science degree at IIUI, where he was awarded a gold medal for attaining the highest position in the social sciences faculty with a perfect CGPA of 4/4. He continued his education by pursuing a Master of Science in clinical psychology at NUST Pakistan and then pursued a career in academia and became a psychology lecturer at Islamabad Model College for Boys H-9. He currently serves as clinical supervisor and academics coordinator at the same institution, where he mentors and guides aspiring psychologists. He is also an Islamic Psychology Research Fellow at the Alkaram Institute. Beyond his academic responsibilities, Shahid's research interests encompass a variety of clinical research fields. He has concentrated on behavioral addictions, sexuality, and positive psychology, with an emphasis on programs that foster positive personality. His extensive knowledge of these topics prompted him to begin his current Ph.D. research, which delves deeper into the domain of positive personality building in Islamic contexts.

Ghena Ismail, Psy.D. holds a doctorate degree in Clinical Psychology from James Madison University and is registered with the College of Psychologists of Ontario as a Clinical and Forensic Psychologist. She held varied clinical positions within Canada's federal and provincial sectors before returning to Lebanon in 2014 to join the faculty ranks of the American University of Beirut (AUB). Currently, she serves as an Assistant Professor in the AUB Psychology Department and is the coordinator of its graduate program. She also serves as a Clinical Associate at the AUB Department of Psychiatry and is the Director of its multidisciplinary Eating Disorders program. Dr. Ismail served on multiple committees at AUB

170

including the Advisory Board for the Islamic Studies program, the Salim Hoss Bioethics committee, the Palliative Care committee and the Health Education committee. She maintains an active clinical practice and is also engaged in community-based initiatives aimed at raising awareness of mental health issues across Lebanon. She supervises psychology interns and residents in clinical training and students completing graduate theses. Her research is focused on the psychology of religion and spirituality which also informs her clinical work and community-based activities. She completed graduate level courses in Qur'anic exegesis and Islamic philosophy at the University of Toronto. Most recently, she participated in a conference coordinated by Dan Mission and the Forum for Contextual Theology in Lebanon whereby she offered a lecture on how contextual theology may be applied to the field of psychology.

Muhammad Tahir Khalily, PhD is a professor of psychology and Dean of the faculty of social sciences at Shifa Tameer-e-Millat University. He is Professor Chair of Psychology and Vice President Academics at International Islamic University Islamabad, Pakistan. He has more than thirty years of national and international teaching, research, clinical, supervisory, academic, administrative, and service development experience. He also worked as Director Academics, Director Quality Enhancement Cell (QEC), Students Advisor, and Director ORIC at International Islamic University Islamabad and was Head and Senior Clinical Psychologist in the Psychology Department of Roscommon Mental Health Service and clinical supervisor of the School of Psychology at the National University of Ireland, Galway, Republic of Ireland. His special interest is the rediscovery of religious perspectives with renewed interest in the current therapeutic approaches of professional psychology and their integration in line with the teachings of the Quran and Sunah. He is the principal author of three books and a study report. He teaches Muslim/Islamic psychology to Masters and PhD students as part of their syllabus and has successfully executed many research projects and subsequently published in international journals.

Sarah Mohr, LCSW is an independent researcher, licensed clinical social worker, and certified drug and alcohol counselor who has lived for most of her life in the San Francisco Bay area - the ancestral and traditional land of the Ohlone people. She received her Bachelor's in Religion from Dominican University (2003), and a Master's in Religion and Psychology from the Graduate Theological Union with a Certificate in Islamic Studies (2009). She has presented at conferences on Muslim Mental Health both nationally and internationally and is the author of multiple works on psychology in peer-reviewed journals including the *Journal of Muslim Mental Health* and the *Journal of Islamic Faith and Practice*. Her book,

Loving the Present: Sufism, Mindfulness, and Recovery from Addiction and Mental Illness was published in 2021. She currently works in mental health and alcohol and drug treatment, is a Visiting Scholar at the Graduate Theological Union, and is a guest faculty in the Islamic psychology program at the Alkaram Institute.

Salua Omais is a doctoral candidate in psychology at the University of Sao Paulo with a visiting research period at the University of Cambridge and Cambridge Muslim College (CMC) in the UK. Her doctoral research in Brazil is on happiness, well-being, religiosity, and spirituality in Islam, using the theoretical perspectives of positive psychology and Islamic psychology. She has a Master's in Health Psychology and Mental Health, an MBA in Positive Psychology and Human Development, a Postgraduate degree in Islamic Psychology (CMC), and a Bachelor's in Psychology. She has been a psychologist since 2008 and has implemented the discipline of happiness and emotional intelligence at the Federal University of Mato Grosso do Sul, working as a voluntary lecturer in this subject. In 2020 Salua created a group of Muslim psychologists in Brazil called PsicoIslam with the aim of giving an orientation about mental health to the Muslim community. She has also published two books in the field of psychology and worked for a newspaper in Brazil as a columnist for two years, writing articles about human behavior. She is a member of the International Students of Islamic Psychology, the International Positive Psychology Association, and the International Society of Neurossemantics. Email: saluaomais@usp.br

Misbah Rafiq, Ph.D. is a Guest Faculty and Senior Research Fellow in the Department of Social Work at University of Kashmir, India. She teaches various courses in psychology like counselling skills, personality psychology, and life-span development. In addition, she has been a part of a research project titled "Domestic Violence in Kashmir". Currently, she is working on a research project which is aimed at designing culturally-tailored primary prevention interventions for mental health in her hometown, Kashmir. She is also pursuing a Diploma in Islamic Psychology from Cambridge Muslim college, UK. She earned her Ph.D. in psychology from University of Kashmir, India. Her Ph.D. was an attempt to integrate religion (Islam) and psychology. Her research problem was "Conceptualising Human Nature in Quran as a Basis for Islamic Counselling". During her Ph.D. she arrived at a theory of human nature in Quran using grounded theory analysis. She also used the Quranic understanding of human nature to develop an Islamic counselling model. Her recent publications include, "Dynamics of Domestic Violence in Kashmir: An Interplay of Multiple Factors" and "A Quranic

Contextualisation of Mental Health Dynamics Involved in Domestic Violence".

Haseena Sahib is a doctoral candidate in Islamic Studies at the University of Virginia. She received her MA in History of Philosophies: East and West from State University of New York at Stony Brook in 2022, in which she immersed herself in classes on Islamic philosophy. She also received an MPH in Environmental Health from Columbia University in 2013. Her research interests include Sufism, Sufi literature and poetry, female Sufi scholarship, comparative religion, and religion and the environment. In her free time, she enjoys writing her own poetry, singing, and playing the traditional Middle Eastern frame drums.

Manoel Antônio dos Santos, PhD is a full professor at the University of São Paulo (USP), Faculty of Philosophy, Sciences and Letters of Ribeirão Preto, Brazil (FFCLRP-USP). He is the Head of the Teaching and Research Laboratory in Health Psychology (LEPPS). He holds a degree in psychology from the Institute of Psychology of the University of São Paulo, a Master's degree and Ph.D. in clinical psychology from the Institute of Psychology of the University of São Paulo. He is also an Associate Professor at the FFCLRP-USP. He is a specialist in family and couple therapy, in clinical psychology and hospital psychology. Since 1987, he has been a professor at the FFCLRP-USP, where he currently holds the position of full professor and Chair of the Department of Psychology. He is a Research Productivity Fellow at Level 1A of the National Council for Scientific and Technological Development (CNPq), Brazil. He is also a member of the São Paulo Academy of Psychology, Brazil. E-mail: masantos@ffclrp.usp.br

Shawkat Ahmad Shah, Ph.D. is a Professor in the Department of Psychology and Director at Directorate of Distance Education at University of Kashmir, Srinagar. He has also served as Former Dean, School of Education and Behavioural Sciences at the same university. After completing a B.Sc. from University of Kashmir, he joined Aligarh Muslim University, India for Post-graduate programme (Psychology) in 1994 and thereafter joined Ph.D. programme in the same university and completed the doctorate degree in 2000. Then he joined University of Kashmir as an assistant professor in 2002. He has around 70 research papers published in various reputed international and national journals. Till date 16 scholars have completed M.Phil/Ph.D under his supervision. Most of the research work has been carried out in the areas of mental health, social psychology, organizational behavior, and Islamic psychology. In addition, the main courses he has taught at the post-graduate level are counselling psychology, psychometry, research methodology and cognitive psychology. He is a member of various academic and administrative committees in the university and also a member of various academic bodies at the national level. At the administrative level he has served as head of the department of psychology for nine years.

Eman Tarif is a research analyst and moderator for an American engineering and scientific consulting firm at Exponent, Inc. She has a Bachelor's of Science degree in Cognitive Science and has co-authored research papers in the field of psychology. She is a designer and researcher who is passionate about creating impactful and effective product experiences. She also has an Associate's degree in teacher education and an Associate's degree in social & behavioral psychology, with experience as a teacher's assistant. Email: etarif21@gmail.com

www.ingramcontent.com/pod-product-compliance
Lightning Source LLC
Chambersburg PA
CBHW062133020426
42335CB00013B/1196